Resurrection · Discipleship · Justice

Jesus Christ,

the faithful witness,

the firstborn of the dead,

and the ruler of the kings of the earth

—Revelation 1:5

Praise for
Resurrection · Discipleship · Justice

"The resurrection of Jesus Christ has been at the center of Thorwald Lorenzen's theology, evidenced in his teaching and preaching. The truth of resurrection demands more evidence, however, and Lorenzen through his involvement in issues of human rights, justice, and ecology, testifies to faith in this mysterious and wondrous truth being not only something you accept but something you do."

ISAM BALLENGER
BAPTIST THEOLOGICAL SEMINARY AT RICHMOND
RICHMOND, VIRGINIA

"*Resurrection–Discipleship–Justice* is one of the most intriguing introductions to the meaning and practical implications of the resurrection of the crucified Jesus currently available. While deeply informed by contemporary theological debate, conservative and liberal alike, this book is written for the general reader. In language free from jargon, obscurity and sentimentality, Thorwald Lorenzen spells out the implications of God's act in raising Jesus from the dead for the life of faith, for the mission of the Church, and for the struggle for justice, peace and sustainable life in a dangerous world. A book not to be missed!"

GRAEME GARRETT
ST. MARK'S NATIONAL THEOLOGICAL CENTRE
CANBERRA, AUSTRALIA

"Thorwald Lorenzen 'connects the dots.' *Resurrection–Discipleship–Justice* and the triangle that emerges proves to be a hermeneutical plateau opening up new perspectives that can help us not only to recapture essential elements of the Christian faith, but also to focus our commitment on the implementation of justice without which the church may prove to be irrelevant in our times. In addition to its theological thrust, the book reflects a profound spirituality and pastoral concern. It is down-to-earth, frank, and honest."

GÜNTER WAGNER
CORRALES, NEW MEXICO

Dedication

Gratefully remembering my parents, Martha and Wilhelm Lorenzen, hoping that Australia's indigenous people will experience justice, and respectfully honoring the leaders, teachers and students at the Kathoolei Karen Baptist Bible School & College, Mae La Refugee Camp at the Thai/Myanmar border.

THORWALD LORENZEN

Resurrection Discipleship Justice

AFFIRMING THE RESURRECTION JESUS CHRIST TODAY

Smyth & Helwys Publishing, Inc.
6316 Peake Road
Macon, Georgia 31210-3960
1-800-747-3016
©2003 by Smyth & Helwys Publishing
All rights reserved.

Library of Congress Cataloging-in-Publication Data

Lorenzen, Thorwald.
Resurrection, discipleship, justice / Thorwald Lorenzen.
p. cm.
Includes indexes.
ISBN 978-1-57312-399-0
1. Jesus Christ—Resurrection.
2. Jesus Chris—Resurrection—History of doctrines—20th century.
3. Christianity and justice.
I. Title.
BT482 .L67 2003
232'.5—dc21

2003012232

Table of Contents

Introduction 3

Setting the Stage
Challenge 11
Joining the Debate 13
Intensifying the Discussion 20
Conclusion 36

The Resurrection of the Crucified Christ: Real and Relational
Construction 43
Toward a Relational Ontology 54
Summary and Conclusions 60

The Cross of the Risen Christ
Continuity 65
Accessing the Life of Jesus. 68
"God" vs. "God" 69
Summary: Crucifixion and Resurrection 77
Ontology 79

The Triumph of God Over the Estranging Forces of Death
The Death of Death 83
Death Has Many Faces 84
At-one-ment 84
Hope for the Individual 89
Hope for Unlived Lives 90
Hope in the Face of Injustice 90
Beyond the Shadow of Time 91
"... In the Lord Your Labor Is Not in Vain" 92
Summary and Conclusion 93

Affirming the Risen Christ Today

Introduction 95
A Community of Equals 96
The Ordination of Women 105
Ecological Responsibility 109
Conclusion 113

Christ and Other Religions

Introduction 119
Challenge 120
Options 123
Dialogue 124
Similarity and Difference 125
God as Creator—the Ground of Being 125
God as Reconciler—the Ground of Salvation and the Norm for Life 127
God as Spirit of Life and Salvation—Presence and Experience 131
Conclusion—By Their Fruits You Shall Know Them! 133

Discipleship

Prelude 137
Options 139
Retrieving a Forgotten Tradition 142
"Witness" 144
Paul Ricoeur 146
Francis Schüssler Fiorenza 148
Beyond the "Objective–Subjective" Dilemma 149
Faith as Discipleship 150
The Content of Discipleship 152
Conclusion 157

Summary and Conclusion

Affirming Life 163
Beyond "Liberal" and "Conservative" 164
The Argument 166

Author and Subject Index 171

Introduction

Many scholarly books are not easily accessible to busy pastors and other Christian leaders. Such books are often long with heavy language and numerous footnotes. In this resource, I have aimed for brevity and clarity. I have tried to give an account of the theology that underlies my ministry as a pastor of a local church, as a part-time theological teacher, and as a person involved in ecumenical and social justice activities. Sunday by Sunday, I enter the pulpit, not as an orator, but as a Christian minister; not trying to tell people what to do, but attempting to preach the liberating gospel of Christ. Week by week, I visit with people, not as a psychiatrist, but as a pastor who would like to speak words of hope, comfort, and challenge into the lives of people. In my ministry, ecumenical involvement, and social justice concerns, I feel the need for a theology that provides grounding, content, guidance, encouragement, inspiration, and promise.

In recent years, I have become increasingly dissatisfied with the way the resurrection of Christ has been "handled" in the pew, in the pulpit, and in the classroom. While early Christians spoke of the power of the resurrection, today it has become a cause for embarrassment or the topic of apologetics. While the earliest resurrection texts speak about a revolutionary change of history in the direction of justice, today resurrection theology is dominated by digging around in the past, trying to affirm or deny an empty tomb. While the New Testament claims that apart from the resurrection of Christ, faith and the forgiveness of sin are illusions, today there is a strange silence about the resurrection in many pulpits. While the first Easter led to an explosion of language from faith "in God" to faith "in Christ," today there seems to be a great hesitancy in many quarters clearly to confess Christ as the object of faith. There is a traditional acknowledgment that the resurrection of Christ is the foundation for Christian faith and for the Christian church, and yet more and more Christians seem to be more comfortable talking about the pre-Easter Jesus—the so-called historical or earthly Jesus—as the ground and content of faith. The earliest Christians who experienced the resurrection appearances of Christ felt renewed, empowered, and sent to mission, but today the resurrection seems to have become the intellectual battleground for those who want to deny or affirm an event that occurred 2000 years ago. A few concerns have led me to enter the contemporary debate on the resurrection.

The debate between "evangelical" and "liberal" theologians has raged since Rudolf Bultmann's pivotal essay on "New Testament and Mythology" (1941).[1] Indeed, it goes further back than that to the days of David Friedrich Strauss (1808–1874). In the nineteenth century, Strauss said what Professor John Dominic Crossan and Bishop John Shelby Spong say today. Our "modern world, . . . after many centuries of tedious research, has attained a conviction, that all things are linked together by a chain of causes and effects, which suffers no interruption."[2] Consequently, in our "modern" or even "post-modern" times, the Christian faith can only be maintained if the miraculous element is eliminated. Reason cannot and therefore must not be contradicted by revelation. Strauss concludes that "either Jesus was not really dead, or he did not really rise again."[3] The debate has not made much progress since. The opponents' focus on each other, and their preoccupation with what can be historically verified or falsified as having happened 2000 years ago, has hindered them from giving due attention to the nature and content of the resurrection of Christ.

The focus on what can or cannot be historically demonstrated or proven has led to a singular concentration on historical reason. Reason and its scientific methods, which often by definition exclude events that do not cohere with the "omnipotence of analogy,"[4] are supposed to give a verdict on the resurrection of Christ. This concentration on human reason is fueled by the human desire to define. The need to define, if it is not counteracted by a genuine attempt to understand, can easily be seen as an attempt to control and rule on our terms. It is therefore of great interest that in modern hermeneutical discussions, knowledge as participation and involvement has gained ground over so-called objective and neutral knowledge.

This leads to a further observation. Much of the resurrection debate takes little account of the essential interrelation of the resurrection with Jesus' life and death on the one hand and with the believer and the community of faith on the other. The focus is on whether the tomb into which Jesus' corpse had been placed was empty or not or whether there was a tomb at all. Yet, the New Testament traditions emphasize that it was the *crucified* One who was raised from the dead, and that he was recognized as Jesus in the event of faith. There were no neutral and, in that sense, objective observers of the resurrection of Christ. Indeed, the New Testament texts, in contrast to extracanonical writings, show a noticeable hesitancy to meet the demands of reason. In contrast, there is the clear intimation that the crucified Christ calls for an existence of faith in which it becomes evident that the resurrection of the crucified Christ established a new reality. This new reality calls for a corresponding lifestyle. The lifestyle has kerygmatic functions. It must in ever-changing situations preserve the memory that the *crucified* One was raised from the dead.

According to biblical authors, through faith and baptism the resurrection of Christ flows into the life of the believer and creates analogies to Christ's life, death, and resurrection. This theology calls for new ways of understanding. We shall try to suggest a relational ontology in which subject and object are no longer separated but interrelated. There may need to be a procedural priority, but we must seek and find ways to say that the resurrection of Christ is not simply an event completed in the past, but the beginning of a revolution that aims to restore beauty and promise to creation. The riches of the resurrection cannot be understood by merely concentrating on the laws of nature, because the resurrection is concerned with celebrating life and opposing the estranging forces of death. Theology must be concerned not only with the question of whether the resurrection occurred or not, but especially what it means for our understanding of life and its challenges.

The resurrection texts witness to the inner dynamic that the risen Christ produces his own history, what German theologians call *Wirkungsgeschichte*. That has to do with process, but it is more than process philosophy. The resurrection of Christ has started a process, but Christ is not dissolved into the process. Christ remains the power, the measure, the meaning, and the end of the process. This dynamic understanding of the resurrection is often missing in the modern debate, while I think it is the main thrust. The power of the risen Christ aims to transform history in the direction of God's *shalom*.

Although the resurrection reality contains many dimensions, I think a proper understanding of the interrelation of the resurrection with Jesus' life and death on the one hand, and an appreciation that the resurrection spells the end to the estranging powers of death on the other, impels us to make the struggle for justice a priority. This biblical and theological insight is intensified by our situation. We cannot overlook that the major causes for the ecology crisis, for the militarization of the world, and for the failure to share resources lie in the West—

we would have to say, in the *Christian* West. The West is that region of the world where traditionally the Christian faith and the Christian church has been of influence. While quoting biblical texts, we have exploited nature, conquered the world, considered the poor to be lazy, and treated the oppressed as being fated. This historical baggage should make us especially sensitive to the caring and liberating thrust of the gospel.

This also raises the question as to the foundation for Christian ethics. For something to be Christian, it needs to be grounded in Christology. This is not meant to show disrespect to other traditions. It is also not intended to make an absolute truth claim for the Christian vision of reality. It simply means that for dialogue in and with the global community, we Christians need to put our cards on the table. We need to demonstrate that we live and work out of a discernible and transparent vision of life. Take the ecological challenge, perhaps the greatest challenge that demands an urgent response from the global community. The Christian contributions are generally grounded in the doctrine of creation. But it would intensify our response, and put ecology on the theological rather than the moral agenda, if we were to ground our social ethics in Christology. The resurrection of Christ makes that possible.

A further challenge that Christians face today is our relationship to adherents of other religions. We need to develop a theology of religions. It is no longer possible to either ignore or demonize other religions. At the same time, we should not merely use the otherwise important virtues of tolerance and humility to say that we live in a pluralistic world, that everything is situational, that every claim to a grand narrative is imperialistic, and that therefore the only thing we can do is to take care of our own backyard. That is naive and simply validates the ever-present tendency to use religious convictions for personal comfort and social, political, and economic interests. In a global crisis of ecological neglect, abject poverty, ethnic hatred, child abuse, and torture, the religions of the world are challenged to demonstrate that they are concerned about human dignity and the value of nature.

For a meaningful Christian response, we need to mobilize the silent majority in the churches. One of the great and lasting achievements of the sixteenth century Reformation was to retrieve the early Christian rejection of law, cult, and hierarchy as fundamental for the Christian faith and its social expression, the church. The Reformers and the left wing of the Reformation rediscovered Paul with his emphasis on Christ as the fulfillment and the end of the law; they acclaimed with the Epistle to the Hebrews that Christ, being the great high priest who died "once for all" for our sins, is the fulfillment and the end of the cult; and with Johannine Christianity they confessed the church as the community of equals, the so-called priesthood of all believers. Today, all denominations realize that the future of the church depends heavily on whether we succeed in allowing more space for the democratizing power of the Spirit of God to mobilize and empower laity. For such empowerment of the laity to have depth, the laity needs to become interested in theological discussions about the origin and nature of faith. We cannot leave such discussions to a small group of experts. It is a mark of a mature community not to ignore conflict, but to deal with it. My intention is to write in such a way, keeping theological jargon and academic ballast to a minimum, that an interested layperson is able to follow the argument.

In all this, we cannot and we must not forget that history points beyond itself. The resurrection of Christ opens a future of hope and delivers us from deadening fatedness and threatening nothingness. Our human experience is aware of the otherness and the future of God by never being quite satisfied with even the best this life has to offer. Just as the process of creation led to the Sabbath rest, so our days in space and time are graced with the anticipation that one day our lives will experience clarity and then be transfigured into the eternal presence of God. Most religions have symbols for what Jews call *shalom* and Christians call salvation. Salvation does not exclude the present, but its reality participates in the ongoing story of Jesus and longs for its fulfillment. The present is therefore marked by a certain restlessness created by the hope for the fulfillment of God's ways with God's creation.

The following argument is my attempt to respond to the above reflections. In the first two chapters, I engage in conversation with representative theologians from both sides of the Atlantic. In dialogue with and as an alternative to liberal (John Dominic Crossan, Gerd Lüdemann) and evangelical (William Lane Craig) theologians, I have argued that the resurrection of Christ is a real event, but that its reality bursts our traditional historical categories and therefore calls for a new appreciation of a relational understanding of life. The relevant biblical texts say that by raising Jesus from the dead, God has started something new, something that is "open" and ongoing, an event that potentially embraces the future of creation. This calls for a relational ontology, an understanding of reality in which subject and object are no longer separate and over against each other, but related and understood only in their togetherness. The resurrection of Christ does not only say something about Jesus and God; it also says something about God and us and the rest of creation.

As far as we humans are concerned, the effect of the resurrection on human history came with the appearances of the risen Christ to the first believers.

The Spirit of God, who according to the earliest sources raised Jesus from the dead, created faith in them and thereby they were drawn into God's passion to reconcile with God what belongs to God. To celebrate and share their faith, the first believers found themselves in a community where Christ in the power of the Spirit was the determining and liberating presence.

In chapters three and four, I examine two central theological assertions for a theology of the resurrection: (1) that it was the crucified One who was raised from the dead and (2) that the resurrection entails the death to death. Both assertions suggest that resurrection faith and a passion for justice are interrelated. Given the tendency of either spiritualizing the resurrection or of transposing its relevance into the past or the future, I have tried to show that the resurrection aims at transforming history in the respective "here and now" in the direction of justice. Although the church has confessed on good biblical and experiential grounds that Christ is present in many ways in the believer's life, in worship, in the Eucharist, in preaching, and in the gathered community, I have argued that a commitment to justice deserves priority. I have argued that case not on narrow biblical grounds (e.g., Matt 25) or on grounds of relevance given by the terrible state of the world around us, but by recognizing the two basic pillars that determine the reality of the resurrection: the defeat of the estranging power of death and the fact that the crucified Christ was raised from the dead. Both emphases point our attention in the direction of reconciling what is estranged, of healing what is broken, and of liberating what is in chains.

Then, in chapters five and six, I apply that discussion to four areas that were controversial in New Testament days and that remain so today: humanity's ethnic, economic, and gender class divisions; the dignity of womanhood; the ecological challenge; and our relationship to other religions. I have tried to show that the resurrection of the crucified Christ establishes a new understanding of reality in which equality is affirmed and in which ecological responsibility and dialogue with other religions is encouraged. The resurrection of Christ therefore has a critical thrust, questioning traditional social patterns and seeking to change social structures in the direction of more justice.

Since it was the *crucified* Christ whom God raised from the dead, and who in the power of the Spirit shapes the lives of believers and the faith community, in the final chapter I raise the question of how we can most appropriately respond to the resurrection of the crucified Christ and implement what justice requires. How can the integrity of the event be preserved in our way of knowing? I have argued that individual piety, doctrinal orthodoxy, or liturgical worship are important but inadequate to capture the nature of the event. The concrete following of Jesus in our everyday life is the most adequate way of responding to the resurrection of the crucified Christ. I have developed my presentation with the help of the Anabaptist emphasis on discipleship and with acknowledging the hermeneutics of testimony by Paul Ricoeur and Francis Schüssler Fiorenza.

In 1995, I published a rather lengthy and detailed book under the title *Resurrection and Discipleship*.[5] Some of the themes mentioned there will recur here. The major differences between that book and this one is that I have tried to be less academic and more focused. The detailed biblical and theological reflections I have provided there will be taken for granted here. I have tried to provide an "evangelical" alternative to the conservative and liberal options that dominate the theological scene today. I mean "evangelical" in the sense of tuning into the dynamic life and history changing reality of the gospel, rather than forcing the gospel into the straitjacket of our understanding or denominational ideologies or theological networks. This has led me to focus here much more on the dominant motifs I detect in the resurrection reality: the risen life of the crucified One and our participation in it.

I want to acknowledge my gratitude for the support of my wife Jill. I am also grateful to my friends Merilyn Carey and Graeme Garrett, who have read the whole manuscript, and to Günter Wagner, who has read parts of it. They have made helpful suggestions. A three-month sabbatical granted by the Canberra Baptist Church and an invitation from the Baptist Theological Seminary at Richmond, Virginia, to give the "Cousins Lectures" in October 2000 provided the initial motivation for this book.

Notes

[1] Rudolf Bultmann, "New Testament and Mythology" (1941), in Rudolf Bultmann et al., *Kerygma and Myth: A Theological Debate*, ed. and trans. Hans Werner Bartsch, rev. ed. by Reginald Fuller (New York: Harper & Row, 1961), 1-44.

[2] David Friedrich Strauss, *The Life of Jesus Critically Examined*, 4th ed. (1840), ed. Peter C. Hodgson, trans. George Eliot (Philadelphia: Fortress, 1972), 78.

[3] Ibid., 736.

[4] Ernst Troeltsch, "Historical and Dogmatic Method in Theology" (1898), in *Religion in History*, intro. James Luther Adams, trans. James Luther Adams and Walter F. Bense. Fortress Texts in Modern Theology (Minneapolis: Fortress, 1991), 11-32.

[5] *Resurrection and Discipleship: Interpretive Models, Biblical Reflections, Theological Consequences* (Maryknoll NY: Orbis Books, 1995).

Chapter 1

Setting the Stage

... two of them were going ... and talking with each other about all these things that had happened. —Luke 24:13f.

Challenge

Christian theologians are engaged in interesting and at the same time far-reaching discussions about the origin, the source, the ground, and the content of Christian faith. There is agreement, of course, that Christian faith has to do with Jesus Christ. But when it comes to the question as to what "Jesus Christ" stands for, the agreement ends. Was "Jesus Christ" the woodworker or stonemason from Nazareth who founded a new religion similar to Islam, which traces its story back to Mohammed? Or was Jesus a wandering prophet, a charismatic leader, an inspiring teacher, a social reformer who wanted to renew and reform Judaism but had no intention of starting a new religion? There are theologians both within Judaism and within Christianity who see Jesus as a radical Jew and who blame his followers, mainly Paul, for leading his reform movement away from Judaism. Is it Jesus' death as the atonement for the sins of the world which is the substantial core of Christianity and the necessary ground for the Christian faith? Was Jesus Christ the incarnation of the divine *logos* (λόγος = "word") or the divine *sophia* (σοφία = "wisdom") and thus the origin of Christianity? Or is the resurrection of the crucified Christ, which then became historically manifest in the appearances of Christ to the first believers, the real ground of the Christian faith?

Such discussions are not new, but they deserve a wider audience. It is interesting that many people in the pew are not aware of these discussions, and many preachers in the pulpit or priests officiating at the Eucharist ignore them. Such ignorance cannot be helpful for the life and future of the churches. We are not dealing with a side issue or footnote to the story of faith. We are not only discussing historical questions about the beginnings of Christianity.

The resurrection concerns the very nature of our faith in Christ, the meaning of our life, and our responsibility in the world.

One important question dealing both with the origin of faith and with the ongoing nature and content of faith is the question of whether the "resurrection of Christ" is an ontological reality or a replaceable metaphor. We shall address that question in this and the next chapter and suggest that "resurrection" is a metaphor—but not a replaceable metaphor. I shall argue that this metaphor is grounded in a new reality that actually happened, although that happening of God raising Jesus from the dead and thereby defeating the estranging power of sin, separation, and death escapes our definition and transcends our rational understanding.

At the same time, I propose that we must learn in our perception and understanding of reality to give procedural priority to the matter we try to investigate. Jesus Christ is not only the faithful witness to God's truth, but he is also "the firstborn of the dead." The Christ whom Christians experience is therefore part of a divine story that goes back to Jesus and beyond to God's plan for God's creation. We therefore look for an understanding of reality that is not centered on the separation of subject and object but on the interrelation between the two.

Such a thesis is controversial today. While Christians through the ages and official church pronouncements have taken their cue from the apostle Paul and seen the resurrection of the crucified Christ as the foundation of Christian faith—1 Corinthians 15—that foundation seems to be giving way. While the apostle insisted that if it were not for the resurrection of Christ, the Christian preacher would have nothing to proclaim, that faith would be empty, and forgiveness would be an illusion, modern theologians of many persuasions say that the validity and integrity of the Christian message does not depend on the resurrection of Christ—at least not the way Paul and the church through the ages have understood it. All we need is Jesus, they say, the historical, the earthly, the pre-Easter Jesus, to give meaning to the great Christian symbol of salvation.[1] While Paul insisted that apart from the resurrection of Christ the nature of God and consequently the nature of faith would be distorted, there are modern theologians who insist that only a distancing from the resurrection can save the concept of God for the modern seeker. Increasingly, there are theologians from David Friedrich Strauss in the nineteenth century to Gerd Lüdemann, Marianne Sawicki, and John Dominic Crossan in our day, who insist in different ways that resurrection faith does not entail an action of God involving the crucified Jesus. Important for many of them is the empowerment of believers to face life's challenges. But is such empowerment more than wishful thinking? Does it have a ground, a foundation? From where is such empowerment nourished? Are there wells grounded in the very being of God that feed the followers of Jesus for the journey of life and faith?

Joining the Debate

In recent decades, there have been a number of lively and at times aggressive debates concerning the nature and content of Christ's resurrection. We cannot mention them all, but a brief sampling may offer an overview of the issues at stake.

"Evangelical" versus "Existential"

In October 1964, over 2000 people from all walks of life gathered into the church of the little country town of Sittensen in Northern Germany to listen to a debate between the "evangelical" theologian Walter Künneth and the "existential" theologian and student of Rudolf Bultmann, Ernst Fuchs. The topic was "The Resurrection of Jesus Christ from the dead."[2]

Walter Künneth emphasized the objective reality of the resurrection of Christ. It is *extra nos*. It precedes our faith, our preaching, and the genesis of the church. Ernst Fuchs, on the other hand, did not want to talk of the resurrection of Christ apart from his own experience and existence. Fuchs invited listeners to imagine a normal family. In such a family, a son would not ask his mother whether his father was really his father. He would simply take it for granted that his father is his father. There would be something strange and indeed wrong if it were otherwise. Related to resurrection and faith, Fuchs argues that the believer presupposes the resurrection and takes it for granted. Indeed, for Fuchs it would be an act of unbelief to ask for historical verification external to the relationship itself, whether it is the relationship of a father and his son, or of Christ and the believer.[3]

If we were to envisage an ellipse with two focal points, one being the resurrection of Christ, the other being the believer, then Künneth would occupy one point. Let us call it the "ontological" or "historical" point. The emphasis would be on insisting that God actually (historically) raised Jesus from the dead by changing his earthly material corpse into a new spiritual body. The tomb into which Jesus' corpse had been placed must therefore have been empty. God actually changed the being of Jesus and thereby changed being itself ("ontological"). This ontological and historical reality, for Künneth, is the necessary and irreplaceable foundation and cause for Christian faith, for Christian proclamation, and for the Christian church.[4]

The other focal point, occupied by Ernst Fuchs, could be named the "existential" or "ontic" focus. Fuchs is primarily concerned with the effect and the relevance of the resurrection. His interest is in the difference faith in the resurrection makes for the life of the believer. He focuses not on the objective ontological change in the being of Jesus, but on the relevance of the resurrection reality in the life of the believer ("ontic"). Fuchs insists that apart from being confronted with the actual questions of life and death, resurrection talk makes little sense: "whoever speaks of resurrection must be concerned with the unity of life and death in love."[5] This "unity of life and death in love has appeared in the world in the love of Jesus," and the believer participates in this reality by believing as Jesus did.[6]

Although the debate conveys the impression of an unbridgeable gulf, I think we need to hear both interpretations. At the same time, I remain dissatisfied and therefore seek to go further. Both theologians affirm that human reason cannot fully grasp the reality of the resurrection and that therefore resurrection and faith belong together. Both allow for ontological (objective) and personal (relational) categories to gather up the full meaning of the resurrection,[7] although Künneth emphasizes the ontological while Fuchs focuses on the personal.

We shall pursue the question of ontology in this book. Ontology (*ontōs* [ὄντως] = being, real; *logos* [λόγος] = word) is the science that wonders why there is something and not nothing, and then sets out to grasp reality or being. It tries to go beyond our experience, knowledge, and perception and think what really *is*. It tries to come to terms with the reality that feeds and nourishes our thinking and feeling. An important question in this regard is whether what *is* (reality) is objectively there, to be perceived by secular reason, or whether what *is* entails also mystery, aiming at relationship and participation. Reason then would not define or postulate reality and would not be secular by definition, but it would *receive* reality, it would be nourished by reality, and it would appreciate its personal and relational dimensions.[8]

When theologians address the question of ontology, they challenge claims of reason that arrogate for themselves the privilege to decide what is real and what is not. Reason in their view must hear, see, and receive what is, but it must not assume the power to postulate what is real and what is not. Since theologians speak about God and creation as being different and yet at the same time as being related, they understand ontology as relational.[9] We shall return to this issue later.

Both Künneth and Fuchs seem to have a fairly romantic and abstract picture of the historical Jesus. There is nothing of the protest, struggle, and torture that was so much a part of Jesus' life. They affirmed of course, as most theologians do, the unity of the life, death, and resurrection of Jesus. They also emphasized that it was the crucified One who was raised from the dead, but the life of Jesus that actually provoked the crucifixion received little or no theological attention during the debate.

The Passion for Historicity

In May 1985, Liberty University in Lynchburg, Virginia, hosted a conference to debate what they considered to be "the most significant topic of our day": "Did Jesus rise from the dead?"[10] In the presence of 3000 people the theologian Gary R. Habermas (in favor) and the philosopher Anthony G. N. Flew (against) debated the issue. Two panels of experts adjudicated the debate. One panel of five philosophers, evaluating the content of the debate, voted 4 to 0 (one draw) for the affirmative position of Habermas. The other panel of five professional debate judges, evaluating the form and method of the debate, voted 3 to 2 for Habermas. Then other philosophers and theologians responded to the debate (among them Wolfhart Pannenberg, Charles Hartshorne, and James I. Packer).

The debaters agreed to understand the resurrection in the following terms:[11] (1) Resurrection refers to the historical, literal, physical event of Jesus being brought back from the dead (which Flew categorized as "miracle"[12]). (2) Such an event, like any historical event, can only be determined by historically reliable evidence. (3) If the resurrection could be established as a historical event, then materialism would be doomed and the existence of a supernatural reality would be demonstrated. (4) The affirmation of a historical resurrection is "the defining and distinguishing characteristic of the true Christian,"[13] and it would have important existential significance for all people. The book concludes with Habermas's assertion: "Our eternal destiny hangs in the balance."[14]

Flew's argument against the historicity of the resurrection[15] rests on two main points, which are interrelated. Firstly, in the universe as we perceive it from our experience and from scientific inquiry, there can be no place for miracles, unless we approach our topic with the presupposition of the existence of an acting and supernatural God who can and does suspend laws of nature. For Flew, the laws of nature are strong and tight. Secondly, such a presumption can only be overturned by solid historical evidence to the contrary. He admits that in theory an emphasis on a universe with consistent natural laws can be modified. But he insists that the historical evidence for the resurrection is inadequate for constructing a resurrection event that would override, suspend, or modify our perception of a universe in which miracles do not happen.

Flew illustrates the historical unreliability of New Testament texts with a discussion of the birth narratives in the Gospels. He also notes the lack of non-Christian evidence for the resurrection, and he argues that even the earliest testimonies to the resurrection are uncertain and in fact they are too far removed from the event to provide a trustworthy basis for a reliable historical verdict.

Habermas turns the table around and accuses Flew of a "naturalistic prejudice" and an "a priori assumption against miracles."[16] He shows that even modern philosophy and modern science do not agree that a possibility of an "external intervention in nature" must be ruled out.[17] If there is even the slightest possibility for the supernatural, then any claim or evidence for a supernatural event cannot be ruled out on principle but must at least be given serious consideration.

He then lists many reasons for the historical evidence of the resurrection. Among them "the original experiences of the disciples" are described as "pivotal."[18] Closely following are the transformation of these disciples after the crisis of the cross and the experiences of the apostle Paul. This historical evidence, in Habermas's view, overturns any presupposition that a resurrection from the dead must be ruled out on principle. Furthermore, he argues, the positive evidence for the resurrection of Jesus is so strong that an unprejudiced observer must affirm its historicity.

From the respondents, let me briefly mention Wolfhart Pannenberg,[19] who basically agrees with Gary Habermas. He affirms the historicity of the empty tomb, but at the same time admits that the appearances are primary—"the judgment concerning the kind of reality that occurred with the appearances cannot be independent of the question of what happened in the tomb."[20] Pannenberg is more aware than the other participants that critical New Testament scholarship has demonstrated many legendary elements in the resurrection narratives in the Gospels, and he is more aware of the powerful fact that we live in a world where "the dead do not rise again" and that therefore the historicity of the resurrection will continue to be a "debated issue."[21]

In listening to the debate, several observations come to mind. I have the somewhat strange feeling that the agenda is not determined by the object of inquiry, but by the needs and interests of the inquirer. Must it not be the first task of interpreters of texts to analyze carefully and listen before they speak? The question of historicity dominates the whole discussion and the impression is conveyed that it is the major topic with regard to understanding the resurrection. Only James I. Packer in his response shows some awareness that this is only one issue and that there are others—Packer refers to "the theological significance of the Resurrection, or its importance for humanity"—that may be closer to the heart of the matter.[22] By forcing the resurrection into the "historicity," "fact," "miracle," "laws of nature" framework, one is in danger of missing the point. It is like me telling someone that I have fallen in love with Jill. The response comes: Does she exist? Is she a woman? How tall is she and what is her hair color? The response is not irrational, but it seems inappropriate to the occasion!

In the debate, there was no appreciation, for instance, that the crucified One was raised from the dead. There seemed to be no awareness that whether faith is based on historically established fact, or created and sustained by the word of the gospel, makes a fundamental difference for the nature of faith.[23] Likewise, there seemed to be no appreciation that it makes an elemental difference for the content of faith, whether the resurrection was some kind of super miracle, or whether it was that particular Jew Jesus who lived a certain kind of life and who in response to that life was opposed and crucified, who was raised from the dead makes an elemental difference for the content of faith.

It is interesting and helpful to know that Habermas won the debate. But it was not a theological debate. It was a historical one. Such debates belong in the forecourts of theology, in what theologians call prolegomena. Theology is much more concerned with appreciating the nature and meaning of the resurrection as it comes to us through the resurrection texts and narratives. Theology allows the text also to question our questions. Although Habermas accepts the authority of the Scriptures, there seems to be little awareness of the difficult problems of interpretation. He assumes that the biblical texts can directly, without hermeneutical considerations, answer *our* historical questions—which is simply not the case!

Engaging with Post-Modernism

In April 1996, Roman Catholic theologians hosted an ecumenical Resurrection Summit in New York that drew together scholars from a variety of disciplines.[24] The basic tenor of most presentations was that the resurrection of Jesus is a historical event, which must not be dissolved into the faith of the disciples. God raised the crucified Jesus from the dead, and Jesus appeared to the disciples. This emphasis is defended against those who—like John Hick, Sallie McFague, and Gerd Lüdemann—understand the appearances of the risen Christ as psychological projections or as depth psychological compensations for guilt feelings. "Easter" for these theologians does not stand for anything really new or for anything God has done to Jesus. It symbolizes the strengthening and intensification of the disciples' admiration for the historical but now dead Jesus. A number of the contributors to the summit point out that these explanations reflect our modern and even post-modern situation where we try to understand the divine within the framework of our human reason.

Three contributions deserve special attention. Francis Schüssler Fiorenza[25] is critical of "foundationalism" and "fundamental theology," which suggest that absolute certainty concerning the foundation for theology can be reached by secular reason, apart from and independent of faith. From a careful analysis of the early New Testament resurrection formulas and narratives, he arrives at the conclusion that the hermeneutical categories of testimony, witness, and praxis are more appropriate to capture the reality to which the resurrection texts witness and from which they come than apologetic interests or historical objectivism. The *Sitz im Leben* of resurrection formulas is worship, and for the resurrection narratives it is calling and mission. The involvement, the participation, is part of the testimony: "the lives of the witnesses were often considered an important factor in the veracity of the testimony."[26] And the authenticity of the testimony is verified in praxis. To answer the question whether our faith is founded on the faith of the early Christians, Schüssler Fiorenza distinguishes between the epistemological and the ontological ground of faith: "the epistemological ground of faith is the New Testament testimonies, whereas the ontological ground is God's act."[27]

Peter Carnley in his response to Gerald O'Collins, SJ[28] argues that neither the resurrection appearances nor the empty tomb narratives provide sufficient evidence for the veracity of Easter. The appearances could have been "subjective visions," and the empty tomb stories may be later creations of faith, rather than reasons for faith. Carnley therefore emphasizes a third dimension associated with the reality of Easter, the experience of the Spirit of the crucified Christ in worship. He considers "the most important challenge facing resurrection theology today" the need to develop "an epistemology that can account for the Christian claim to identify the presence of the raised Christ as a religious object in present experience."[29] This is an important reminder we must not forget. The challenge is, however, to bring together "worship" with the "crucified" Christ. Healthy suspicion needs to remind us that the church has more often than not domesticated the cross[30] and failed to remember and actualize that the Spirit of Christ includes Jesus' commitment to the poor and oppressed.

Brian V. Johnstone, CSsR[31] observes correctly that the resurrection of Christ, though at the center of Christian faith, has seldom been used as the basic reference point for Christian ethics. That is probably due to the dominant influence of reason and anthropology in Christian ethics. If, however, it is true that by raising Jesus from the dead, God has established a new reality, then this must have consequences for our understanding of life and our involvement in life.

By encountering the risen Christ, the believer will learn "to transcend oneself in the service of others," create space for the victim, and thereby participate "in the divine reality itself."[32] By raising Jesus from the dead, God unmasks the false peace of the world that actually was a cause for Jesus' death (John 11:50). That peace was founded on violence. By raising Jesus from the dead, God established an ontology of peace. Christian ethics is therefore committed to peace rather than war, to nonviolence rather than violence, to relationships of love rather than enmity. By being drawn into the resurrection reality, the believer shapes presumptions of peace, justice, freedom, nonviolence, and ecological justice. These then need to be applied to each ethical challenge. By affirming an ontology of peace, resurrection ethics has the resources to be transformative in a world often marked by violence and competitiveness.

Conclusion

These and many other such gatherings bring to the surface what boils underneath. There is no consensus in sight. These summits are the public manifestations of what goes on in many theological classrooms—indeed, in the hearts and minds of most theologians and thoughtful Christians. There is a challenge in the air and it touches the very ground and content of our faith.

Christian thinkers who for the most part are also intentional and responsible members of Christian churches find themselves being torn between two claims. On the one hand, there is the strong biblical evidence and the declared faith of the church through the ages and around the world, both of which witness to the central role that the resurrection of Christ plays in the genesis and formation of Christian faith. It seems arrogant to deny such overwhelming community consensus and go against it by wanting to build another foundation for Christian faith today. One may question the centrality of the "virgin birth" or the "preexistence" of Christ or his "ascension." These incidents are only found in parts of the New Testament traditions. But to question the centrality of the resurrection seems to remove the foundation that is universally claimed as necessary by all the New Testament traditions and affirmed by the major Christian creeds and all the churches through the ages. A theologian must have good reason to question the legitimacy of such massive support for the importance, indeed necessity, of the resurrection of Christ for Christian faith and the Christian church.

On the other hand, thoughtful Christians cannot escape their own situation. They are powerfully aware of the fact that in our experience dead people do not rise. They want to recognize and take seriously the scientific worldview taught at the university and presupposed by experiments in the laboratory. We cannot live in two philosophical worlds. Thus, whatever we say about the resurrection of Christ must inform our worldview. It must be defended at the dinner table and in the university seminar. It must inform our preaching, our pastoral care, and our prophetic ministries.

The problem is, of course, that at least in the Western world the dominant scientific worldview of our time is by definition secular. It is permeated by the "omnipotence of analogy" and seems therefore to have no room for a *novum*, and much less for new and surprising activities of God. Are we compelled to opt for one or the other, for the secular or the sacred? Or must something new emerge? We must certainly try to break the deadlock of "objective" *or* "subjective." Our responsibility is to put our cards on the table and enter into an open and fearless dialogue with others for the best interpretation of what constitutes reality.

In that sense, every crisis is also a challenge. For Christian theologians who confess God not only as redeemer and reconciler, but also as "maker of heaven and earth, of all that is, seen and unseen," it is not advisable to retreat into the safe harbor of one's own scholarly "networks" or theological communities. We must try to listen, analyze, and understand. Every theologian, every pastor, every theological student, every church leader must at some point enter the debate and occupy his or her own space in it. The matter is too important to leave to a few experts. The community of faith is challenged to become aware of and then accept responsibility for the very ground and content of its faith.

So far, then, two important questions have emerged. First, what do we actually mean when we speak of the resurrection of the crucified Christ; and second, how can we bring our affirmation of the resurrection into correlation with our experience of life?

Intensifying the Discussion

We shall now intensify our discussion by entering into a brief dialogue with recent publications by three representative theologians from both sides of the Atlantic. Their writings have found widespread attention in both religious and secular media. American John Dominic Crossan and German Gerd Lüdemann represent what may be called the "post-modern" or "liberal" paradigm, while American William Lane Craig is a good representative of the conservative "evangelical" approach. Their views featured in a public debate between representatives of the "Jesus Seminar" (mainly John Dominic Crossan) and Evangelicalism (mainly William Lane Craig) that took place in Moody Memorial Church in Chicago in 1994.[33]

Preparing the Way

It is difficult to sketch the modern theological landscape.[34] The views are so diverse and the philosophical and cultural presuppositions so different that a meaningful dialogue or an empathetic conversation seems impossible. If one listens to the conversation between Walter Künneth and Ernst Fuchs, or between William Lane Craig and John Dominic Crossan, or between Gerd Lüdemann and Wolfhart Pannenberg, one inevitably becomes frustrated at the unwillingness or inability to appreciate the other's views and the lack of communication that actually takes place.

These debates do not concern a controversy about an exegetical detail or a marginal issue of the Christian faith. Scholars, who are diametrically opposed in their conclusions, share the same amount of basic knowledge—they know modern exegetical methods, they are aware of contemporary exegetical findings, they know different models, approaches, and paradigms. Yet, their theological conclusions are often diametrically opposed. The problem obviously goes much deeper than a scholarly interpretation of texts.

It has to do, for instance, with the philosophical presuppositions and the personal experiences scholars bring to their work. Does our vision of reality allow room for an affirmation that "God is," that this God can and does give "life to the dead and calls into existence the things that do not exist," and who therefore can and does justify the "ungodly" (Rom 4:5, 17)? I know, of course, that we cannot escape the life-world in which we find ourselves. However, do we have to join fundamentalists and liberals who tend to absolutize our modern Western scientific worldview and then interpret and evaluate the past in light of the present? In our attitude and approach to ancient texts, should we not display some hermeneutical humility and allow for the possibility that reality may be wider and even different than our perception of it? I have met Christian theologians from Africa who experience our Western way of filtering theological symbols through our scientific sieve as cultural imperialism.

When it comes to topics like the resurrection of Jesus from the dead, we must confront our own death, our preparations for it, and our hopes beyond it. I am confronted with the question of whether the resurrection of Jesus has anything to say about the unfulfilled life of my brother, who was killed by the violence of war at the age of six months. I cannot avoid the question of what the resurrection of Christ has to say to my experience of church as at times inflexible, dogmatic, selfish, loveless, and unjust. I cannot ignore the experience that often I find meaningful and inspiring companions for the journey outside the Christian community, with friends who have a passion for justice, who celebrate freedom, and yet, who seem to believe in other or in no gods. If a theology book is more than a manual for classroom discussion or ecclesiastical indoctrination, it also serves to help theologians deal with their own experiences and struggles in life.

Nevertheless, neither our philosophical presuppositions nor our personal experiences are the most significant stuff of theology. As theologians, we have to deal with texts. Texts can bring something new into our lives. In order to allow for that possibility and to hear the message of the text, we have to protect the text against our invasive self-interest and against our unbending self-will.

To achieve that purpose, it is important to utilize the historical critical method for interpreting biblical texts. That method has been controversial in recent years and people have tried to replace or supplement it with other approaches.[35] Yet, it is the only method that actually attempts to protect the text against ourselves. It is not critical of the texts; it is critical of the texts' interpreters. Furthermore, this method takes seriously that Christian faith is bound to a historical person. The historical critical method properly understood is the only method available to us to ascertain that in our reading of texts, our faith, its nature, and its content remains in substantial continuity with Jesus. At the same time, Karl Barth's warning should always be kept in mind: "Kritischer müßten mir die Historisch-Kritischen sein!"[36] We must accept that there is a hermeneutical gulf between "then" and "now" and try, ever anew, to discern the reality to which the biblical texts introduce us. The main purpose for using a transparent methodology is our intention not to postulate reality but to understand it.

That reality for Christians is faith in a person, not in historical facts or dogmatic propositions. We need historical inquiry and theological reflection in order to assure the continuity between our faith and its ground and to understand the content of our faith. Theological inquiry must carefully and sensitively guard against distorting this fundamental identity mark of the Christian faith—that it is faith in a person, not in a fact or a proposition.

Here the authenticity and liberating quality of faith in Christ is at stake. We know that Easter entailed an explosion of new language. Jesus, the historical Jesus, never called for faith in himself.[37] Faith before Easter meant trust and reliance on God. Such faith is narrated in the Hebrew Bible (for instance, in Gen 15:1-6; Isa 7:3-9; 28:14-22), and during Jesus' earthly life it is encouraged and made possible by his physical presence. But what was implicit before Easter had to become explicit with Easter. What was taken for granted during Jesus' earthly life, that in his presence people could and did experience God, had to be gathered into language when he was no longer physically present. Therefore, part of the Easter reality is the confession of faith "in Christ."

This raises the question of whether the confession of "faith *in Christ*" is a mythological statement meaning that faith is faith in the God of Jesus or whether it is a real statement meaning that Christ can actually be addressed and worshiped as the object of faith. Our answer to that question depends on our understanding of the resurrection. I hope this is not seen as theological nit-picking, but I intend to argue that the liberating and saving quality of faith is at stake with our understanding of the resurrection of Christ. Since theology is a church discipline and can therefore only be done in community, let us now turn to the discussion.

John Dominic Crossan[38]

For John Dominic Crossan, all theological language is metaphorical, symbolical or figurative. He distinguishes between those theologians (e.g. conservative evangelicals) who believe "that everything in the Gospels that can be taken literally and historically should be so taken" and those, like himself, whose exegetical experience has led them to the conclusion "that some stories that could be taken literally were intended to be and should be taken symbolically instead."[39]

I agree that God-talk is by necessity metaphorical. Human language cannot directly and with immediacy locate and name God. We must acknowledge the qualitative difference between God and us. We need to be aware of the fact that we are limited to the language of our human experience. When we talk of God and of God's ways, we do so in word pictures that tease intimations of God into our minds and hearts, without actually grasping or defining the totality and wholeness of God. We may say, for instance, that "God is father or mother" or that "God acts like a shepherd or a lion." Thereby we suggest that God has created us, that God cares for us, that God is strong, and that God uses God's strength to look after us. All that is true. But at the same time, God is "more" than what we have gathered up in these word pictures. Keeping that in mind, I want to foreshadow two questions: first, is "resurrection" a *replaceable* metaphor; and second, does the use of metaphor rule out that in its depth there is an *event* that feeds the metaphor and to which the metaphor relates and witnesses?

Is resurrection "but one way, not the only way, of expressing Christian faith"?[40] Does it stand for something else, like Willy Marxsen's continuing cause of Jesus (*die weitergehende oder weiterlebende "Sache Jesu"*),[41] or Crossan's continuing and empowering presence of Jesus in communities of justice, peace, and resistance?[42] Or was "resurrection" the best, the most adequate, and as such the only metaphor available to gather into language that God has acted in the life and death of Jesus and that God's action was for the welfare of humanity and the cosmos?

We know, of course, that the word "resurrection" was adopted by the early Christians from the realm of their human experience. It could mean such things as "arising" or "waking up" from sleep, "resuscitating" a dead person, "rising" in order to speak, or "installing" a person to an office.[43] But given the fact that we only have the language of human experience to describe an event, we must still ask whether our language captures and defines the event, or whether an event can give new meaning to our language. How can the "more" of an event be captured unless we allow for a transfiguration of language? The event of the resurrection is only accessible through the experiences and the words that witness to it, and yet, neither the experiences nor the words can adequately capture the event. We must be aware of this hermeneutical challenge and attempt to give priority to the event, so that the event determines the language and not vice versa. Acknowledging that "resurrection" is a metaphor, we do not limit the event to the traditional meaning of "resurrection," but we allow for the event itself to determine and indeed give new and added meanings to words.

So when we disagree with Crossan, Marxsen, and others who say that "resurrection" is one, but not the only metaphor that tries to capture what Christians mean by "Easter," then we are not saying that the language of human experience can adequately capture this new, unexpected, and divine event. We are saying that "resurrection" is the most adequate metaphor to focus our attention that God has acted with regard to the dead Jesus and that God has done so for our good.

Applied to the question at hand, when the earliest Christians used "resurrection" language, they certainly did not want to say Jesus was "raised from unconsciousness" or "delivered" from pain or agony. For them, Jesus was dead, and then, through his appearances, he was revealed or he revealed himself as the Living One. For the early Christians, the resurrection of Jesus was also different from resurrections of which they had heard in their Hebrew Scriptures or from Hellenistic-Jewish writings. Jesus' resurrection for them was not like the resurrection of Lazarus (John 11:38-44), the resurrection of Jairus's daughter (Mark 5:21-24a, 35-43), or the resurrection of the widow's son at Nain (Luke 7:11-15). These were understood to be supernatural miracles: uncommon, but not unheard of. It was clearly understood that these individuals were raised back to earthly life and that, consequently, they would have to die again. They were not delivered from the power and realm of death. Romans 6:9—"We know that Christ, being raised from the dead, will never die again; death no longer has dominion over him"—does not apply to them. We may say that theirs was resuscitation from death to earthly life, which is a life unto death; it was not a resurrection from death into the eternal presence of God.

While John Dominic Crossan sees "resurrection" as one metaphor among others to express the continuing empowering presence of the historical Jesus, and while Crossan argues that the Christian emphasis on this one metaphor "resurrection" comes from Paul,[44] we maintain that "resurrection" is the most adequate metaphor for saying that God has raised Jesus from the dead, and that this event is not only central for the apostle Paul, but for all major traditions in the early church.

This leads to the other controversial question. Does the metaphor "resurrection" point to a reality that has event character, a reality that modifies being? Concretely, did God act in the life, death, and resurrection of Jesus and thereby do something for us and for our salvation that needed to be done and that we could not do for ourselves?

Although Crossan, in his attempt to demarcate himself clearly from the conservative Evangelical position, remains somewhat nebulous, my reading of him indicates that his theological focus is the historical Jesus and the effect the historical Jesus had on the ongoing believers and the continuing Christian communities.[45] The historical Jesus empowers people and communities in their way of peace, resistance, and justice. Easter is not dependent on what happened to Jesus after his death. Important is that companions and communities experience Jesus' presence after his death. At the same time, Crossan insists that the "real Jesus" is "much bigger than the historical Jesus."[46] The "real Jesus" includes the historical Jesus and his *Wirkungsgeschichte* (the ongoing effect Jesus has on people and on history). At this point, theologians must show their cards! Is the difference between the "historical" Jesus and the "real" Jesus in the reception and the empowering remembrance of Jesus by his followers and their communities, or did God do something with the dead Jesus, and as such provide an ontological foundation for remembrance and empowerment? Communities of resistance, peace, and justice struggle against the manifestations of the estranging and dehumanizing forces of death in our world. Yet the important theological question is whether their struggle is grounded in what God has done in defeating the estranging forces of death, or does "resurrection," the triumph of life over death, actually happen in their human activity?

John Dominic Crossan rejects the literal, physical, bodily resurrection of Jesus. Following his death, scavengers either devoured Jesus' corpse or it was thrown into a common grave or a lime pit. Crossan approvingly quotes Marianne Sawicki: "Lime eats the body quickly and hygienically."[47]

The birth of Christianity for Crossan was therefore not when Jesus after his death appeared to his disciples. According to Crossan, "the birth of Christianity is the interaction between the historical Jesus and his first companions and the continuation of that relationship despite his execution."[48] Christian faith is not Easter faith. Indeed, "the first Christian" happened to be before Easter. It was the nameless woman in Mark 14:3-9 because she saw God in Jesus and believed the passion-resurrection predictions of Jesus as recorded in Mark 8:31, 9:31, and 10:33f.[49]

Nevertheless, Crossan does not want to avoid the language of "bodily," even "fleshly" resurrection. He rejects the Hellenistic dualism between flesh and spirit as un-Christian and dehumanizing, and he is critical of what he perceives as St. Paul's compromise with Hellenism. Although resurrection for Crossan has nothing to do with Jesus' dead body, he insists on its "fleshliness": "Resurrected life and risen vision appear as offered shelter and shared meal. Resurrection is not enough. You still need scripture and eucharist, tradition and table, community and justice; otherwise, divine presence remains unrecognized and human eyes remain unopened."[50]

What leaves me uncertain, whether or not I have done justice to John Dominic Crossan, is his comment that resurrection "is not enough." What does he mean? If he means that what God has begun with raising Jesus from the dead is the intensification of a process of liberation, peace, and justice that continues after Jesus' death in the same power that raised Jesus from the dead, I would readily agree. But I find Crossan somewhat unclear at that point. Picking up Paul's seed metaphor from 1 Corinthians 15, Crossan says:

> From seed to grain is a combination of absolutely the same and yet totally different. So with the resurrection. It is the same Jesus, the one and only historical Jesus of the late 20s in his Jewish homeland, but now untrammeled by time and place, language and proximity. It is the one and only Jesus, absolutely the same, absolutely different. He is trammeled, of course—then, now, and always—by faith. Bodily resurrection has nothing to do with a resuscitated body coming out of its tomb. And neither is bodily resurrection just another term for Christian faith itself. Bodily resurrection means that the *embodied* life and death of the historical Jesus continues to be experienced, by believers, as powerfully efficacious and salvifically present in the world.[51]

Perhaps the apologetic and confrontational climate in America with the seemingly unbridgeable gulf between conservative Evangelicals and the "Jesus Seminar" scholars has led to formulations that appear to be unclear and one-sided. What does it mean to say that Jesus is untrammelled by time and place, but trammelled by faith? We would readily agree, of course, that "bodily resurrection has nothing to do with a *resuscitated* body coming out of its tomb" and "neither is bodily resurrection just another term for Christian faith itself," but the question remains: does faith produce the risen Christ, or is the risen Christ the ground of faith?

Let me summarize. Crossan shows theological insight and sensitivity by marveling that God has revealed God's self in a Galilean peasant who lived in an occupied territory and showed solidarity with the oppressed and marginalized. This concern for justice is shaped in communities of resistance who continue after Jesus' death and who are empowered for the struggle by remembering the historical Jesus.

My concerns are not with Crossan's portrayal of the pre-Easter Jesus. His description of the life of Jesus is incisive and helpful. My fear is that by focusing all attention on that part of the Christ-event, he has in fact distorted the whole. A Christology that brackets out God's defeat of death in the cross and resurrection fails to gather not only the surface meaning of the New Testament texts but also their theological intentions. The Pauline verdict stands: "If Christ has not been raised, your faith is futile and you are still in your sins" (1 Cor 15:17).

A second point is related to Crossan's claim that the historical Jesus is experienced as "powerfully efficacious and salvifically present." I do not doubt, of course, that this can be the case. But I seriously doubt whether Crossan's theological foundation allows for that conclusion. Indeed, I suggest that by focusing all theological attention on the historical Jesus, Crossan's conclusion leads to a fundamental distortion of the Christian faith. Jesus is thereby inevitably understood in terms of an example, a hero, a good and noble human being. There is no doubt that we need examples such as Jesus to shape a meaningful human life. At the same time, an example becomes a burden and even produces guilt when we become aware that we can't measure up to it. An example cannot liberate us from what the Bible calls sin. Christian faith therefore confesses Christ not only as friend, hero, and example, but also as life-giving, liberating, and empowering savior. Christian faith lives from the awareness that in Christ, God has not only shown us how to live, has not only loved the world, but has in fact reconciled the world with God's self and thereby laid the foundation on which we can build our lives.

My basic objection to Crossan's view of the resurrection is that his "real Jesus" does not seem to include the necessity of God doing for us what needed to be done and what we could not do for ourselves: that he died for our sins and rose for our justification (Rom 4:24f.). If Jesus is primarily an example, then faith is reduced to morality and thereby contravenes the very intention of Crossan—to portray a spirituality of empowerment. I suggest therefore that both "liberals" and "conservatives" encourage a reduction of faith. While Crossan is in danger of moralizing faith, conservative evangelicals are, as I will show later, in danger of intellectualizing faith. Crossan's insights are important for understanding the *content* of faith. He underestimates the importance of uncovering the liberating *ground* of faith.

Gerd Lüdemann

What scholars have called the "subjective vision hypothesis" has recently been revived by the German theologian Gerd Lüdemann. The hypothesis is old,[52] but Gerd Lüdemann has redressed and presented it in contemporary psychological categories. His book, published in 1994, and subsequently followed by a more popular version,[53] immediately hit the headlines of both the religious and the secular media.

Lüdemann's approach is interesting because his conclusions claim to be the results of serious exegetical scholarship. His exegetical deliberations move within the generally accepted radius of contemporary New Testament scholarship. The various results are neither unknown nor uncommon. One may quarrel about a detail here and there, but on the whole Lüdemann uses the same methodology practiced by contemporary exegetical scholars. This fact shows clearly that the major theological decisions have to be made not in the interpretation of texts, but in the interpretation of reality.

Although the subtitle of Lüdemann's book is "History, Experience, Theology," in fact he is primarily interested in history, although one gains the strong impression that his conclusions are prefigured by experience. He accepts uncritically the modern Western secular understanding of history. When it comes to experience, his main concerns are with the experiences of Peter and Paul, and, in relation to them, with some modern analogies that may shed light on their experiences. But he shows no interest in the experiences of Christians who received, adapted, and passed on the earliest traditions, and he pays no attention to the experiences of Christians through the ages and around the world. His own experience is probably the determining factor for his scientific conclusions. When it comes to theology, the results are meager, limited to what fits his understanding of history and his experience. He claims a primary interest in history: ". . . the investigation which follows will look in a purely historical and empirical way at the historical context of the testimonies of the resurrection . . . ."[54]

Given the modern Western scientific worldview, which does not allow for a literal physical resurrection from the dead, and given Lüdemann's conviction that according to the New Testament texts Jesus' resurrection can only be understood in material, physical terms, the conclusion is preprogrammed. The resurrection as portrayed in the New Testament cannot be true. The criterion for truth is not found in the texts, but in our modern Western view of natural science. It is *our* understanding and experience of reality that serves as the hermeneutical filter for the reality to which the texts witness.

This leaves us with the questions as to why and how the appearance stories and the empty tomb stories came into being. For Lüdemann, the appearance stories came into being when the early Christians told the stories of Peter's and Paul's primal "Easter" experiences. God did not cause these experiences. They did not result from an external influence like an act of God or an appearance of Christ. They were visions, internal psychological processes, that can be understood, explained, and interpreted within Peter's and Paul's biographies and states of mind. The appearance narratives therefore explain and thereby objectify what happened in the experience of Peter, Paul, and others. Lüdemann, like Crossan, says that "the tomb of Jesus was not empty, but full, and his body did not disappear, but rotted away,"[55] but in contrast to Crossan, Lüdemann recognizes the importance of primal "appearances" to Peter and Paul. He interprets these "experiences" in terms of depth psychology.[56]

The pre-Christian Paul had a Christ-complex.[57] As a practicing religious Jew, he found the Christian emphasis on a crucified Messiah and the Christian critique of Torah and temple offensive. At the same time, he was subconsciously attracted by the witness of Christians to the story of Jesus as the manifestation of God's universal and unconditional love. Paul overplayed this subconscious attraction by an increased zealousness for the law. The unresolved conflict between the subconscious attraction to the gospel and his zealous commitment to the law issued in aggression. Paul became a religious fanatic and as such a persecutor of Christians. Finally, however, Paul's "inner build-up . . . was formally released in a vision of Christ."[58] Paul's subconscious religious longings won the upper hand over his zealousness for the law. He found the fulfillment for his religious longing by centering his conscience on the story of Jesus. He experienced Christ as the liberation from the prison of law, sin, and death. The Damascus vision of Christ brought into consciousness the story of Jesus as the answer to Paul's suppressed religious needs.

In Peter's case,[59] the unexpected death of his Master and friend threw him into a crisis. It would normally take a long process of mourning before the living memory of Jesus would slowly fade away. This process of mourning was interrupted and frustrated by Peter's memory, and the guilt-feelings associated with it, that he had denied Jesus in the hour of crisis. The conflict of memories became too painful to endure, and consequently "he breaks off the mourning process abruptly by replacing the dead Jesus with a living picture of Jesus which is true to reality."[60] This happened in an inner vision—again without any external influence—in which God's unconditional grace and forgiveness, already present in the life of Jesus, were newly experienced and confirmed. The availability and certainty of grace replaced his guilt feelings and made up for the interrupted process of mourning.[61]

The appearance to the 500 brethren (1 Cor 15:6) for Lüdemann is the same as the Pentecost gathering (Acts 2) and needs to be understood in terms of a "mass ecstasy" or "mass psychosis" initiated by the experiences of Peter and Paul and the preaching that followed their experiences.[62] Within the wider radius of the mass psychosis, we also have to place the appearance to James and to the twelve.

The primal visions of Peter and Paul, confirmed and intensified by the mass ecstasy and the individual vision of James, led to the general conclusion that God had raised Jesus from the dead.[63] But, to Lüdemann, in light of our modern understanding of reality, such a conclusion cannot stand the test of time. The people then believed it to be true, but we must judge their belief to be an illusion. The visions have no external referent. Historically speaking, Jesus' body decayed.[64] Consequently, "God must no longer be assumed to be the author of these visions. . . . Rather, these were psychological processes which ran their course with a degree of regularity—complete without divine intervention."[65]

Nevertheless, given the objectification and rationalization of their experience, they still needed to explain the question as to what happened to Jesus' corpse. In answer to potential Jewish opponents and also to give expression to their own conviction, the tradition that lies behind the empty tomb narratives evolved.

What then, according to Gerd Lüdemann, is the origin and meaning of "Easter" if there was no external catalyst to the experiences of the disciples? Easter is located in the primal visions of Peter and Paul. They experienced Jesus as forgiving and liberating after failing to honor him through denial or by the persecution of his followers. The understanding and analysis of these "Easter appearances" is decisive because they in fact constitute the beginning of Christianity. Our faith in Christ would be in trouble if it cannot be shown that the experiences of Peter and Paul do not contain some universal religious significance.

In his books on the resurrection, Lüdemann still argues that it is possible for us today to maintain a meaningful Christian faith: "So to the question 'Can we still be Christians?' the answer is a confident 'Yes.'"[66] Christian faith here is not based on the resurrection of Jesus, nor is it based on the subjective visions of Peter, Paul, and others. It is based, as with Crossan, on the *objective* reality of the pre-Easter historical Jesus.[67] Focusing our faith on the historical Jesus as he is reconstructed for us from the Gospels will assure us that God is a gracious, forgiving, liberating God. Nevertheless, on reflection, Lüdemann realized that faith in Jesus still implied a "resurrection,"[68] which consequently led him to having to say farewell not only to the resurrection but also to Jesus.[69]

We must conclude therefore that in Lüdemann's view the appearances of Christ had no ontological depth. The appearances were not grounded in God's raising Jesus from the dead. They were grounded in Peter's and Paul's psychological makeup, their needs and desires. Again, we note the shift of emphasis. While for Crossan the shift was from the resurrection to the historical Jesus, for Lüdemann it was from the resurrection to the psychological constellations of Peter and Paul. In both cases, a modern understanding of history, determined by the "omnipotence of analogy"[70] and therefore not allowing for an act of God, has served as a hermeneutical filter for interpreting the New Testament resurrection texts.

Where are we? I suggest that both John Dominic Crossan and Gerd Lüdemann reduce reality to their "liberal" view of history, which is dominated by the "omnipotence of analogy" and therefore has no room for a *novum*.[71] With Lüdemann's intention to undertake a historical investigation, and given his understanding of history, his results were preprogrammed. How can a methodology that in principle excludes acts of God and events that have no analogy in our human experience understand and explain the earliest Christian confession that "God raised Jesus from the dead"? At stake here is not the interpretation of texts, but the understanding of reality with which we approach and read the texts. It is the task of the theologian not to reduce God-talk to our modern understanding of reality, but to insist that God is "more" than our understanding postulates. The theologian is primarily interested in that "more."

I suggest therefore that Lüdemann and, less clearly, Crossan operate with an alternative that in fact leads to a reduction of reality. Their alternative seems to be that either Jesus was physically resurrected from death, with the implication that the tomb into which his corpse had been laid must have been empty, or "resurrection" does not refer to any action of God with reference to Jesus. In such a scheme, "resurrection" can only be a metaphor for the significance of the historical Jesus or for the experience of the disciples.

The same unsatisfactory reduction of reality is the failure to distinguish between central and marginal symbols in the New Testament. Lüdemann throws everything in the same basket: the bodily resurrection, the bodily ascension, the bodily return. His citation from Emanuel Hirsch adds to the caricature: "Where is he, if he really emerged from the tomb through a divine resuscitation into a transfigured healthy human body which is now different from the old body that existed before the crucifixion only by the addition of some miraculous extra properties?"[72] It is my contention that the resurrection is not just one miraculous event among others, but that it is the one decisive foundational event from which many other symbols are derived. Although Lüdemann is aware of the distinction between historical and eschatological[73] categories, he dismisses it too easily.

This leads to a reduction of reality, which the biblical resurrection texts already recognized and opposed. The resurrection narratives in the Gospels on the one hand speak of the massive bodily presence of the risen one, and on the other hand they portray him as walking through closed doors. Not only faith, but also doubt, uncertainty, surprise, and wonder are important motifs in the resurrection narratives (Matt 28:17; Luke 24:41; Mark 16:14). The apostle Paul, trying to answer the questions "How are the dead raised? With what kind of body do they come?" (1 Cor 15:35), speaks of continuity and of discontinuity.

To illustrate continuity, Paul uses the metaphor of a seed. You sow a bare seed, "perhaps of wheat or of some other grain," and then "God gives it a body as he has chosen, and to each kind of seed its own body" (1 Cor 15:37f.). The fact that all "bodies" have a "flesh" and a "glory" that is specific to them assures that within the discontinuity between the "perishable" and the "imperishable" there is also continuity. Paul argues:

> Not all flesh is alike, but there is one flesh for human beings, another for animals, another for birds, and another for fish. There are both heavenly bodies and earthly bodies, but the glory of the heavenly is one thing, and that of the earthly is another. There is one glory of the sun, and another glory of the moon, and another glory of the stars; indeed, star differs from star in glory. So it is with the resurrection of the dead. What is sown is perishable, what is raised is imperishable. It is sown in dishonor, it is raised in glory. It is sown in weakness, it is raised in power. It is sown a physical body, it is raised a spiritual body. If there is a physical body, there is also a spiritual body. (1 Cor 15:39-44)

Within this description there is already enough fluidity to resist any rationalization and objectification. This becomes even clearer with Paul's emphasis on discontinuity:

> Listen, I will tell you a mystery! We will not all die, but we will all be changed, in a moment, in the twinkling of an eye, at the last trumpet. For the trumpet will sound, and the dead will be raised imperishable, and we will be changed. For this perishable body must put on imperishability, and this mortal body must put on immortality. (1 Cor 15:51-53)

Between the brief discussion on continuity and discontinuity, there is Paul's strong warning against any crude materialism or objectification: "What I am saying, brothers and sisters, is this: flesh and blood cannot inherit the kingdom of God, nor does the perishable inherit the imperishable" (1 Cor 15:50).

Paul's insightful and sensitive God-talk is based on his conviction of God's sovereignty (v. 38). That question will continue to remain with us. How can we in our reflection remain cognizant of God's sovereignty? If there is a God, and if God's being together with us and with God's creation is not dissolved into God's creation, then there must be room for mystery, for *novum*, for surprise. And if the resurrection texts and the experience of Christians through the ages and around the world so powerfully witness to that mystery, that *novum*, and that surprise, what right do we have to reduce reality to our perception of it? With both Crossan and Lüdemann I have the impression that their will to define reality on our terms has in fact reduced it.

In fact, their argument dissolves the christological basis for salvation. What is left are the words of Jesus and the memory of a life that is past. But Jesus' words—be they the Lord's prayer or the parables or the wisdom sayings—are bound to his person. His words of forgiveness, his call to discipleship, his revolutionary suspension of Torah and cult, his solidarity with publicans and sinners make no sense apart from his actual personal presence. One cannot reduce Jesus to his words and deeds. The words and deeds hang in the air apart from his person. We shall have to ask whether there is a way beyond a crude materialism on the one hand and a groundless subjectivism on the other. Can we find ways to understand and elaborate the New Testament insistence that resurrection did not mean Jesus was brought back to this life but that by raising Jesus from the dead God defeated death itself? "We know that Christ, being raised from the dead, will never die again; death no longer has dominion over him" (Rom 6:9; compare 1 Cor 15:54-57).

Before we develop that further, however, let us look at the other extreme of the theological spectrum.

William Lane Craig[74]

In portraying the conservative "evangelical" approach, we can be considerably briefer because that approach has a long tradition in the Christian church, it is fairly well known, and it is widely accepted by many or most intentional Christians. In a conversation with John Dominic Crossan, the conservative "evangelical" theologian William Lane Craig calls Crossan's view atheistic.[75] For Craig, resurrection describes what God has done with the dead corpse of Jesus. Craig believes "that Christ was literally, bodily, physically raised from the dead."[76]

He offers this conclusion as "the best explanation" of four historical facts that, in his view, the majority of New Testament scholars, both of the "conservative" and of the "liberal" persuasion, affirm:[77]

1. "After his crucifixion Jesus was buried by Joseph of Arimathea in his personal tomb."
2. "On the Sunday following the crucifixion, the tomb of Jesus was found empty by a group of his women followers."
3. "On multiple occasions and under various circumstances different individuals and groups of people experienced appearances of Jesus alive from the dead."
4. "The original disciples believed that Jesus was risen from the dead despite their having every reason not to."

For Craig, then, the resurrection became historically manifest and can therefore be verified in the historical facts that the tomb into which Jesus' corpse was laid was found empty and that the risen Jesus appeared to people after his death. All of this is considered necessary for salvation. Consequently, 1 Corinthians 15:17 is frequently quoted: "If Christ has not been raised, your faith is futile and you are still in your sins." A denial of the literal, physical resurrection of Jesus would reduce Christianity to "a fairy tale which no rational person should believe."[78]

Responding to Craig, I appreciate the shift of emphasis, that "resurrection" has to do with Jesus *first* and only then with the disciples and the community of believers. The various resurrection traditions in the New Testament concur in the one point: that God acted with reference to the dead Jesus and that act of God is the basis for our salvation.

Things become somewhat nebulous when Craig says, "The Christ of faith, who lives in my heart today, is the *same* person who once walked the shores of Galilee, hung on a Roman cross, and rose triumphantly from the tomb for our salvation."[79] Craig's intentions are clear and justified. He wants to safeguard the *content* of faith as being Christian by affirming the *continuity* between the Christ of faith and the Christ-event.[80] But the only way to distinguish between the Christ of faith and the "Christ of National Socialist Germany or the Christ of Catholic Ireland . . . the Christ of Jim Jones or David Koresh . . ."[81] is to capture and understand the vision that became discernible in Jesus' life and ministry. For that the work of John Dominic Crossan can actually be quite helpful. Craig considers it necessary that Jesus' life vision—what Craig calls Jesus' "radical personal claims to divinity"[82]—is confirmed by the resurrection, and he maintains that resurrection can only be conceived in literal physical terms.

Where I disagree with Craig and the theologians of his persuasion is not only in the arrogance of questioning the faith of their colleagues, but primarily in their assertion that Jesus' resurrection was literal, bodily, physical and as such open to rational historical analysis. Here Craig goes beyond New Testament claims. He satisfies human longings for rational proof. There are traces of such a quest in the New Testament, but the first clear expression of it we have in the *Gospel of Peter* (c. AD 150), which was not accepted into the Christian Canon.[83] There we read that after the death and burial of Jesus the tomb was carefully sealed with a "great stone" and "seven seals" and guarded by soldiers who "pitched a tent and kept watch" "lest his disciples come and steal him away and the people suppose that he is risen from the dead." Also scribes and elders and crowds from Jerusalem and the surrounding country witness this safety operation. The text then continues:

> Now in the night in which the Lord's day dawned, when the soldiers, two by two in every watch, were keeping guard, there rang a loud voice in heaven, and they saw the heavens opened and two men come down from there in a great brightness and draw nigh to the sepulchre. That stone which had been laid against the entrance to the sepulchre started of itself to roll and gave way to the side, and the sepulchre was opened, and both the young men entered in. When now the soldiers saw this, they wakened the centurion and the elders—for they also were there to assist at the watch. And whilst they were relating what they had seen, they saw again three men come down from the sepulchre, and two of them sustaining the other, and a cross following them, and the heads of the two reaching to heaven, but that of him who was led of them by the hand overpassing the heavens.

All of this climaxes in the confession (which in Mark 15:39 is made in front of the crucified Christ!): "In truth he was the Son of God."

In the New Testament itself, there are no impartial spectators to the resurrection, and where there are intimations to the contrary—as with Mary and Thomas in John 20—the evangelist sets the record straight: "Blessed are those who have not seen and yet have come to believe" (John 20:29). Theologians must carefully distinguish gospel and faith from fact and reason. Replacing the former with the latter leads to a fundamental distortion of faith.

Conclusion

So far we have engaged with contemporary theological voices about the resurrection of Jesus Christ. The discussion leaves us with the following impressions.

For many, the discussion is dominated by the question of what happened to Jesus' corpse after he was crucified and buried. Even when it was not explicitly stated, the empty tomb narratives were the main focus of the debate. "Evangelical" theologians insist that the empty tomb stories contain reliable historical information, while "liberal" and "existential" theologians suggest that these narratives are creations of the early church to meet certain apologetic challenges. For "liberal" theologians, Jesus corpse was devoured by scavengers or rotted away in a mass grave, while for "evangelical" theologians it was transfigured into a spiritual body. We shall have to ask whether the New Testament portrayal of the resurrection allows or encourages us to give such heavy theological emphasis on the empty tomb narratives.

This presupposes, of course, that we accept biblical authority and with it the theological emphases of the biblical traditions. This is a serious hermeneutical challenge. On the one hand, we live in totally different cultures than the biblical authors and communities did, but on the other hand we also do not want to absolutize our own cultural worldview. We have to oscillate sensitively. Our intention is to give priority to the theological intentions of the New Testament witnesses to the resurrection.

At that point, we find the "liberal" portrayals of Crossan and Lüdemann lacking. For them, revelation can only happen within the framework of a modern Western scientific worldview, a worldview intentionally designed to do without the hypothesis "God," which therefore has no room for an event that claims to be an act of God. In their view, all God-language has to be interpreted within categories of immanence that can be verified by our human experience. One is reminded of the famous encounter between Pierre Simon de Laplace and Napoleon. Napoleon asked the scientist where God featured in his system, to which Laplace replied, "I have no need for that hypothesis." In such a closed immanent system, divine appearances can only be interpreted as internal visions without any external catalyst, and the Christ-event can only include what we can ascertain about the historical Jesus and his death. What the Christian theological tradition has tried to capture in words such as the "atoning death of Jesus" and the "novum of his resurrection"—that, to use the words of the apostle Paul, Christ "was handed over to death for our trespasses and was raised for our justification" (Rom 4:25)—receives scant attention by these theologians. We miss the ontological depth of the event of salvation that is necessary to deal with the seriousness of human estrangement, self-interest, and sin.

With the evangelical theologians we affirm, therefore, that God has acted with respect to the dead Jesus. The early Christian confession that "God raised Jesus from the dead" points to an act of God that actually modified being. With the help of many different metaphors, the Bible and Christian tradition claim that by raising Jesus from the dead, God has defeated the estranging power of death and has therefore done something for us that we could not do for ourselves. Resurrection, therefore, is not a replaceable metaphor. It is a metaphor with ontological depth.

The metaphorical dimension of all God-language reminds us, however, that although "resurrection" may be the best metaphor available, yet, at the same time, the event must determine the language and not vice versa. Since the resurrection of Christ is an unexpected and new event, the metaphor "resurrection" must be open to new content. It must somehow gather up and express the Trinitarian reality that God, through the agency of the Spirit, raised Jesus from the dead. That is the ontological foundation for Christian faith and its social dimension, the Christian church.

I am dissatisfied with the theological importance that "evangelical" theologians assign to the literal, bodily, physical resurrection; and with their insistence that unprejudiced reason can prove the tomb was empty and that therefore Jesus must have risen from the dead. We saw that such argumentation is motivated more by a human need or desire for rational security rather than by the intentions of the biblical narratives. Here we need to proceed carefully. We shall need to ask whether the resurrection appearances are *sufficient* cause for confessing that God raised Jesus from the dead, and whether the empty tomb stories are *necessary* for that affirmation.

Our basic criticism against the historical objectivism with its emphasis on historical reason is twofold. First, their emphasis cannot be sustained from the message of the New Testament sources; and second, it would lead in fact to a fundamental distortion of the Christian faith.

Faith is not merely intellectual assent to historical truth. Faith is voluntary and liberating obedience to the gospel; it is repentance and a change of consciousness. Its seat is not the intellect, but the human conscience. The resurrection of Christ is not a divine suspension of the laws of nature and history, but it is God's way of dealing with the estranging forces of sin and death: "We know that Christ, being raised from the dead, will never die again; death no longer has dominion over him" (Rom 6:9).

The New Testament sources never narrate the resurrection as such, and they resist objectification. The risen Christ can be massively present and at the same time walk through closed doors and disappear. There are no neutral and disinterested observers to the resurrection appearances. It is only in the extracanonical *Gospel of Peter* that the human desire for objectification is given sway.[84]

Having raised and begun to discuss the major issues with regard to the resurrection of Christ, we must now examine the pillars of which a theology of the resurrection is built.

Notes

[1] John Dominic Crossan actively encourages a shift of theological emphasis from Paul to Jesus. He fears that Paul has been unduly influenced by a dehumanizing Hellenistic dualism, and he stipulates that the sixteenth century Reformation, rather than first-century Christianity, has moved Paul into the center of Christian theology. "If you begin with Paul, you will interpret Jesus incorrectly; if you begin with Jesus, you will interpret Paul differently" (*The Birth of Christianity* [New York: HarperCollins, 1998], xxi, compare xx-xxvii).

[2] Ernst Fuchs, Walter Künneth, *Die Auferstehung Jesu Christi von den Toten: Dokumentation eines Streitgesprächs,* Nach einer Tonbandaufzeichnung herausgegeben von Christian Möller (Neukirchen-Vluyn: Neukirchener Verlag, 1973).

[3] Ibid., 53f.

[4] Künneth's theses are summarized ibid. 12 and then dealt with throughout the book.

[5] Ibid., 13 (my translation).

[6] Fuchs's theses are summarized ibid. 13 and then explained throughout the book.

[7] For Künneth, see ibid. 118; for Fuchs, see ibid., 53.

[8] I still find Paul Tillich's distinction between ontological and technical reason helpful. Ontological reason receives reality, while technical reason ("reasoning") rationally digests what has been received. Technical reason becomes destructive when it is separated from ontological reason (*Reason and Revelation, Being and God,* Systematic Theology, vol. 1 [Chicago: University Press, 1951], 71-75).

[9] This is helpfully developed by Gerhard Ebeling, *Dogmatik des christlichen Glaubens,* Band 1 (Tübingen: J. C. B. Mohr, 1979), 219-24, 346-55.

[10] Terry L. Miethe, ed., *Did Jesus Rise From The Dead? The Resurrection Debate: Gary R. Habermas and Anthony G. N. Flew* (San Francisco: Harper & Row, 1987). The quote is taken from ix and xi.

[11] Ibid., ix, xif., 3.

[12] Ibid., 4 and often afterward.

[13] Ibid., xii, 3.

[14] Ibid., 180.

[15] Ibid., 3-13, 33-37, 49-72, 75-121.

[16] Ibid., 16. Habermas's contributions are found in ibid., 15-32, 39-47, 49-72, 75-121, 153-83.

[17] Ibid., 17.

[18] Ibid., 20, 25.

[19] Wolfhart Pannenberg's response is found in ibid., 125-35.

[20] Ibid., 131.

[21] Ibid., 135.

[22] James I. Packer's response is found in ibid., 142-50. The above quote is found on 145.

[23] Habermas says quite emphatically that "facts . . . are actually the foundation for a faith commitment" (Ibid., 153).

[24] Stephen T. Davis, Daniel Kendall, Gerald O'Collins, SJ, eds., *The Resurrection: An Interdisciplinary Symposium on the Resurrection of Jesus* (New York: Oxford University Press, 1997). Further conversations include C.F.D. Moule and Don Cupitt, "The Resurrection: A Disagreement," *Theology: A Monthly Review* 75/628 (October 1972): 507-19; Paul Avis, ed., *The Resurrection of Jesus Christ* (London: Darton, Longmann, and Todd, 1993); Stephen Barton and Graham Stanton, eds., *Resurrection: Essays in Honour of Leslie Houlden* (London: SPCK, 1994); Alexander Bommarius, ed., *Fand die Aufesrtehung wirklich statt? Eine Diskussion mit Gerd Lüdemann* (Düsseldorf: Pererga Verlag, 1995); Gavin D'Costa, ed., *Resurrection Reconsidered* (Oxford: Oneworld, 1996).

[25] "The Resurrection of Jesus and Roman Catholic Fundamental Theology," in Davis et al., eds., *The Resurrection: An Interdisciplinary Symposium*, 212-48.

[26] Ibid., 248.

[27] Ibid., 245.

[28] Gerald O'Collins, "The Resurrection: The State of the Question," in Davis et al., eds., *The Resurrection: An Interdisciplinary Symposium*, 5-28; Peter Carnley, "Response," in ibid., 29-40.

[29] Ibid., 40.

[30] This is well explicated by Jürgen Moltmann in *The Crucified God: The Cross of Christ as the Foundation and Criticism of Christian Theology*, trans. R. A. Wilson and John Bowden (London: SCM, 1974), 32-81.

[31] "Transformation Ethics: The Moral Implications of the Resurrection," in Davis et al., eds., *The Resurrection: An Interdisciplinary Symposium*, 339-60.

[32] Ibid., 346.

[33] Paul Copan, ed., *Will the Real Jesus Please Stand Up? A Debate between William Lane Craig and John Dominic Crossan*, moderated by William F. Buckley Jr. (Grand Rapids MI: Baker Books, 1998).

[34] I have made an attempt to do so in *Resurrection and Discipleship: Interpretive Models, Biblical Reflections, Theological Consequences* (Maryknoll NY: Orbis, 1995), pt. 1, 7-111, where I have portrayed and discussed four models for understanding the resurrection of Christ: the "traditional" approach, the "liberal" approach, the "evangelical" approach, and the "liberation" approach.

[35] For a survey, see Anthony C. Thiselton, *New Horizons in Hermeneutics* (London: HarperCollins, 1992).

[36] Karl Barth, *Der Römerbrief*, 2d ed. (München: Chr. Kaiser Verlag, 1924), XII. The English translation fails to convey the pathos: "The critical historian needs to be more critical" (Karl Barth, *The Epistle to the Romans*, trans. Edwyn C. Hoskyns, preface to 2d ed., in 6th ed. [London: Oxford University Press, 1968], 8). Compare Friedrich-Wilhelm Marquardt, "Exegese und Dogmatik in Karl Barths Theologie. Was meint 'Kritischer müßten mir die Historisch-Kritischen sein!?," in Karl Barth, *Die Kirchliche*

Dogmatik. Registerband unter Mitarbeit von Wolfgang Eck und Marcel Pfändler, hrsg. von Helmut Krause (Zürich: EVZ-Verlag, 1970), 649-76 (this essay has been omitted from the English translation).

[37] The "in me" in Matthew 18:6 is most likely a post-Easter editorial interpretation of Mark 9:42, which in its earliest version probably did not have the phrase.

[38] From the many writings of John Dominic Crossan, I concentrate on *The Birth of Christianity* (New York: HarperCollins, 1998); Paul Copan, ed., *Will the Real Jesus Please Stand Up? A Debate between William Lane Craig and John Dominic Crossan* (1998), 33-39, 45-67, 71, 147-55; "Historical Jesus as Risen Lord," in John Dominic Crossan, Luke Timothy Johnson, and Werner H. Kelber, *The Jesus Controversy: Perspectives in Conflict* (Harrisburg PA: Trinity Press International, 1999), 1-47; *Jesus: A Revolutionary Biography* (San Francisco: Harper, 1995).

[39] *Will the Real Jesus Please Stand Up?*, 148, compare 35.

[40] Crossan, *Jesus: A Revolutionary Biography*, 160.

[41] Willy Marxsen, *Die Sache Jesu geht weiter* (Gütersloh: Gerd Mohn, 1978); "The Resurrection of Jesus as a Historical and Theological Problem," in C. F. D. Moule, ed., *The Significance of the Message of the Resurrection of Faith in Jesus Christ*, Studies in Biblical Theology, 2d series, 8 (London: SCM, 1968, 15-50) 38; *The Resurrection of Jesus of Nazareth*, trans. Margaret Kohl (Philadelphia: Fortress, 1970), 147f. Compare the discussion of Marxsen's view by Gerhard Friedrich, "Die Auferweckung Jesu, eine Tat Gottes oder ein Interpretament der Jünger?" *KuD* 17 (1971), 153-87, and Bertold Klappert, *Die Auferweckung des Gekreuzigten: Der Ansatz der Christologie Karl Barths im Zusammenhang der Christologie der Gegenwart* (Neukirchen-Vluyn: Neukirchener Verlag, 1971), 36-53.

[42] Compare Crossan, *Jesus: A RevolutionaryBiography*, chs. 3–5.

[43] For details, see Albrecht Oepke, "ἀνίστημι κτλ.," in *Theological Dictionary of the New Testament* (*TDNT*) 1 (1964 [1933]): 368-72, and "ἐγείρω κτλ.," in *TDNT* 2 (1964 [1935]): 333-39.

[44] Crossan, *Jesus: A Revolutionary Biography*, 163.

[45] Crossan says, "There is . . . only one Jesus, the embodied Galilean who lived a life of divine justice in an unjust world, who was officially and legally executed by that world's accredited representatives, and whose continued empowering presence indicates, for believers, that God is not on the side of injustice. . . . There are not two Jesuses, one pre-Easter and another post-Easter, one earthly and another heavenly, one with a physical and another with a spiritual body. There is only one Jesus, the *historical* Jesus who incarnated, for believers, the Jewish God of justice. . . ." ("Historical Jesus as Risen Lord," 45).

[46] Crossan, *Will the Real Jesus Please Stand Up?*, 33.

[47] Crossan, *Birth of Christianity*, xxvii, see 528; *Will the Real Jesus Please Stand Up?*, 29; "Historical Jesus as Risen Lord," 17f., 25f.

[48] Crossan, *Birth of Christianity*, xxi.

[49] Crossan, *Birth of Christianity*, 558; "Historical Jesus as Risen Lord," 11f.; *The Historical Jesus: The Life of a Mediterranean Jewish Peasant* (San Francisco: HarperCollins, 1991), 416. As an aside, it is interesting to note that for most critical scholars these predictions are at least in part creations of the early church.

[50] *Birth of Christianity*, xi.

[51] Ibid., xxxf.

[52] I have presented and discussed the Subjective Vision hypothesis of David Friedrich Strauss (1808–1874) in *Resurrection and Discipleship*, 50f., 61f., 122-24, 142, 295.

[53] Gerd Lüdemann, *The Resurrection of Jesus: History, Experience, Theology*, trans. John Bowden (London: SCM, 1994); Gerd Lüdemann in collaboration with Alf Özen, *What Really Happened to Jesus: A historical approach to the resurrection*, trans. John Bowden (London: SCM, 1995); Gerd Lüdemann, "Die Auferstehung Jesu," in Alexander Bommarius (Hrsg.), *Fand die Auferstehung wirklich statt? Eine Diskussion mit Gerd Lüdemann* (Düsseldorf: Pererga Verlag, 1995), 11-29.

⁵⁴ *Resurrection of Jesus*, 14f.

⁵⁵ *What Really Happened to Jesus*, 135, italicized in the original.

⁵⁶ *Resurrection of Jesus*, 81.

⁵⁷ *Resurrection of Jesus*, 79-84, 96f.; *What Really Happened to Jesus*, 102-30.

⁵⁸ *Resurrection of Jesus*, 83.

⁵⁹ *Resurrection of Jesus*, 95-100; *What Really Happened to Jesus*, 83-94, 129f.

⁶⁰ *What Really Happened to Jesus*, 94.

⁶¹ *Resurrection of Jesus*, 96.

⁶² *Resurrection of Jesus*, 100-108; *What Really Happened to Jesus*, 99-102.

⁶³ *Resurrection of Jesus*, 26.

⁶⁴ Ibid., 180.

⁶⁵ *What Really Happened to Jesus*, 130.

⁶⁶ Ibid., 136, italicized in the original.

⁶⁷ *Resurrection of Jesus*, 180-84.

⁶⁸ Gerd Lüdemann, "A letter to Jesus," in *The Great Deception* (Amherst NY: Prometheus Books, 1999, 1-9), 7: ". . . I now know that in my attempts to attach myself to you and understand you as the basis of my life, I was still secretly living from Easter, from your Easter image, which is based on the church's dogma." Lüdemann writes of "the collapse of the idea of a creation from nothing, . . . the hoax of your 'resurrection' and the impossibility of ethics on the basis of your preaching. . . . My attempts to define your 'resurrection' as a [*sic*] experience of forgiveness, as an experience of eternity and an experience of life had to fail, because these experiences can also be had apart from your person and your 'resurrection', and do not depend on what you called God" (8).

⁶⁹ Gerd Lüdemann, "A letter to Jesus," in *The Great Deception*, 1-9. He speaks of "a dream which freed me from this super-father, not to say superstition" (6). "So, Lord Jesus, an end to all that. I can no longer bear the totally confused situation of theology, the church and the Bible" (8f.).

⁷⁰ For more details, see my *Resurrection and Discipleship*, 39-42.

⁷¹ For more detail concerning "liberal theology" and the importance of the *novum* in resurrection theology, see my *Resurrection and Discipleship*, 36-63, 116-26.

⁷² *Resurrection of Jesus*, 181.

⁷³ Ibid., 180.

⁷⁴ Paul Copan, ed., *Will the Real Jesus Please Stand Up?*, 25-32, 40-44, 48-70, 156-79; Craig's major work on the resurrection is *Assessing the New Testament Evidence for the Historicity of the Resurrection of Jesus*, Studies in the Bible and Early Christianity 16 (Lewiston NY: Edwin Mellen, 1989).

⁷⁵ In *Will the Real Jesus Please Stand Up?*, 174.

⁷⁶ Ibid., 43.

⁷⁷ Ibid., 160f., 26-29.

⁷⁸ Ibid., 25, 31, 69.

⁷⁹ Ibid., 32 (emphasis mine), compare 43f.

⁸⁰ Ibid., 43f.

⁸¹ Ibid., 43, 69.

⁸² Ibid., 25, compare 40, 157-71.

⁸³ Of the *Gospel of Peter*, only a fragment has been found. It was probably written around AD 150 in Gnostic circles in Syria. Text and introduction in Edgar Hennecke, *Gospels and Related Writings*, vol. 1 of

New Testament Apocrypha, ed. Wilhelm Schneemelcher, trans. R. McL. Wilson (Philadelphia: Westminster, 1963), 179-87; the text to which I refer is found on 185f. In the New Testament, there are traces of the same tendency in those Gospel texts in which the tomb is guarded by soldiers (Matt 27:62-66), or where male witnesses authenticate the empty tomb tradition (Luke 24:12,25; John 20:2-10). But these texts do not acquire independent value. They are part of a story that emphasizes the *reality* of the resurrection *without objectifying* it. Similar to the text in the *Gospel of Peter* is a text from the *Gospel of the Hebrews* (AD 150?): "And when the Lord had given the linen cloth to the servant of the priest, he went to James and appeared to him. . . . And . . . the Lord said: Bring a table and bread! And immediately it is added: he took the bread, blessed it and broke it and gave it to James the Just and said to him: My brother, eat thy bread, for the Son of man is risen from among them that sleep" (§7, Hennecke, *Gospels and Related Writings*, 165).

[84] For details, see my *Resurrection and Discipleship*, 30f., 174-76.

Chapter 2

The Resurrection of the Crucified Christ: Real and Relational

. . . in fact Christ has been raised from the dead, the first fruits of those who have died. —1 Corinthians 15:20

Construction

Where do we go from here? Is there a way beyond the dilemmas with which the debates between "liberal," "existential," and "evangelical" theologians have left us? Can we take seriously that God has acted in raising Jesus from death and at the same time avoid "freezing" the resurrection into the past? We must, however briefly, revisit the main pillars on which a theology of resurrection is built and ask what understanding of ontology the resurrection of Christ calls for.

As we proceed, we must remain aware of certain limitations. Theological humility is in order when we approach and try to understand the divine. What we know and experience and say may not be identical with what really is. There is always some distortion, for instance, between who God really is and how we experience and express God in our lives. We must resist human attempts to define "being" because when we try to do so, we too easily subject "being" to our categories and our interests. Theologians, for instance, are in constant danger of trying to define God and thereby functionalize God for their own interests and thereby offend against the second commandment. Definitions may be attempts to understand, but they can also be means to control and, as such, they reveal an attitude inappropriate in relation to God. It belongs to the work of the theologian, therefore, to guard the mystery of God by reminding us to take off our shoes when we come into the presence of the divine.

At the same time, as Christian theologians, we claim that God has revealed God's nature in terms that invite and enable human understanding.[1] God-language is therefore possible, although it must be carefully chosen. Yet the conviction that *God* has chosen to share God's life with Jesus not only enables us to speak of God, but it also empowers us to make ontological claims. Naturally, we must avoid idolatry. We do that by refusing to make claims of infallibility for our very human and therefore very fallible theological attempts to grasp the divine and then gather into words what we have seen and felt and understood. Nevertheless, our theological statements do *imply* an ontology. The theological challenge is to figure out what kind of ontology God's revelation in Jesus Christ calls for. Let us visit again the major pillars of a theology of the risen Christ and ask how close we can get to the event and what way of understanding and of speaking is appropriate to the event.

The Appearances

Among those who agree that "resurrection" is not a replaceable metaphor but the ontological foundation for Christian faith, there is a wide consensus that the appearances of Christ after the death of Jesus are the *primary* data for confessing that God raised Jesus from the dead.

With the appearances, the event of the resurrection reaches out and begins to manifest what God has established in the Christ-event. The Christ-event includes both the *event* of reconciliation and the *ministry* of reconciliation. This becomes explicit in 2 Corinthians 5:17-21:

> . . . if anyone is in Christ, there is a new creation: everything old has passed away; see, everything has become new! All this is from God, who *reconciled* us to himself through Christ, and has given us the *ministry* of reconciliation; that is, in Christ God was *reconciling* the world to himself, not counting their trespasses against them, and entrusting the *message* of reconciliation to us. So *we* are ambassadors for Christ, since *God* is making his appeal through *us*; we entreat you on behalf of Christ, be reconciled to God. For our sake he made him to be sin who knew no sin, so that in him we might become the righteousness of God.

God the creator reclaims God's creation. Although humanity has separated itself from God by arrogating divinity to itself, God continues to love the *world* (John 3:16), and since God "desires *everyone* to be saved and to come to the knowledge of the truth" (1 Tim 2:4), therefore God has reconciled the *world* with God.

Here the fact that God *is* love and that God has concretely displayed that divine love in Jesus Christ becomes historically manifest. By sharing God's life with the human person Jesus and by raising him from death, God has made God's nature known as the one who is with and for others. The resurrection appearances are not the resurrection itself. They are implied in the resurrection in the sense that what God does, God does for others. In a helpful formulation, Michael Welker says, "An appearance is essentially a 'being for others.'"[2] With the appearances, the resurrection begins to influence and shape history.

The appearances are grounded in the resurrection. They are not themselves the ground of faith. They point to the crucified and risen Christ as the ground of faith. At the same time, they reveal the resurrection as an "open" event. The New Testament uses various images to underscore that the resurrection is not a closed event, finished and frozen into the past. It is the outworking of something new. The risen Christ is therefore understood as "the *first fruits* of those who have died" (1 Cor 15:20, 23) and as "the *firstborn* from the dead" (Col 1:18, compare Rom 8:29; Rev 1:5). Indeed, there is a saying in the Matthean passion story that was originally part of the resurrection tradition. It paints a dramatic apocalyptic picture about the consequences of the resurrection of Jesus: "The tombs also were opened, and many bodies of the saints who had fallen asleep were raised. After his resurrection they came out of the tombs and entered the holy city and appeared to many" (Matt 27:52f.). The power of death is broken. Reality has been changed and this change has consequences for the living and the dead.

The well-known resurrection tradition in 1 Corinthians 15:3-5 makes the same point in a more subtle manner. Most of the verbs are in the aorist tense describing events that have concluded: "Christ *died* [aorist tense] . . . he was *buried* [aorist tense] . . . he *appeared* [aorist tense] . . . ." But then, in ostentatious difference from the aorist tense of the surrounding verbs, we have an assertion in the *perfect* tense: "he has been raised." The use of the perfect tense stands out. It is intentionally used to underline the "continuing effect"[3] of the event of resurrection.

This is an important point. The resurrection is portrayed as the beginning of the end when God will be all in all, when the defeat of death and its life-destroying forces will be consummated. In biblical and theological terms, life and death cannot be reduced to their material aspects. Life and death have to do with the formation and sustaining of relationships. On the basis of the resurrection of Christ, the believer can and does confess with the apostle Paul that *nothing* can break the relationship between God and God's people: "For I am convinced that neither death, nor life, nor angels, nor rulers, nor things present, nor things to come, nor powers, nor height, nor depth, nor anything else in all creation, will be able to separate us from the love of God in Christ Jesus our Lord" (Rom 8:38f.).

This *relational* and *universal* dimension of the resurrection is underlined by the fact that the appearances, which make the resurrection manifest, contain two motifs: the coming to faith and the sending to mission.

The correlation of God and faith is a biblical maxim. There were no neutral observers to the resurrection appearances. Even Paul and James, who were drawn into the Christ-event as opponents and unbelievers, emerged from it as followers. The resurrection does not presuppose faith, and faith does not postulate or create the resurrection. The Spirit of God who raised Jesus from the dead is in being for others and therefore aims at the creation of faith. The New Testament writings insist therefore that an encounter with the risen Christ creates faith. To recognize the risen Christ implies acknowledging him as "Lord."

The creation of faith is closely interrelated with the call to mission. The reason for this is that the God who creates faith is the God who wants to implement what God has established in the Christ-event—the salvation of the world. Resurrection faith does not encourage a private and individualistic piety as an end in itself. It draws the believer into God's passion for the world.

This can be illustrated well with the testimony of the apostle Paul. Paul interweaves the appearance of Christ with his call to faith and mission:

> ... when God, who had set me apart before I was born and called me through his grace, *was pleased to reveal his Son to me, so that I might proclaim him among the Gentiles*, I did not confer with any human being, nor did I go up to Jerusalem to those who were already apostles before me, but I went away at once into Arabia, and afterwards I returned to Damascus. (Gal 1:15-17, emphasis mine)

The same interlocking between the resurrection appearances and the call to faith and mission is also evident from the Gospel narratives:

> ... Jesus came and said to them, "All authority in heaven and on earth has been given to me. Go therefore and make disciples of all nations, baptizing them in the name of the Father and of the Son and of the Holy Spirit, teaching them to observe all that I have commanded you; and lo, I am with you always, to the close of the age." (Matt 28:19f.)

There are other similar texts in which the resurrection of Christ and the call to mission are interrelated: Mark 16:15; Luke 24:46-49; Acts 1:8; John 20:21. Through Christ, God the creator has reconciled creation with the creator. But since God is love, reconciliation calls for voluntary agreement. It cannot be coerced and it cannot be automatic. The bearers of the good news must manifest the content of the gospel in their existence. Freedom, nonviolence, and the appealing request—"we appeal to you (δεόμεθα) on behalf of Christ, be reconciled to God" (2 Cor 5:20)—shape the content and form of reconciliation.

We conclude that the appearances of the risen Christ reveal the resurrection as a *relational* event. It is an event *for others*. It gives expression to the fact that God *is* love. To share the reality, which God has established by raising Jesus from the dead, belongs to the very nature of the resurrection. The gift of faith and the call to mission of the early disciples are therefore an inherent part of the reality of the resurrection. But within the experience and activity of faith and mission the *extra nos* is never forgotten:

> For *we do not proclaim ourselves; we proclaim Jesus Christ as Lord* and ourselves as your slaves for Jesus' sake. For it is the God who said, "Let light shine out of darkness," who has shone in our hearts to give the light of the knowledge of the glory of God in the face of Jesus Christ. (2 Cor 4:5f., emphasis mine)

It is therefore inadequate and indeed self-defeating to describe the experiences of the earliest witnesses merely in historical or psychological terms. One can do that, of course. And in certain situations one may have to do it for apologetic purposes. One may have to argue that a worldview and a methodology in which the dimensions of God and faith are excluded in principle are inadequate to gather up human experience. But the emphasis in the resurrection texts and narratives is on God's defeat of the estranging powers of death. This triumph of God over death is revealed in the resurrection appearances that are received in faith, obedience, and ministry. They are the necessary and sufficient ground for asserting that ultimately we are not surrounded by death, but by life; not by darkness, but by light; not by sorrow, but by joy. This divinely established reality becomes the content of our faith and the imperative for our mission.

The theological emphasis of the resurrection is therefore not on what happened in the tomb 2000 years ago, nor is it on the future—when, whether, and how we shall rise—but it is on the process of God winning back what God has created. That process is grounded in God's defeat of the estranging powers of death, and it lives from the conviction that the crucified Christ will be the measure and the purpose of history. The process involves those who through faith become disciples of Christ. They are active participants—συνεργοί θεοῦ ("God's fellow workers" [1 Cor 3:9])—in God's great plan of salvation. This in no way questions the sovereignty of God or relativizes the emphasis on *sola gratia* ("by grace alone") and *sola fide* ("through faith alone"). It simply recognizes that grace and faith do not bypass human obedience, but bring it to life, channel it, and empower it.

The "Empty Tomb" and Its Theological Significance

This brings us to a second "pillar" on which resurrection theology is often built: the empty tomb narratives. All four Gospels narrate the story about women and men visiting the tomb into which the corpse of Jesus had been laid and finding it empty.

Let me say at the outset that I found Crossan's and Lüdemann's arguments to dismiss the historical claims of the empty tomb narratives unconvincing. Given their understanding of reality, their conclusion was preprogrammed. At the same time, I also think theologians should not intentionally seek conflict with the predominant view of reality. I therefore find the suggestion attractive that the empty tomb narratives are late traditions occasioned by the early church's need to assure themselves and at the same time explain to others that the appearances were not merely psychological and subjective phenomena.

Nevertheless, the arguments for the historicity of the empty tomb are strong.[4] If the early church, for apologetic or other reasons, created the empty tomb narratives, why are women portrayed as the main witnesses? The testimony of women was not regarded highly in those days, and we can observe the clear tendency of linking men (Peter and the beloved disciple [John 20:2-10, Luke 24:12]) with the empty tomb traditions. Wolfhart Pannenberg asks whether the resurrection could have been proclaimed in Jerusalem if people could have immediately invalidated such a claim by pointing to the corpse of Jesus.[5] Most theologians argue that during the time of the beginning of the church in the ancient Orient, resurrection could only be conceived of as physical. Of course, there are also arguments to the contrary, but at this point I only want to say that we cannot dismiss the historical discovery of an empty tomb too easily.

At first sight, it would probably have been helpful for the earliest Christians to be able to refer to the empty tomb narratives as a way of demonstrating that the resurrection appearances were not merely subjective visions, but that they were unexpected interruptions in their lives coming to them as an act of God. Through the ages these narratives have certainly served as an important reminder that resurrection is not a nebulous abstraction, but that it has to do with flesh and change. Nevertheless, since for many people in the pew, and on a more academic level, for many evangelical theologians, there is the tendency to argue that the empty tomb is *necessary* to affirm the resurrection of Christ, we need to examine the *theological* significance of the empty tomb carefully.

Among those who affirm the resurrection of Christ, three positions can be identified with regard to the empty tomb. First, there are those who say that Jesus' corpse was raised from the dead and that therefore the tomb into which his corpse had been placed must have been empty. Consequently, the affirmation of the empty tomb is considered *necessary* for affirming his resurrection. This argument is strengthened by the soteriological concern that *all* of Jesus, not just his soul or spirit, but also his flesh and bones, has been raised. Conservative Evangelicals and traditional Roman Catholic theologians, and on a less reflective level, most intentional Christians would probably fall into this category.

Then there are those who say that the empty tomb is *supportive of* but at the same time *secondary to* the appearances. The strong biblical support for the empty tomb virtually compels Christian theologians, whose primary text, after all, is the Bible, to give utmost attention to these narratives in their interpretation of the resurrection. We saw that this is the position Wolfhart Pannenberg holds. He claims that an unprejudiced approach to Scripture can only lead to the conclusion that the empty tomb narratives contain a historical core. His theological sensitivity and historical awareness comes to the fore in these two sentences: "The empty tomb never provided the decisive evidence of Jesus' resurrection. But without the empty tomb, the Christian proclamation of Jesus' resurrection *at Jerusalem* of all places would have been in serious trouble, because it could have been easily falsified by just pointing to the place where Jesus had been buried."[6] Pannenberg affirms the bodily resurrection of Jesus, but at the same time he notes that the primary datum for that verdict is not the empty tomb, which he considers to be of "secondary importance,"[7] but the appearances of Christ.

Third, there are those who say that the empty tomb narratives are later apologetic legends created to explain and proclaim the reality of the resurrection. We saw that Crossan and Lüdemann belong in that camp.

What is our response?

At the outset, we must note a hermeneutical shift between the way the resurrection is narrated in the New Testament and the way it is debated in contemporary theology.

At its genesis, the confession "God raised Jesus from the dead" was given as part of and in response to the appearances of Christ. God was understood to be the subject in raising Jesus from the dead. By raising Jesus from death, God added value to Jesus, which we try to gather up by calling him "Christ." With the appearances of Christ, God created faith in those who experienced the risen Christ. There were no neutral and uninvolved observers to the resurrection appearances. The divine creation of faith and with it the call to mission were integral to the resurrection appearances. In these experiences, Christ was recognized and identified as Jesus of Nazareth. Yet the continuity between Jesus and Christ was not in his physical, literal body, but it was in the sameness of identity and of personhood. These experiences were new, strange, and frightening. On the one hand, they empowered Peter and others to return to Jerusalem and become courageous witnesses, but on the other hand, doubt, mystery, and fear accompanied their newly found faith. Nevertheless, we would have to conclude that according to the biblical testimonies, the appearances of Christ were *necessary* and *sufficient* as the ground for the confession that "God raised Jesus from the dead."

With the empty tomb narratives, it is different. They presuppose faith in Christ. Apart from the embellishment in John 20:8 (". . . the other disciple . . . went in, and he saw and *believed*"), there is no claim that the discovery of the empty tomb led to faith. Theoretically, it is at least possible that the women went to the wrong tomb or that the corpse of Jesus was stolen. However, given the primary datum of the appearances, the empty tomb stories helped interpret and give content to the experiences of the risen Christ. The appearances were primary; the empty tomb was secondary and supportive.

A brief revisit to the earliest available empty tomb narrative—Mark 16:1-8—confirms this. The women walk into the tomb and as "they entered the tomb," we are not told that the tomb was empty and that therefore they have to believe Jesus had risen from the dead. Rather, ". . . they saw a young man, dressed in a white robe, sitting on the right side; and they were alarmed. But he said to them, 'Do not be alarmed; you are looking for Jesus of Nazareth, who was crucified. He has been raised; he is not here.'" And only then, after the message of the resurrection had been proclaimed to them by the divine messenger and had caused astonishment, wonder, and fear at this new and unexpected state of affairs, are they pointed to the empty tomb: "Look, there is the place they laid him." But that did not create faith. Indeed "they went out and fled from the tomb, for terror and amazement had seized them; and they said nothing to anyone, for they were afraid." But the text reveals where they will "see"[8] the risen Christ: "he is going ahead of you to Galilee; there you will see him."

The narrative in the *Gospel of Peter* provides an informative contrast:

> . . . they went and found the tomb open, and they went near and looked in there, and saw there a young man sitting in the middle of the tomb, handsome, and dressed in a brilliant robe. And he said to them, "Why have you come? Whom do you seek? Not him who was crucified, for he has risen and gone. *But if you do not believe it, look in and see the place where he lay,* that he is not here. For he has risen and gone to the place from which he was sent." Then the women were afraid and fled. (§13:55-57, emphasis mine)

From the Markan narrative, intensified by the contrast with the text from the *Gospel of Peter*, we would have to conclude that the attempt to use the empty tomb narrative as a *proof* for the resurrection of Jesus is closer to the post- and extra-canonical *Gospel of Peter* than it is to the earliest New Testament account.

I would suggest that this tendency to look and long for historical verifications is part of the human longing to verify divine events on human terms. It underestimates the self-authenticating power of revelation and faith, and as such it is an accommodation to our human weakness. In fact, its helpfulness is overrated. It is an illusion to think that by enumerating all the reasons one can find for the historicity of the resurrection one adds anything significant to the experience of faith. Indeed by the constant focus on the longing for facts, one creates uncertainty and causes a subtle shift from faith, obedience, and mission to historical inquiry. It is certainly fatal to claim that historical fact is the basis for faith. The apostle Paul insists rightly that "faith comes from what is heard, and what is heard comes through the word of Christ" (Rom 10:17, compare 2 Cor 4:5f., 13f.), and in the Gospel of John we find the same insistence: "Very truly, I tell you, anyone who hears my word and believes him who sent me has eternal life, and does not come under judgment, but has passed from death to life" (5:24).

I suggest that here we can locate a danger that modern evangelical theology must face. There—against their intention, of course, since evangelical theologians affirm biblical authority!—the emphasis has shifted from faith to reason. The empty tomb narratives no longer serve primarily to interpret the appearances, but their function is to demonstrate or even prove the literal, physical resurrection of Jesus.

This hermeneutical shift is theologically fatal. While the appearances can be interpreted in terms of God, in the power of the Spirit, making Jesus known to those who believe, an emphasis on the empty tomb as a *primary* theological datum or as a datum on an *equal* level with the appearances implies a shift from faith to reason. But reason cannot deliver the goods humans need to satisfy their deepest longing for God. A shift of emphasis from the ministry of the Spirit in creating faith to the affirmation of a historical fact would deliver the quest for soteriological certainty into the hands of historical research. Discussion, dissent, and arguments about the historicity of the empty tomb may be historically interesting, but they should have no influence on the certainty that is an inherent dimension of faith in Christ.

Reason objectifies and distances an event. It keeps an event at arm's length. Historical fact is interesting, but it is not liberating. If the primary trajectory is resurrection - appearances - faith - community - mission, then a theological emphasis on the empty tomb will be a dangerous detour. It may subvert the liberating power of the resurrection and slow down the process it has begun.

I maintain therefore that the resurrection was affirmed on the basis of the appearances of Christ. The appearances were *theologically* necessary and sufficient to confess that "God raised Jesus from the dead." The empty tomb, whatever its *historical* status may have been, was not theologically necessary. This still leaves us with Pannenberg's assertion: ". . . unless it can be shown that the Jewish community of that time in history could conceive of a resurrection from the dead without being concerned with what happened to the dead body, it must be judged extremely implausible that the Christian congregation at Jerusalem proclaimed Jesus' resurrection while his body was resting in his tomb."[9]

In response we make the following observations:

- The apostle Paul developed a sophisticated theology of "bodily" resurrection, without reference to the empty tomb. Indeed, he insists that "flesh and blood cannot inherit the kingdom of God" (1 Cor 15:50).

- Jewish anthropology may not be as clear and as coherent as has been thought. Besides a crude belief in a material and recognizable continuity between the earthly body and the resurrection body, there are other views that speak of a new and transformed resurrection body and even of a spiritual resurrection without a body.[10] John J. Collins, in his recent commentary on the Book of Daniel, reflects on the belief in the resurrection in Judaism of the first century AD: "Belief in some form of resurrection was widespread in Judaism by the first century CE. Even then, however, the form of the resurrected body was controversial. . . . The stereotypical assumption that resurrection in a Jewish context was always bodily is in need of considerable qualification."[11]

- The early Christians made a clear distinction between the resurrection of Lazarus and the resurrection of Jesus. For them, Jesus was not resuscitated, but he was transformed and exalted to the right hand of God.

- Finally, there is the fact that *our* tombs are not or will not be empty. And yet, with the church through the ages,[12] we believe in the "bodily" resurrection from the dead. Therefore, if *our* hope of resurrection does not exclude but includes the fact of a full grave where our physical bodies will disintegrate (or no grave as in the case of cremation), then this can in principle also be true for Jesus.

I conclude that in dealing with the theological significance of the empty tomb narratives, we need to distinguish between historical and theological reasoning. Historically, it is possible or even likely that Mary and one or more other women found the tomb into which Jesus' body had been laid empty. Theologically, the appearances of Christ were *sufficient* reason for confessing that Jesus is alive.

But, given the conviction that Jesus is alive, the empty tomb narratives, whether grounded in historical fact (which I consider to be most likely in light of the biblical evidence) or whether created for apologetic or other theological purposes, proved to be increasingly helpful in showing that the resurrection of Jesus was not merely of inner personal or subjective relevance, but that it in fact meant a change of being. It is the narrative way of saying that "Death has been swallowed up in victory" (1 Cor 15:54), without forgetting that "flesh and blood cannot inherit the kingdom of God" (1 Cor 15:50). By raising Jesus from the dead, God has conquered the estranging power of death: "Thanks be to God, who gives us the victory through our Lord Jesus Christ" (1 Cor 15:57). This event is the basis for the Christian life: "Therefore, my beloved, be steadfast, immovable, always excelling in the work of the Lord, because you know that in the Lord your labor is not in vain" (1 Cor 15:58).

The Holy Spirit

In a pre-Pauline tradition—Romans 1:3b-4—Christ's resurrection from the dead is attributed to the activity of the "Spirit of holiness." Through this event, Jesus Christ "was declared to be Son of God with power," and the apostle interprets that the risen Christ creates faith, apostleship, and mission (Rom 1:5f.).

The role of the Holy Spirit in raising Jesus from the dead has not been sufficiently recognized in the theological debate.[13] It is important. It adds the Trinitarian dimension of the Father and the Spirit being involved with the work and with the verification of the Son. It emphasizes that Christ is an ever-present reality, which is effectively "near" in the power of the Spirit. Since the Spirit is the *ruah* (רוּחַ) of the Hebrew Bible, she (רוּחַ is feminine) binds the story of Jesus into the story of Israel, and beyond it into the life-giving story of the creator God. The Spirit of God is not only the Spirit that empowered Israel's judges and kings; she is not only "breath" and "wind" and "storm," but she is the very "power of creation" and the "wellspring of life."[14] By interlocking the resurrection with the work of the Spirit, the resurrection becomes part of God's great passion for life.

The Holy Spirit stands for God's power and God's self-giving. The Christian symbol gives expression to the Christian conviction that God *is* in being for and with others. In the power of the Spirit, God relates the reconciliation that God has established in Christ to humanity and beyond.

It is promising to explore further this relational dimension of God's being. If with evangelical theologians and against Crossan and Lüdemann we assert that "resurrection" is not a *replaceable* metaphor, but the ontological foundation for faith; if against evangelical theologians we argue that the resurrection cannot be "frozen" into the past and cannot be verified by historical reason; if we agree that the empty tomb neither was nor is *theologically necessary* to affirm and confess that "God raised Jesus from the dead"; if we agree with Crossan and Sawicki that the risen Christ empowers people to a life of solidarity and courage—how then can we bring these different strands together? Perhaps a reminder of the activity of the Holy Spirit can pave the way.

Toward a Relational Ontology

The Holy Spirit is relationship par excellence. The Holy Spirit brings together what belongs together. The Holy Spirit makes what happens *between* people interesting. When a group of individuals comes together and creates a community, something *new* happens. Individuals no longer absolutize their views, but they submit their opinions to the group with the anticipation that by everyone doing it something new will emerge. Not domination of one individual over the other, but edification of the whole becomes the prevailing interest. Not isolation, but relationship becomes the overriding theme. That is the work of the Holy Spirit.

We must learn to understand reality in relational terms. Neither God, nor humanity, nor nature are simply "there." They "are" in their relationship to the rest of reality. Is it not true that the Judeo-Christian understanding of life fits more comfortably with a relational ontology than with an understanding of reality that works on the separation and over-againstness of subject and object? Let us look at a few Christian symbols to illustrate our point.

"God Is Love"

For Christians, the confession that "God is love" is central. It gathers up the nature of the God of Abraham, Isaac, and Jacob, the God of the covenants, and the God who has shared God's being with Jesus Christ. "God is love" is an ontological statement! Love is not merely an attribute of God; it is the designation of God's very being. Therefore, when the "is" in "God is love" is given due attention, we have to seek language that does not portray God as being "there" or as living in splendid isolation, but that portrays God as being "for" and "with" others: ". . . the LORD said, 'I have observed the misery of my people who are in Egypt; I have heard their cry on account of their taskmasters. Indeed, I know their sufferings, and I have come down to deliver them from the Egyptians, and to bring them up out of that land to a good and broad land, a land flowing with milk and honey . . .'" (Exod 3:7f.).

This "observing" is not "looking at"; this "hearing" does not just happen with ears; this "knowing" is not the knowledge of the mind. These verbs—verbs rather than nouns indicate activity—express the very being of God, which with ontological necessity leads to "coming down" and "bringing up" the oppressed. The passion for liberation issues from the ἔρως ("*erōs*"—passionate love) of divine ἀγάπη ("*agape*"—self-giving love).

In Exodus, the God who calls Moses to participate in liberating the people of Israel from slavery is introduced as אֶהְיֶה אֲשֶׁר אֶהְיֶה) (= imperfect of הָיָה "to be," Exod 3:14). This divine self-revelation is difficult to render in English because Hebrew, unlike English, does not have past, present, and future tenses. In Hebrew, the verb describes an action that is either completed in the past (perfect) or incomplete (imperfect). Applied to the above sentence, God is described as an "open" or "relational" reality. Perhaps the best translation would be, "I am the One who I will show myself to be in your ongoing history."[15] The self-introduction is therefore immediately followed by the promise: "I promise that I will bring you up out of the affliction of Egypt" (Exod 3:17).[16] This promise is not arbitrary. It is grounded in God's nature, and it relates God's passion to liberate people from oppression.

Knowing *this* God does not call for a theoretical affirmation of God's existence. Such intellectual acknowledgment would presume that a place could be occupied outside and over against God, from which God's existence can be observed, affirmed, or denied. In a relational ontology, that is not possible. The existence of God is presupposed. Referring to the analogy that Ernst Fuchs used,[17] in a healthy family situation, when the son or daughter kisses their father, they do not ask their mother whether their father is really their father. That is presupposed. In God's economy, hearing means obeying; believing means accepting responsibility for what one knows.[18] In a relational ontology, to know the God who is love would mean believing and obeying God by tuning into God's promises and thus joining God in shaping history as a story of liberation.

God as "Trinity"

For Christians, the symbol "trinity" seeks to express their specific understanding of God. Whatever else this symbol means, it expresses the Christian conviction that God is a relational and a personal reality. Through the humanity of Christ and through the life-giving work of the Spirit, creation—humanity, nature, cosmos—is understood in its relationship to God. God's being is distinct but not separate from God's creation. God *is* in being together with God's creation. In this relational reality, God is creator, redeemer, enabler, and sustainer, while the world is creation, in need of redemption, dependent, and yet able to receive grace and give thanks. It belongs to the very being of God to love, to come, to heal, to save, to liberate, to gather up into God's *shalom* what God has created. The Christian God cannot be thought apart from, but only together with God's creation. But this being together with God's creation has its ground in the togetherness of Father, Son, and Holy Spirit. Each of the divine persons is distinct, yet at the same time they are not what they are apart from the other. God is relational, both in the inward journey and in the outward journey.

Σῶμα πνευματικόν ("Spiritual Body")

We are also pointed toward a relational ontology when we consider the transition from our earthly life to our life in the presence of God. When the apostle Paul talks about the nature of the resurrection body, he speaks of a "spiritual body," a body of "glory," a body "chosen and given by God" (1 Cor 15:35-57). Since in his argument Paul interrelates the resurrection of Christ (1 Cor 15:48f.) with the resurrection of believers, we may assume that his discourse on the resurrection body applies both to Christ and to believers. This raises the important question as to what Paul means by "spiritual body," especially in light of the fact that he contrasts it with a "physical body" (1 Cor 15:44), and keeping in mind his insistence that "flesh and blood cannot inherit the kingdom of God" (1 Cor 15:50).

When the apostle thinks about resurrection existence, he seeks to avoid two extremes. There is the extreme of spiritual abstraction on the one hand and of historical materialism on the other. Paul cannot think of a "naked" or "unclothed" existence (2 Cor 5:1-5). An existence for him must be identifiable. It must have a "body." It must be "embodied." According to Mark 12:25, even angels have "bodies." On the other hand, Paul knows that matter and human estranged existence, "flesh and blood," are not concomitant with the realm of the divine.

His alternative is "relationship." Let us try to follow that thought.

For us, it is difficult to understand what Paul means by his use of "body" (σῶμα). For us, body has matter. It is made up of flesh and bones and skin and cells. But Paul's use of "body" is different. We therefore have to try to rid ourselves of the persistent linguistic prejudice that links "body" with matter. Σῶμα ("body") is never used to describe a corpse, and it is not used as a contrast to ψυξή ("soul"). It is true, of course, that we can't think of our present existence apart from a physical body. Yet our physical body at a certain point of time is not who we really are. Our flesh and bones and cells change and renew themselves. Our σῶμα is not merely what we can feel and see when we are twenty or forty or eighty years of age.

Our "body" is who we are as the product of our genetic determination and our relationships. Our physical body connects us with the world around us. Our eyes see, our ears hear, our noses smell, our hands touch, our mouths eat, our minds digest and discern, our wills decide and act. With our bodies, we relate to God in prayer and worship; with our bodies, we relate to each other in affection and support; with our bodies, we relate to nature in work and artistry; with our bodies, we relate to history by participating responsibly in public life. We are in being related to nature, to friends, to culture, to God. These relationships and their interactivity with our genetic predisposition determine who we are. And what we are is called σῶμα ("body").

What, then, happens at death? We know what happens to our physical remains. They become dust—"the earthly tent we live in is destroyed" (2 Cor 5:1). And yet, at the same time we are promised eternal life. Not that there is an immortal soul within us that will continue to exist when our body disintegrates. Not that there is an immortal soul that can and will take on different bodies in a chain of incarnations. No, God—*sola gratia* ("by grace alone")!—gives us a new "body," a spiritual body, a body of glory, "a building from God, a house not made with hands, eternal in the heavens" (2 Cor 5:1). In this new, God-given existence our identity is remembered and preserved. But the form of that existence is no longer the form necessitated by an existence in time and space. Instead, it is concomitant with the new existence in the divine presence.

While we live in the world, in the context of time and space and matter, our σῶμα ("body") includes a physical body. It is a body limited by time and space and matter. On the other side of death, in the new presence of God, another body, a spiritual body, will be given by God to manifest our σῶμα ("body").

What is important for our inquiry is that "body" is a relational concept. Our identity, our σῶμα ("body"), is not simply what we are in isolation from God, friends, culture, and nature, but what we are in relationship to our environment. Yet even "environment" is an inadequate description, because God, friends, culture, and nature are not merely "around" us, but they are part of us and we are part of them. We cannot live and survive without them. They are part of our being. We are ontologically interwoven with them.

The "Body of Christ"

Let us apply the same way of thinking to Christ, who is different from us in that his resurrection has been revealed and has, in unity with his life and death, been made the ground and content of our faith. Let us ask how and why the apostle Paul came to designate the church as the "body of Christ."[19]

The idea of using the concept "body" (σῶμα) for a group of people, for the state, or even for humanity and for the world was known in the ancient world.[20] But what caused the apostle to name the church as the "body of Christ"?

"Body of Christ" has a colorful variety of meanings. With this concept Paul interweaves several realities: the church, the Lord's Supper, Jesus Christ, and even the world. In Romans 7:4, "body of Christ" refers to Jesus' self-giving on the cross. In other texts, "body" refers to the Lord's Supper: "This is my body" (1 Cor 11:24; 10:16); and from there it flows over to designate the church: "we who are many are one body" (1 Cor 10:16f., compare 1 Cor 12:12-30; Rom 12:3-8). An early Christian hymn even celebrates Christ as the head of the "body," the world, or the cosmos (Col 1:18; "the church" is a later interpretation). Our question focuses on the use of "body of Christ" for the church or for the cosmos. How can that be understood?

We remember that the earthly Jesus fulfilled human destiny by radically living a life for God and, at the same time, a life for and with others. Jesus cannot be understood, Jesus would not be Jesus, apart from his intimate relationship with God, his liberating authority, his solidarity with and his commitment to the poor, and his friendship with publicans and sinners. Those relationships in their interplay with his genetic disposition constituted his being, his identity, his "I," his "body." God, other people, the social and geographical context were part of his identity. He freely submitted himself as son to the father, and his authority was voluntarily accepted and recognized by his followers. His identity was not apart from, but a result of his being together with God and friends and life-world.

His radical openness to God and his life for and with others clashed with the religious, economic, and political structures of his time. He was captured, tried, and killed. But death was not the end. God, the master over life and death, confirmed Jesus' vision of life by raising him from the dead. The resurrection is not a negation or cancellation of Jesus' life and death, but a confirmation and a verification. Indeed, Jesus' death and resurrection had a further dimension. It included the soteriological demonstration that now, in consequence to Jesus' death and resurrection, *nothing*, "neither death, nor life, nor angels, nor rulers, nor things present, nor things to come, nor powers, nor height, nor depth, nor anything else in all creation, will be able to separate us from the love of God in Christ Jesus our Lord" (Rom 8:38f.).

It was important to spell out the continuity between Jesus' life and death, his acceptance by God, and then his resurrection. It had to be shown that there was continuity of Jesus' openness to God and his being for and with others, before and after the resurrection. His identity, his "I," his "body" must therefore include those who believe in him. Just as God and friends were part of Jesus' identity before Easter, so they were part of his identity after Easter. Indeed, ultimately Jesus' identity as savior of the world must include all people and the whole cosmos. God's shalom is universal; otherwise God would not be God. There was an early Christian hymn (Col 1:15-20) that celebrated that Christ "is the head of the *body*," meaning the body of God's creation, the whole cosmos. Realizing, however, that such a universal salvation has so far only been implemented where Christ is believed and obeyed, the author of Colossians adds the caution that Christ "is the head of the body, *the church*." At the same time, he reminds his readers that they must "continue in the faith" and that the gospel is destined to be "preached to every creature under heaven." The potential Lordship of Christ over the whole cosmos has become tangible and is celebrated in the church, and through the church's mission it is becoming actual in all parts of God's creation.

Therefore, Christ's σῶμα ("body"), Christ's identity, Christ's "I" includes those for whom he lived and died. This relational interpretation must be guarded against two misunderstandings. One such misunderstanding tends to identify the body of Christ with the church and thereby dissolves Christ into the church. The church then understands itself as the continuing incarnation. It arrogates infallibility to itself and consequently relativizes the Lordship of Christ over the church. To avoid this misunderstanding the post-Pauline tradition emphasizes that Christ is the "head" of the body, the church (Col 1:18, 24; 2:19; Eph 1:22f.; 4:15f.; 5:24), and at the same time we have the emphasis that Christ's Lordship extends beyond the church to all of creation.[21] The other misunderstanding arises when Christ's resurrection body is understood in terms of the Gospel narratives where the risen Christ is portrayed as an individual who can eat and speak and touch, but who at the same time can walk through closed doors. Such narratives about the risen Christ serve a different purpose. With the hermeneutical possibilities of that time, they emphasize the reality of the resurrection, not its physicality.

Summary and Conclusions

Advancing beyond the conversation with recent representative theological voices (chapter 1), I have sought to show that "resurrection" is not a replaceable metaphor, but that it is a metaphor that is grounded in and witnesses to the ontological foundation of the Christian faith and its social dimension, the Christian church.

The resurrection of the crucified Christ is the foundational event for Christian faith. Apart from it, faith is either a psychological illusion or it dissolves into sterile morality. By raising Jesus from the dead, God has broken the estranging power of death and thereby provided the divine ground for the confession that *nothing* "will be able to separate us from the love of God in Christ Jesus our Lord" (Rom 8:38f.). The resurrection of the crucified Christ marks the triumph of love and life over the estranging forces of death.

By giving uncritical credence to a scientific worldview that by definition excludes God and an act of God, we cannot understand the reality that produced the Easter texts and to which these texts point. The Christian understanding of Easter necessarily includes God and faith, and I contend that apart from that divine foundation there is no ontological basis for our personal hope beyond the grave and for our struggle for peace and justice here and now. On the basis of the resurrection, we can affirm that history can be changed in the direction of truth, justice, and *shalom*, and that God is involved with such change.

With the appearances of the risen Christ, God, who through the power of the Spirit raised Jesus from the dead, reached out and as such included the first Christian believers in God's *shalom*. This happened by creating faith and with it the community of believers, the church.

The experience of faith included and continues to include the call to mission. This is to be expected, since the God who raised Jesus from the dead and thereby broke the estranging power of death is the creator of heaven and earth. Faith therefore includes a universalizing tendency and issues into love and justice. Since the history of Christian missions is replete with examples of how the call to mission has been interpreted in imperialistic terms, it needs to be emphasized that such an interpretation is made impossible by our suggestion that with raising Jesus from the dead, God has established an ontology of love, peace, and nonviolence.

The resurrection cannot be limited to its anthropological consequences. The symbols of "ascension" and "exaltation to the right hand of God" express the fact that the resurrection has ecological and cosmic implications. God, the creator, claims back God's creation. However marred and distorted creation may appear, it stands under the eternal and colorful rainbow of God's grace and it is graced with the promise of God's salvation.

The empty tomb stories remain controversial. Modern thinking has removed them from their original intention to underline and emphasize the reality of the triumph of love and life over the estranging forces of death by assigning to them the intention of wanting to demonstrate or even prove that Jesus was literally and physically removed from the tomb. Both liberal and evangelical theologians have adopted the false alternative that either Jesus was literally, physically raised or he was not raised at all. I have argued that according to the biblical testimonies, the empty tomb was not necessary for affirming that God raised Jesus from the dead, and in light of our own human experience that our tombs are not empty, it may even add to the promising reality of the incarnation if the empty tomb narratives assume secondary significance in our theological arguments. On the other hand, it must be maintained that the historical evidence for the discovery of an empty tomb remains strong. Nevertheless, its affirmation or denial cannot be made the test case for affirming or denying the resurrection of Christ.

Conservative evangelicals have not been able to explain how the apostle Paul can develop the most sophisticated theology of the resurrection in the early church without explicit reference to the empty tomb. To say that given his anthropology Paul must have implied an empty tomb when he cited the formula that Christ "died" and "was buried" (1 Cor 15:3f.) is an argument from silence presupposing a religio-historical situation that is not as clear as people make out.

On the other hand, liberal theologians who tend to shift the theological emphasis from Paul to Jesus are equally distorting the intention of the New Testament traditions, except possibly for the so-called Q-source or Q-tradition. But then, it may not be an accident that the Q-source or Q-tradition, just as it was with the pre-Markan traditions and with the special material of Luke and Matthew, was not granted independent theological dignity, but was woven into the Gospels that confess and celebrate that the risen Lord was none other than the Jesus who was killed on the cross. Theologically the Gospels and Paul are on the same level. One cannot use the Gospels to play Jesus over against Paul. The Gospels are not biographies of Jesus. Like Paul's letters and like our sermons today, they are stories of Jesus that aim in the power of the Spirit to create and sustain faith. Jesus, the pre-Easter Jesus, is the important criteria for Christian truth and as such the measure of faith. The historically constructed Jesus is important for the content of faith; he is not the ground of faith!

I have tried to argue that "resurrection" is a metaphor, but it is not a replaceable metaphor. It is the verbal symbol for the ontological foundation of Christian faith and its social dimension, the Christian church. Its reality is grounded in God who actually and who alone raised Jesus from the dead. But since that event is a divine event, an event without analogy, we are confronted with the question as to what ontology and what language is available to understand and communicate that event.

My suggestion, based on the first available witnesses to the resurrection, is that we must understand the resurrection of Christ as an "open", relational event; an event that implies and at the same time anticipates the new heaven and the new earth, when God will be all in all. Between its genesis and its fulfillment is the time of discipleship and mission where faith is understood as participating in God's passion to reconcile with God what God has created. But before we talk about Christian discipleship and mission, we shall seek to unravel more clearly the ground and the content of our faith in Christ.

Notes

[1] Compare the helpful essay by Eberhard Jüngel, "Anthropomorphism: A fundamental problem in modern hermeneutics," in *Theological Essays*, trans. with introduction by J. B. Webster (Edinburgh: T&T Clark, 1989), 72-94.

[2] Michael Welker, "Resurrection and the Reign of God," *The Princeton Seminary Bulletin*, supp. issue, no. 3 (1994, 3-16): 10.

[3] F. Blass and A. Debrunner, *A Greek Grammar of the New Testament and Other Early Christian Literature*, trans. and ed. Robert W. Funk (Chicago: Chicago University Press, 1961), 176 (§342).

[4] For details, see my *Resurrection and Discipleship: Interpretive Models, Biblical Reflections, Theological Consequences* (Maryknoll NY: Orbis, 1995), 166-81.

[5] Wolfhart Pannenberg, "History and the Reality of the Resurrection," in *Resurrection Reconsidered*, ed. Gavin D'Costa (Oxford: One World, 1996, 62-72): 69f.

[6] Ibid., 69.

[7] Ibid., 70.

[8] The text shifts terminology, which may be significant. In Mark 16:4 the Greek verb θεωρέω is used to describe the women "seeing" that the stone was rolled away, while in vv. 5 and 6, where they "see" the young man who is clearly designated as a heavenly messenger and where they "see" the "place where they laid him," the verb ὁράω is used. It is interesting that ὁράω is deeply embedded in the appearance tradition (compare 1 Cor 15:5-8; Luke 24:34; Acts 9:17; 13:31; 26:16; 1 Tim 3:16). It is therefore possible or even likely that the text wants us to differentiate between what can be seen with the eyes of reason and the eyes of faith.

[9] Ibid., 69f.

[10] Details can be found in my *Resurrection and Discipleship*, 172f., footnote 17.

[11] John J. Collins, *Daniel: A Commentary on the Book of Daniel* (Minneapolis: Fortress Press, 1993), 398. Further literature is mentioned in my *Resurrection and Discipleship*, 177f., footnote 28.

[12] The Niceno-Constantinopolitan Creed of AD 381: "We look for the resurrection of the dead, and the life of the world to come." The Apostles' Creed: "I believe in . . . the resurrection of the body (flesh)." The Athanasian Creed: "At whose coming all men shall rise again with their bodies."

[13] Yet there are significant exceptions: Eduard Schweizer, *The Holy Spirit*, trans. Reginald H. and Ilse Fuller (Philadelphia: Fortress, 1980); Peter Carnley, *The Structure of Resurrection Belief* (Oxford: Clarendon Press, 1987); Jürgen Moltmann, *The Way of Jesus Christ: Christology in Messianic Dimensions*, trans. Margaret Kohl (London: SCM, 1990); idem, *The Spirit of Life: A Universal Affirmation*, trans. Margaret Kohl (London: SCM, 1992).

[14] See Jürgen Moltmann, *Spirit of Life*, 35.

[15] The Septuagint translates ἐγώ εἰμι ὁ ὤν (*ego eimi ho ōn*). Here a Hebrew verb (imperfect, denoting incomplete action) is made into a Greek participial noun. This has often been interpreted as a move from historical thinking to a metaphysical ontology in which God is perceived in terms of transcendence, separation from the world, and non-involvement with history. Such a change in emphasis may have been implied in the Greek worldview of that time, but it should not lead to a rejection of ontology altogether. The challenge is not to reject and replace ontology, but to reshape it in a way that it takes God and history seriously.

[16] This is, of course, a common motif in Old Testament thinking. Compare Exod 20:2f.; Deut 5:6f.; Hos 13:4.

[17] See above p.13 (chapter 1).

[18] Compare Jas 2:14-26 and 4:17.

[19] Every New Testament theology and every treatment of Paul deals with this topic. Of fundamental importance are the treatments by Eduard Schweizer ("σῶμα κτλ.," *TDNT* 7 [1971]: 1024-44, 1049-94) and Ernst Käsemann, "The theological problem presented by the motif of the Body of Christ," in *Perspectives on Paul*, trans. Margaret Kohl (London: SCM, 1971), 102-21.

[20] The religio-historical parallels are gathered by Eduard Schweizer, "σῶμα κτλ.," *TDNT* 7 (1971): 1036-39, 1054f.

[21] See below, pp. 109-113, section on ecology.

Chapter 3

The Cross of the Risen Christ

. . . he showed them his hands and his feet . . . —Luke 24:40

We now move to the heart of the matter. In the next two chapters, I aim to show that resurrection faith and a passion for justice are interrelated, and they are grounded in a solid theological basis. My argument is essentially built on two pillars.

First, there is the Christian conviction that Jesus was not only willing to die for a good cause, but that God actually raised Jesus from the dead and thereby broke the estranging powers of death. Jesus' resurrection implies the end to the ultimate threat of death. On the basis of the resurrection, we can affirm that at the center of reality there is not death but life, not war but peace, not injustice but justice. We shall remind ourselves of that important Christian affirmation in the next chapter.

The second pillar, which we shall address in this chapter, is concerned with the *content* of faith in Christ. We seek to take seriously that it was the *crucified* Christ who was raised from the dead. Thereby the resurrection is not only portrayed as the death of death, but its meaning is interwoven with the life and passion of Jesus. The implied consequences of the resurrection will then be discussed in chapter 5.

Continuity

The foundational Christian symbols of "cross" and "resurrection" would become abstract, empty, and distorted if it were not to become clear that *Jesus* was killed on the cross and raised from the dead—that particular Jew, Jesus, who lived a certain kind of life, and who as a direct result of that specific life met opposition, conflict, trial, torture, and execution. Only with that focus on Jesus can we ascertain that resurrection faith is not used to validate our human needs and desires, our political and national ideologies, our economic and cultural interests.[1] And we must not forget that Jesus did not die of old age or of a heart attack; nor was his death the result of a judicial error. He was crucified for discernible reasons that must be considered in any attempt to understand the meaning of his death and resurrection. With the resurrection, Jesus' life and death are not relativized or left behind—as the popular slogan "from cross to crown" may suggest—but in, with, and through the resurrection, the theological and soteriological dignity of Jesus' life and death is revealed and effectively manifested.

Christians must therefore be aware of the danger that the word "God" is easily usurped to validate political, cultural, economic, and ecclesiastical ideologies. We are often unwilling to admit that our manifold attempts to detour around the "foolishness" and the "stumbling block" of the cross (1 Cor 1:18–2:5) has led to the domestication of the cross and to a spiritualization of the resurrection. The desire for cheap grace has been used to empty cross and resurrection of the dangerous memory of Jesus.

With regard to the cross, that can be done quite naively by thinking that we have done justice to its symbolic power when we hang silver and golden crosses around our necks or place crosses in our religious spaces and processions. Or we employ a cross as a sign of victory by which we conquer other nations and other religions. On a more sophisticated and theological level, we may develop complicated theories of atonement in which the poverty of Jesus' life, his liberating solidarity with marginal groups, his revolutionary but nonviolent attacks on the political and religious establishment of his day are given no theological status. We may be moved by J. S. Bach's *St. Matthew's* and *St. John's Passion*, by Handel's *Messiah*, or by a negro spiritual about being there when they crucified my Lord, and miss altogether that Jesus was the Messiah of the poor and oppressed and that his passion included opposition, torture, and murder.

With regard to the resurrection, any attempt to relativize or play down that the crucified Jesus was raised from the dead should raise our theological suspicion. When the Gospels portray the risen Christ as establishing his identity by pointing to the marks of the crucifixion, they use this story-language to insist on the theological continuity between his life, death, and resurrection. The resurrection is more than the coming of faith to the disciples. The resurrection is different from a depth-psychological explanation that after the death of Jesus the early disciples through different crises came to a new awareness of the power of Jesus' personality. The resurrection must also not be objectified and frozen into the past, merely calling for an intellectual response of "yes" or "no" to a historical question. And we must certainly resist limiting the relevance of the resurrection to what happens after our life here on earth. With the resurrection of the *crucified* Christ, God has changed reality, God makes a claim upon us, God has initiated faith, and God has given us the content of that faith.

Very early, Christians and Christian churches began to protest against the separation of faith from the poverty and from the particularity of Jesus' life and its consequences. Paul in his protest against the Christians in Corinth, where charismatic self-edification had become more important than waiting for and sharing with the slaves and wharfies and nannies, emphasized that the *crucified* Christ is the host at the Lord's Supper (1 Cor 11:23) and that it was therefore inconceivable (1 Cor 11:20) that a Christian church would not wait for the "latecomers." The earliest Gospel, the Gospel of Mark, was written forty years after Jesus' death to protect the identity of Christian faith against the distortions of the ever-present religious instincts of Christians. By interweaving the miracle stories with the passion story of Jesus, the Gospel of Mark is a narrative protest against spiritualizing Christian faith. According to the first evangelist, Jesus can only be known "on the way," and this way is the way of following Jesus in radical discipleship (Mark 8:27–9:1). Indeed, the evangelist "Mark" makes the point that it was not the disciples but the ὄχλος, the common people and the lower classes, whose relationship to Jesus was theologically significant.[2]

If we, therefore, want to understand the "cross" and "resurrection" as foundational symbols of the Christian faith, we must see them in their essential togetherness with the life of Jesus. Apart from the life of Jesus, his death may be interpreted in terms of an abstract theory of atonement that emphasizes bridging the gulf between God and humanity through a perfect sacrifice, but that at the same time loses sight of the particularity of Jesus' life, his poverty, and his prophetic critique of the dehumanizing structures of his day. Again, apart from the life of Jesus, the resurrection would tempt believers, indeed has tempted believers from New Testament days to the present time, to view Jesus in terms of being "superman" or a miracle worker, while the offense that his life provoked and the subsequent way to Gethsemane and Calvary become theologically irrelevant. In order to avoid a distortion of "cross" and "resurrection" as central identity symbols of the Christian faith, it is essential to give theological dignity to the historical Jesus, to see the "cross" as the result and consequence of a certain way and vision of life, and to understand the "resurrection" not as a negation of Jesus' life and death, but as a confirmation and effective implementation of that life and death.

Accessing the Life of Jesus

This raises the much-debated problem as to how we can access and understand the life of Jesus. Scholars talk about various "quests" for the historical Jesus.[3] I am not entering that debate, and for the present investigation I am not interested in the various historical details that a host of scholars are discovering about Jesus' life and times. I am mainly interested in two related matters: first, that the gospel and faith are essentially interrelated with the historical Jesus; and second, that the vision of Jesus' life for which he was prepared to die has to do with the establishing of justice.

I am still persuaded that the distinction between the ground, the subject, and the object of faith on the one hand[4] and the content of faith on the other is theologically important. That distinction was introduced by Ernst Käsemann[5] and Gerhard Ebeling[6] in response to Rudolf Bultmann. It seeks to maintain that faith is created by the Holy Spirit through the word of the gospel. Faith is "heard" and "comes" to the believer and through the ministry of the Holy Spirit creates the "obedience of faith" in the believer (Rom 1:5; 10:17; Gal 3:23-26). That faith-creating word of the gospel is grounded in what God has done in the life, death, and resurrection of Jesus. In consequence of the resurrection, the risen Christ can be both the object and the subject of faith. Nevertheless, the faith created by the word of the gospel is essentially linked to the actual Jesus of history (the Jesus behind the New Testament writings), because the gospel tells the story of this *particular person Jesus*. The gospel is not a history lesson *about* the Jesus of history, but the identity of the gospel lives from its *continuity* with Jesus. That is the great claim and obstacle of the Christian faith: the fact that in a free and sovereign act of God, God has tied the riches of God's grace to the poverty of that particular Jew, Jesus from Nazareth. As such, the *content* of faith must be in continuity with Jesus. Not with his nationality and maleness. Not just with the details of his teachings or actions, not just with his character, not just with his God-consciousness, but with his very being, with the vision that constituted his life. Faith does not need to repeat in every detail what Jesus said or how Jesus lived. Indeed, that is impossible. We don't know the exact words of the historical Jesus, and the cultural gulf between Jesus' time and our time is virtually unbridgeable. But what faith must do and what faith can do is continue the history of truth, freedom, peace, and justice, of *shalom* and salvation, that is grounded in the very being of God, that was at the heart of the vision and mission of God's people through the ages, and that was renewed and intensified by Jesus Christ. For Christians, God's will and plan for this world is therefore tied to the story of Jesus.

What Christians think and do may and must be different in *form* to what Jesus did and said. That awareness goes right back to the beginnings of Christianity as the developments of the Gospel narratives illustrate. It is part of the work of the Holy Spirit that keeps the Jesus story alive in different cultural contexts. Nevertheless, within the discontinuity of time and culture, there must be *continuity in content* to that for which Jesus lived and died.

In what follows, I therefore hope to sketch the particular understanding of God and of life that undergirded Jesus' ministry and was the cause for being opposed, captured, condemned, and crucified. I therefore seek to provide some contours for a living faith in Christ and thus avoid faith that separates itself from Jesus and ends up in abstraction and myth or is domesticated into a personal piety, lifeless dogma, or convenient ecclesiology.

It is generally agreed that the Gospels are not biographies. They say nothing about Jesus' early life—except the birth narratives and a verse in Luke that speaks of Jesus visiting the temple at twelve years of age (Luke 2:41-52). His life comes into focus as he sets out on his messianic mission, a mission that met fascination and opposition. It ended within a short span of years with crucifixion. When the crucified Jesus was raised from the dead, the cross, as the intensification of Jesus' life, became the theological center of early Christianity. This echoes throughout the New Testament. The apostle Paul, for instance, in his struggle for Christian identity and relevance with the church in Corinth, states his central theological interest in this way: ". . . I decided to know nothing among you except Jesus Christ and him crucified" (1 Cor 2:2). The Letter of the Hebrews tells us that "Jesus also suffered outside the gate in order to sanctify the people through his own blood" (13:12). In the Book of Revelation it is "the lamb who was slain" who rules and who alone is worthy to reveal God's plan for the world (Rev 5). In the Gospel of Mark the first adequate christological confession arises in view of the crucified Christ: "This man was truly a Son of God" (15:39), whereby the "was" ties the crucified One to the particular life that he lived. In the Gospel of John the glorification of Jesus takes place on the cross (12:23; 17:1). These texts make clear that the early Christians viewed the life of Jesus in its essential interrelation with the cross. It is in the cross where the intention of Jesus' life becomes centered.[7]

"God" vs. "God"

Viewing Jesus' life from the perspective of the cross means that his death resulted neither from an accident nor from a judicial error. Given the religious, economic, and political situation of Jesus' day, his death was the "natural" and predictable consequence of his way of life. The opposition against him, his capture, and his execution were a response to his understanding of God and the resultant unconditional love for and solidarity with human beings.

Can this interrelationship between Jesus' life and death be made more transparent? What factors raised suspicion and opposition against Jesus and then finally led to his crucifixion? We may not know what Jesus thought and felt. Many details of his life escape us. The gulf of time, language, and culture is tremendous. Yet, like in a woodcut, some features emerge from a careful and critical reading of the Gospel narratives that may explain why Jesus met such fierce opposition.

Jesus' life was ruled by voluntary obedience to the first commandment (Exod 20:2f.). He had no other passion than to recognize God as God, and therefore to have no other gods besides God. This recognition of God as God included the passion for justice, because according to the first commandment, God's Godhood is displayed in liberating God's people "out of the house of bondage." The third Evangelist is therefore correct when he has Jesus voicing the overture to his messianic life:

> The Spirit of the Lord is upon me, because he has anointed me to preach good news to the poor. He has sent me to proclaim release to the captives and recovering of sight to the blind, to set at liberty those who are oppressed, to proclaim the acceptable year of the Lord. (Luke 4:18f.)

This commitment to the first commandment and its interpretation in the light of the coming of God to God's creation shaped the vision, the activities, and the words of Jesus. At the same time, Jesus' words and especially his deeds raised the suspicion and opposition of the religious and political authorities of his day. This finally led to his capture, trial, torture, and execution. Behind this conflict stands the explosive question: who is God and what is God doing in the world? We shall therefore have to ask what kind of activities raised the opposition of the establishment. Why was Jesus charged with blasphemy and with leading people astray? What were the many activities in his life that finally intensified the opposition to have him captured and killed? Jesus' activities manifest an understanding of God that obviously caused great offense to the dominant political, economic, and religious forces of his day.

The Immediacy of the "Reign of God"[8]

It is clear that for Jesus, "God" was a good and dynamic word, pointing to a personal and transformative reality. Addressing God with the intimate "abba" is considered to be "the most important linguistic innovation" of Jesus.[9] The God who comes to expression in Jesus' life is a dynamic personal reality that changes things in the direction of freedom and justice. Jesus manifests the rule or reign of God that is always near (Mark 1:16), because God is always near. This nearness becomes an actual present reality when the demons are exorcised, when the poor are fed, when the oppressed receive hope, when the lame can walk, when the blind begin to see, and when the deaf start hearing (Luke 11:20; Matt 11:2-6). Since I have been critical of John Dominic Crossan's understanding of the resurrection, let me say that I have found his portrayal of the historical Jesus helpful.[10] This is what he says about Jesus and the reign of God:

> He not only discussed the Kingdom of God; he enacted it, and said that others could do so as well. . . . To remove . . . that which is radically subversive, socially revolutionary, and politically dangerous from Jesus' *actions* is to leave his life meaningless and his death inexplicable."[11]

The Solidarity of Grace

Jesus shared his life with the marginal people of his day, and he spoke the promises of God into their lives. His healing hand touched the religiously unclean leper. To the tax collectors who were not only morally suspect but also religiously disqualified because they collected taxes from God's people (the Jews) on soil that God had given to them, and they did it for the Gentiles (Romans), Jesus offered forgiveness and friendship. He called people of the lower classes (fishermen) and even women into his circle of disciples (Luke 8:1-3). In a patriarchal society, he raised the status of women and children. With the beatitudes he pronounced the eschatological blessings of the kingdom not on the wise and religious, but on battlers and others who struggle. He was accused of being a friend of publicans and sinners (Matt 11:19/Luke 7:34). That was not merely a moral criticism. It was a religious charge, claiming that Jesus had misrepresented God's activity in the world.

Miracles of the Kingdom

Although some of the miracles (especially the nature miracles and raising people from death) pose a problem for us today, this was not so in the ancient world. Miracles were unusual but not unheard of. There are parallels to Jesus' miracles in the Hebrew Bible and in the religious surroundings of Jesus' day. It would certainly amount to a post-Enlightenment domestication of Jesus if we were to erase all miracles from Jesus' life and ministry. Miracles are part of Jesus' life just as are his baptism, his solidarity with sinners, his sayings, his critique of cult and temple, his capture, and his crucifixion. Which miracles have a historical basis or a historical core will have to be decided from case to case. But to eliminate all miracles to make Jesus more acceptable to the modern skeptic is highly problematic and cannot be done on historical grounds.[12]

For our purpose, it is important to note that the miracles of Jesus were not primarily demonstrations of power or proofs of his divinity, but they were the actual demonstrations that the "reign of God" had arrived in human lives and in history. They manifest that God's passionate concern is to make human life whole. This passion longs especially to restore what is marginal, to heal what is sick, to liberate what is in chains. A word that most likely comes from the historical Jesus summarizes his activity: "the blind receive their sight, the lame walk, the lepers are cleansed, the deaf hear, the dead are raised, and the poor have good news brought to them" (Matt 11:5). What was offensive in the eyes of the religious establishment was not the fact that Jesus performed miracles. That was nothing new in the ancient world. What caused opposition was the fact that Jesus' miracles implied a theological claim. Jesus performed them in his role as messenger of the "reign of God." The miracles were part of the arrival of the "reign of God." Adding to the provocation was that Jesus exorcised demons from people who were shunned, that he healed the mute, the blind, the lame, the lepers—people who were religiously disqualified and whose disabilities, if at all, would be removed by God in the eschaton. By performing miracles of grace then and there, Jesus claimed to act in God's stead, which was considered blasphemy.

Ethos and Truth

In a society where several religious movements sought to worship and obey God by meticulously interpreting and observing the religious law (the Torah), Jesus' reference point for his attitude and activity was the "reign of God," which, for Jesus, was not correlative with the Torah or with the then-popular interpretation of the Torah. He called people to radical discipleship even when this conflicted with the demands of the Torah (Matt 8:21f./Luke 9:59f.). He questioned traditional family ties and began to shape a new family of brothers and sisters who share a common faith (Mark 3:31-35). He protected the dignity and affirmed the equality of women by criticizing divorce laws that were heavily slanted in favor of the male. He accused the religious establishment for not practicing what they preach (Matt 23:3) and for being concerned with tithing of "mint, dill, and cummin" while neglecting "the weightier matters of the law: justice and mercy and faith" (Matt 23:23=Luke 11:42). He questioned the "eye for an eye" mentality that was deeply embedded in the Torah (Gen 9:6; Exod 21:23-25;

Lev 24:20f.; Deut 19:21), and he tried to break the vicious spiral of violence, domination, and submission by seeking a new lifestyle in which even the enemy deserves love and respect (Matt 5:38-48). For Jesus, "otherness" and "difference" was not a threat to his identity but a potentially interesting reflection of the colorful grace of God.

Sacred and Profane

When Jesus affirmed the goodness of creation and placed the source of evil in the hearts of people (Mark 7:15), he thereby suspended the whole religious mentality that divided reality into clean and unclean, holy and profane. According to Israel's Holiness Code, life was to be viewed in terms of what pleased and displeased God. Jews were holy; Gentiles were worldly. Women during their time of menstruation were considered unclean. Some animals were clean and others were unclean. Some meats could be eaten; others couldn't. The uneducated people of the land, who had not been trained in the Torah, were considered less worthy in the sight of God than the Pharisees and scribes and rabbis and priests. When Jesus undermined this view of life, the implication was, of course, that no religious ritual or sacrifice is able to deal with the problem of evil, but only the forgiveness of God spoken into the hearts of people. Unless the human heart is changed, no "good fruits" can be expected. This was a fundamental critique on the whole system of law and cult that surrounded him. It raised the fierce opposition of the establishment.

Gift and Responsibility

During Jesus' time, there were people who had conveniently forgotten that the purpose of the law was not to protect the interests of the rich and powerful but to safeguard human dignity, to show a way forward for slaves, orphans, widows, and foreigners, and to use the land for the common good. When Jesus said to a man "who had great possessions" that he needed to "sell what you have, and give it to the poor" and follow Jesus if he wanted to have "treasure in heaven," the man "went away sorrowful" (Mark 10:17-22). He had not and he could not understand that God's ways have to do with justice for all rather than with personal and private piety.[13] Such an interpretation of the Torah would not have been welcome by the powerbrokers of Jesus' day.

The Sabbath

A further reason for conflict between Jesus and the religious forces of his day was his attitude toward the Sabbath.[14] Keeping the Sabbath had become the most important demand of the Torah. It was the identity celebration of Israel. It was the sign of God's election and it was designated to manifest that Israel is the people of God. To be an Israelite was synonymous with obeying the Sabbath rules. Offenders were punished heavily (including the death penalty, Jub 2:25; 50:8). Jesus showed no disrespect for the Sabbath as such. But he wanted to reclaim it as the day when the ways of God are celebrated. The "kingdom of God" is celebrated when love becomes an event. Jesus therefore relativized the then-current Sabbath laws in order to "do good" and to "save life" (Mark 3:4). He healed people on the Sabbath even when there was no medical emergency. This was an intentional provocation. Where love longs to become an event, there religious laws and practices must be suspended. How can the God who liberated his people from slavery and whose commandments are structures of liberation be confined to religious rules when human life needs to be healed? The response of the religious people was to hold counsel as to "how to destroy him" (Mark 3:6).

The Temple

Jesus' treatment of the Sabbath went hand in hand with his critical attitude toward the temple.[15] He questioned the paying of temple tax (Matt 17:24-27), and in a prophetic protest, he interfered with the proceedings of the temple to demonstrate that the temple establishment had led the people in wrong directions (Mark 11:15-19). Not ritual and sacrifice, but repentance, prayer, and commitment to justice were elements that would restore the temple to become again the house of God.[16] "And the chief priests and the scribes . . . sought a way to destroy him" (Mark 11:18).

Meddling in Politics

Jesus was confronted with the question of whether "it is lawful to pay taxes to Caesar, or not" (Mark 12:13-17; Matt 22:15-22; Luke 20:20-26), and the Lukan version of the trial against Jesus includes the accusation: "We found this man . . . forbidding us to give tribute to Caesar" (Luke 23:2).[17] This was a highly sensitive and potentially inflammable topic. Palestine was under Roman occupation. Some groups, like the Sadducees and the tax and toll collectors, aligned themselves with the occupation forces, while others, like the Zealots, were refusing to cooperate and were engaged in a struggle for liberation from the Romans. Where did Jesus stand? Would he be drawn into this highly political issue? Some of his contemporaries must have associated him with the Zealots since he had Zealots among his disciples.[18] But Jesus' emphasis on nonviolence and his encouragement to love one's enemy would suggest that he rejected the Zealot option. That does not mean, however, that Jesus was politically neutral.

When confronted with the question of paying tribute to Caesar, Jesus asked his investigators to hand him a coin. The coin had on one side the picture of the emperor with the inscription "*Tiberius Caesar Divi Augusti Filius Augustus*" (Tiberius Caesar, Augustus, Son of the Divine Augustus). On the other side was the image of the emperor's mother as the incarnation of the heavenly peace. The coin was a symbol of the Roman deity. It signified Rome's power over the Jews. Zealots would therefore not handle such a coin. Jesus took it into his hands, but at the same time he transfigured its significance by reminding his listeners that while they may give "to the emperor the things that are the emperor's," they must give "to God the things that are God's" (Mark 12:17). The coin belonged to the emperor, but the human being belonged to God. Jesus therefore adopted a middle position between violent opposition on the one hand and passive accommodation on the other. The human conscience finds its ultimate concern in God, and therefore the claim of political authorities can only be of secondary significance. The amazement of the people (Mark 12:17) can only be interpreted as the recognition that with Jesus they had encountered a transfiguration of politics.

Word Events

Among the religious groups of Jesus' day there were some who expected the "reign of God" to arrive as a result of political action in liberating Israel from its occupation forces. Others perceived the "kingdom of God" as a future reality. In intentional contrast to these, Jesus claimed that the "reign of God" became a present reality when demons were exorcised, when the sick were healed, when the oppressed were liberated, and when forgiveness happened in the event of word and faith.

Jesus' distinctive mode of communication was the telling of parables. He communicated the "reign of God" through stories. The "reign of God" is like the story of a man who had a hundred sheep, and when one of them got lost, he had no other passion than to find his lost sheep. Or the ways of God are like the story of a father who had two sons, both of whom lost their ways, one in immorality and one in moralism, but the father welcomed both of them back into his fatherly care. Or the "reign of God" is like the story of a farmer who was plowing his field when he came across an unexpected treasure, and like a pearl expert who came across the pearl of his dreams, the joy of the discovery drove them to sell all in order to acquire the one thing that counted. In telling these stories, Jesus invited the hearers to find and accept their place in the story and thus be initiated into the accepting and liberating presence of God. The claim that in these word-events the kingdom of God would come to people and include them in God's reign was an offense to those who expected the kingdom in the future or in political action or by obeying the law and keeping the cult. The nature of the parables as language events was another reason for firming up the opposition against Jesus. This also means, of course, that the message of the parables can only be understood in their relation to the passion of Jesus.

Forgiving Sins

Jesus assumed the place of God when he forgave sins (Mark 2:1-12). He did so without reference to the requirements of the law or to the mediation of the sacrificial system of the temple. What in then-popular expectations only God could do either through law and cult in the present or directly at the end of time, Jesus did there and then on his own authority. This act as such, and by implication the transfiguration of the prevalent understanding of God, was considered blasphemy (Mark 2:7) and added fuel to the religious opposition.

Liberating Authority

The freedom to forgive sins is related to the inherent authority that Jesus manifested in granting faith to people who in the ethos of that day were religiously suspect. Jesus said to a Gentile officer what he did not even say to his closest disciples: "Truly, I say to you, with no one in Israel have I found such faith" (Matt 8:10/Luke 7:9). He interpreted the attitude of a Canaanite woman (a foreigner), a blind man, and a healed leper by saying: "Your faith has made you well" (Mark 5:34; 10:52; Luke 17:19). The ἐξουσία ("authority") and the παρρησία ("confidence," "frankness," "courage," "fearlessness") that Jesus manifested by granting faith, and by granting it to those who were religiously suspect, caused great offense to the religious establishment.

The Call to Discipleship

The same is true for Jesus' authoritative call to discipleship. The idea and practice of following a religious leader was well known in the ancient world. But the audacity of calling people into a life of radical discipleship where traditional morality was suspended and the study of the law replaced with a personal attachment to Jesus was unknown. This new reality of the "reign of God" could not be contained in the old wineskins of traditional religion.

Jesus and John the Baptist

We finally mention Jesus' break with John the Baptist. There can be little doubt that Jesus was baptized by John the Baptist and that at least for some time he joined the Baptist's movement. Jesus may have learned some of his theological emphases from John, like the coming of the reign of God, his disappointment with Israel's sinfulness, and the importance of turning to God. Nevertheless, soon it must have become evident that their understanding of God diverged in important emphases. While John the Baptist preached repentance and baptism as the way to escape from God's imminent judgment, Jesus announced the arrival of the "reign of God" that brings joy, liberation, and hope to people.[19] While John focused on the necessity of repentance to escape punishment, Jesus called disciples to follow him in the celebration of joy and salvation. Again the distinctive message of Jesus becomes apparent.

Summary: Crucifixion and Resurrection

It has not been my intention to write or even sketch a biography of Jesus. I intended to show the inner connection between Jesus' life and death and that this inner connection has to do with Jesus' passion for justice.[20] In word and deed, Jesus displayed an authority and a παρρησία ("inner freedom," "courage") that people rightly interpreted as a claim to act on God's behalf. The "reign of God" became present in the words and deeds of Jesus. The content of the "reign of God" is love. Therefore Jesus' partiality for the marginal people, his passion to restore human life where it is broken, his criticism of the loveless morality of law and cult, his call to radical discipleship—all have their ground and their content in Jesus' understanding of the "reign of God" as love.

This brought Jesus into conflict with the authorities of his day. The religious leaders charged him with being a friend of publicans and sinners. To them it was presumptuous that Jesus (rather than God) would grant faith and forgiveness to people; that in the name of God he would restore people and convey to them hope and dignity; that he would claim those who were socially suspect and religiously unqualified to be the object of God's saving and liberating passion. His opponents rightly understood his lifestyle as questioning and even attacking the final and absolute authority of the foundational pillars of the contemporary Jewish religious establishment: the Torah, the temple, and the cult. What offended the religious establishment was not that Jesus understood and interpreted the regulations of the law and the rules of the cult differently but that he in fact *acted* upon his understanding. Under certain circumstances, when human need was evident and calling, he assumed the authority to break the Sabbath and suspend the cultic rules of ritual purity and fasting. To his religious opponents, he was a blasphemer and seducer of the people (Deut 13 and 17), and as such he deserved the death penalty (Lev 24:16).

By blessing the poor and oppressed, by showing solidarity with the wretched of the earth, and by proclaiming their liberation, he also challenged the economic interests of those in power. Anyone who suggested that the fate of the poor may not be their own fault or may not be the will of God but might indeed be the byproduct of societal structures that favor the interests of the rich and powerful was perceived as dangerous by the establishment.

This would also explain why Jesus' activity was brought to the attention of the political authorities of his day, whose interest it was to maintain social stability, and who readily cooperated in removing one person in order to maintain law and order for the rest of society.

Jesus threatened the religious, political, and economic structures of his day by his radical obedience to God and the resultant radical commitment to make human life human. This understanding of God and the resultant vision of reality clashed with the views and interests of the religious, economic, and political establishment. They could not contain and incorporate the newness of Jesus' vision of the "reign of God." In their understanding of reality, condemning Jesus to death was not only an act of self-preservation, but it was perceived to be a necessary act of obedience to their perception of the will of God.

He was captured, tortured, tried, and crucified. We must not forget that in the ancient Graeco-Roman world, crucifixion was not only "an utterly offensive affair, 'obscene' in the original sense of the word," that it was not only "a horrific, disgusting business," but that it also "was and remained a political and military punishment." It was "as a rule reserved for hardened criminals, rebellious slaves and rebels against the Roman state."[21] Its purpose was to punish and at the same time serve as a public deterrent to discourage other rebellious forces.

When this particular Jesus, who with his life fleshed out a specific understanding of God and of the dignity of human life, was raised from the dead, this life and the subsequent death were revealed as having divine and eternal dignity. By raising the crucified Christ from the dead, God revealed that this particular person, Jesus of Nazareth, and the life he lived must serve to define the content of "divinity" and therewith the content of resurrection faith. Concretely, this means that the deity of Christ is revealed in his radical obedience to God and his radical commitment to the healing and liberating of broken humanity. Deity, therefore, does not withdraw from the world, but it manifests its healing and reconciling reality in the world. It does not in the first place mean commitment to religious institutions and religious rules and dogmas, but the concrete engagement in the alleviation of human need.

What does this mean for our faith in Christ, for our understanding of being the church, for the understanding of our mission in the world? By raising the crucified Jesus from the dead, God declared an end to any religious or cultic ways to please or even impress God. Paul therefore proclaims Christ as the fulfillment and therefore the end of the law, and the Epistle to the Hebrews does the same with respect to the cult. The only adequate way of response to what God has done in Christ is to present our "bodies as a living sacrifice, holy and acceptable to God, which is your spiritual worship" (Rom 12:1). Jesus was crucified because the religious forces with their emphasis on Torah, temple, and cult could interpret Jesus' vision of God only as blasphemy and as leading people astray. "So Jesus also suffered outside the gate in order to sanctify the people through his own blood. Therefore let us go forth to him outside the camp and bear the abuse he endured" (Heb 13:12f.). Not sacrifice or ceremony, but worshiping God in our everyday life is the most adequate response to the resurrection of the crucified Christ.

Ontology

The interlocking of the life, death, and resurrection of Jesus Christ and its relationship to the Holy Spirit and to our life and the life of the world needs to be explored on an even deeper level. The resurrection of Christ enacted a transfiguration in ontology.

The crucifixion as the consequence of Jesus' life reveals the "world" as being determined by violence. The cross unmasks the world as "world"—bereft of love and therefore of God, driven by selfishness, self-interest, and violence. The world as "world" could no longer hear the word of God. The Johannine Prologue (John 1:1-14) most eloquently narrates the tragic destiny of the λόγος ("logos" = "word"): "He was in the world, and the world came into being through him; yet the world *did not know him*. He came to what was his own, and his own people *did not accept him*." How could they know him? How could they accept him? They had turned away—away from faith in God, away from friendship with fellow humans, away from partnership with nature. Humanity had turned into itself, and then it needed to find ways to protect what it found.

Where the "world" remained true to itself by forcing Jesus to the cross, God remained true to God's self. God, being love, identified with the victim, took the crucified One into God's own being, and thereby created new life out of death.

The violence of the world was transfigured into a new ontology: an ontology of justice. That means that at the center of life, in the foundation of being, there is not nothing but God; there is not violence but nonviolence; there is not war but peace; there is not hatred but love. Those who recognize this, those who believe what is true for all, experience the miracle of a new birth! The resurrection of Christ issues into the story of faith: "to all who received him, who believed in his name, he gave power to become children of God, who were *born*, not of blood or of the will of the flesh or of the will of man, but *of God*" (John 1:12f.).

This new ontology, grounded in a free and sovereign act of God, provides the basis and the content for Christian hope and praxis. On the basis of the resurrection of the crucified One, we can now believe that ultimately love and peace and justice will triumph. Not the lion of Judah, but the lamb of God can unlock the mysteries of life (Rev 5). In a world where too often we hear that only the strong will be free and that only the fit will survive, we have now an ontological basis for tuning into the passion of Jesus for bringing hope and liberation to the poor and oppressed.

By raising Jesus from the dead, God has given theological depth and dignity to the life and death of Jesus. In sharing his life with the dead Jesus, God once for all declares that nothing, not even death, can separate us from God. Christ now is our "peace"; in him God reconciled the world with himself. All theological symbols—"atonement," "expiation," "sacrifice," "redemption," "representation," "reconciliation," etc.—and all soteriological theories—ransom, substitution, moral influence, etc.—are valid if they give expression to this foundational theological reality that God has raised the crucified Christ from death and thereby established the event of salvation. Symbols and theories become distorted if they "detach" themselves from that central theological reality and seek to ground the meaning of the death of Jesus elsewhere. This in no way restricts our theological creativity. Indeed we need different theories and symbols because we are all different people and we all experience God's saving action in many different ways. But it must be clear which foundational event we are trying to explain, confess, and communicate.

The resurrection of the crucified Christ is the divine reality that becomes actualized in the event of faith and in the praxis of discipleship. The resurrection of the crucified One and his victory over death has intensified a process toward the gathering of all things, when love will have its way and when God will be all in all.

As part of that process, the story will continue to be told, believers will joyously respond to God in worship, and the gathered community will celebrate the presence of Christ in the elements of bread and wine and in the brother and sister. But all of this will remain partial and lopsided unless it is carried out in the awareness of the new ontology that entails the imperative of the struggle for justice, because it was the *crucified* Jesus who was *raised* from the dead.

Notes

[1] In the first volume of his excellent books on the historical Jesus, John P. Meier says correctly, "Properly understood, the historical Jesus is a bulwark against the reduction of Christian faith in general and christology in particular to 'relevant' ideology of any stripe" (*A Marginal Jew. Rethinking the Historical Jesus. Vol 1: The roots of the problem and the person*, The Anchor Bible Reference Library [New York: Doubleday, 1991], 200, compare 196-200).

[2] Jürgen Moltmann in his recent account of his own theological journey makes this point and elaborates on its significance for the present (*Experiences in Theology: Ways and Forms of Christian Theology*, trans. Margaret Kohl [Minneapolis: Fortress, 2000] III/4, 249-67).

[3] The debate has been summarized often, most recently by William R. Herzog II in *Jesus, Justice, and the Reign of God: A Ministry of Liberation* (Louisville: Westminster John Knox Press, 2000); Luke Timothy Johnson, "The Humanity of Jesus: What's at Stake in the Quest for the Historical Jesus," in John Dominic Crossan, Luke Timothy Johnson, and Werner H. Kelber, *The Jesus Controversy: Perspectives in Conflict* (Harrisburg PA: Trinity Press International, 1999), 48-74.

[4] "The Jesus of history is not and cannot be the object of Christian faith" (Meier, *A Marginal Jew, vol. 1*, 197).

[5] Ernst Käsemann, "The Problem of the Historical Jesus" (1953), in *Essays on New Testament Themes*, trans. W. J. Montague, SBT 41 (Naperville IL: Allenson, 1964), 15-47; "Blind Alleys in the 'Jesus of History' Controversy" (1964), in *New Testament Questions of Today*, trans. W. J. Montague (Philadelphia: Fortress, 1969), 23-65. Compare Rudolf Bultmann's essay, "The Primitive Christian Kerygma and the Historical Jesus" (1959), in Carl E. Braaten and Roy A. Harrisville, eds., *The Historical Jesus and the Kerygmatic Christ: Essays on the New Quest of the Historical Jesus*, trans. Carl E. Braaten and Roy A. Harrisville (New York/Nashville: Abingdon, 1964), 15-42.

[6] Gerhard Ebeling, *Theology and Proclamation: A Discussion with Rudolf Bultmann*, trans. John Riches (London: Collins, 1966); "The Question of the Historical Jesus and the Problem of Christology," in *Word and Faith*, trans. James W. Leitch (London: SCM, 1963), 288-304.

[7] I take some encouragement for this approach from John P. Meier's expertise on the historical Jesus when he says, "Whatever the exact order of Jesus' events and sayings, as a whole they precede and somehow precipitate the final confrontation with the enemies in Jerusalem, resulting in his crucifixion" (*A Marginal Jew, vol. 1*, 409). One of Meier's criteria for determining words and deeds of the historical Jesus is related to Jesus' rejection and execution: "A Jesus whose words and deeds did not threaten or alienate people, especially powerful people, is not the historical Jesus" (*A Marginal Jew. Rethinking the Historical Jesus. Vol. 2: Mentor, Message, and Miracles*. The Anchor Bible Reference Library [New York: Doubleday, 1994], 6).

[8] The reference is of course to the βασιλεία τοῦ Θεοῦ, a concept that is difficult to render into English. It is often translated as "kingdom of God" or "kingly rule of God." If the reader is not familiar with this concept, any good book on the historical Jesus or on the parables will explain it.

[9] Joachim Jeremias, *New Testament Theology: The Proclamation of Jesus*, trans. John Bowden (New York: Charles Scribner's Sons, 1971), 36.

[10] John Dominic Crossan, *The Historical Jesus: The Life of a Mediterranean Jewish Peasant* (San Francisco: HarperCollins, 1991); *Jesus: A Revolutionary Biography* (San Francisco: HarperCollins, 1994).

[11] Crossan, *Jesus: A Revolutionary Biography*, 93.

[12] Of great interest in this regard is the monumental analysis of the Jesus miracles by *A Marginal Jew, vol. 2,* part 3.

[13] For details, see Herzog, *Jesus, Justice, and the Reign of God,* 157-67.

[14] The major texts are Mark 1:21-28 (Luke 4:31-37); Mark 2:23-28 (Matt 12:1-8; Luke 6:1-5); Mark 3:1-6 (Matt 12:9-14; Luke 6:6-11); Mark 6:1-6 (Matt 13:53-58; Luke 4:16-30); Luke 13:10-17; 14:1-6.

[15] For details, see Herzog, *Jesus, Justice, and the Reign of God,* 219-21, 233-38.

[16] William R. Herzog II concludes his analysis of Jesus and the temple with the words: "The destruction of the oppressive institution that the temple had become was one step towards the coming justice of the reign of God . . ." (*Jesus, Justice, and the Reign of God,* 143 and ch. 6, 111-43). In ch. 9 (191-216), Herzog argues on the basis of some of Jesus' parables that Jesus counseled a break between the "temple" and the "land," suggesting that a major reason for the poverty of the people of the land was not the unfruitfulness of the land but the exploitation by the temple. That being the case would of course question the relevance of the whole cult system for the "people of the land."

[17] For details, see Herzog, *Jesus, Justice, and the Reign of God,* 219-32.

[18] Simon the Zealot in Luke 6:15 and Acts 1:13 is probably identical with Simon the Cananaean in Mark 3:18. Judas Iscariot may also have been a Zealot. Although the meaning of "Iscariot" is unclear, one possibility is that it derives from σικάριος, meaning "bandit, assassin."

[19] Compare *A Marginal Jew, vol. 2,* 134, 1042, 1044.

[20] In his recent book on the historical Jesus, William R. Herzog II describes Jesus as a peasant prophet of the justice of the reign of God. As such, Jesus authoritatively interpreted the Torah by retrieving its original humanitarian meaning and seeking ways to protect the people from the exploitation by the temple system and the Roman occupation (*Jesus, Justice, and the Reign of God*).

[21] Martin Hengel, *Crucifixion in the Ancient World and the Folly of the Message of the Cross* (1977), in *The Cross of the Son of God,* trans. John Bowden (London: SCM, 1986), 91-185; the quotations are from 114, 127, 178, and 175.

Chapter 4

The Triumph of God over the Estranging Forces of Death

"Death has been swallowed up in victory...."—1 Corinthians 15:54

The second pillar in our argument that the resurrection of Christ is interrelated with justice and its implementation is God's defeat of the life-denying powers of death. Justice is understood here in its broadest terms. It has to do with what is due to every human being: the fulfillment of human destiny in the context of nature and history. It is a relational concept. Human beings find their fulfillment in creative and life-giving relationships to themselves, to others, to nature, to history, and to God. These relationships are distorted and threatened by the forces of death. Death isolates. Death breaks down relationships. By raising Jesus from death, God has broken the ultimate threat of isolation and thereby provided the basis for the struggle for justice.

The Death of Death

The resurrection of Christ is God's protest against death and its many messengers—against estrangement, oppression, and exploitation. The Swiss theologian and poet Kurt Marti composed the following funeral oration:[1]

> it might readily suit many lords of this world
> if everything would be settled at death
> if the dominion of the lords
> and the servitude of the slaves
> would be confirmed forever
>
> it might readily suit many lords of this world
> if in eternity they would remain lords
> in expensive private tombs

and their slaves would remain slaves
in rows of common graves

but a resurrection is coming
quite different from what we thought
a resurrection is coming which is
god's rising up against the lords
and against the lord of lords—death

The resurrection of Jesus Christ implies the death of death: "For we know that Christ being raised from the dead will never die again; death no longer has dominion over him" (Rom 6:9). Jesus Christ therefore is "the resurrection and the life" (John 11:25). By raising Jesus from death, God has demonstrated God's victory over death and its estranging powers.

Death Has Many Faces

What is death? In Western cultures we tend to limit our understanding of death to the end of our physical life here on earth. That may be the most ostentatious aspect of death, but death is much more. Death isolates. Death individualizes. Death intimates the possibility of being cut off from the sources of life. Death estranges us from the relationships that sustain life: from God, from our fellow human beings, from nature, and from history. The very knowledge of death and the uncertainty and fear created by it can cripple our living. The dead cannot praise God, and they cannot love and be loved by their neighbor. Such isolation becomes most clearly visible in the physical death of a person. But the forces of isolation from the sources of life are already there in the midst of life.

We have to realize, therefore, that death has many faces. It spells the end to one's earthly life, but it is not only that. Death also spreads its odor in the midst of life. Gerhard von Rad says this about Israel's understanding of death: ". . . for Israel death's domain reached far further into the realm of the living. Weakness, illness, imprisonment, and oppression by enemies are a kind of death."[2] A fundamental challenge of life is addressing the threat of death.

At-one-ment

The early Christians and the church through the ages have used a number of metaphors and theories to say that what has been rent asunder by the powers of death, God has brought together again. In his search to find a proper translation for the New Testament word καταλλαγή, which is usually rendered as "reconciliation," William Tyndale (1483–1536) created the word "atonement" ("at-one-ment"), meaning "making one with God."

The implication is, of course, that what belonged together had become estranged and even separated. Human destiny is to live in relationship with God, but this relationship has gone wrong and many symbols and concepts—Satan, principalities, authorities, powers, death, sin, law—have been engaged to explain why the togetherness between God and humanity had issued into estrangement and separation.

Still, where humanity had become unfaithful, God remained faithful. As a free and sovereign act of love, God raised Jesus from death and thereby renewed God's relationship with humanity and creation. This reality of bringing together what had become separated, this at-one-ment, has its ground in the Christ-event. When people meet Christ in the event of faith, they experience forgiveness and reconciliation. When the early Christians sought language to express that experience and to confess at the same time that their experience was not merely immanent and psychological but that it was grounded in an act of God, they used a great variety of symbols. They spoke of expiation (Rom 3:25), sin offering (Rom 8:3; Heb 9:11-14, 28), ransom (Mark 10:45; Rev 5:9), reconciliation (Rom 5:10f.; 2 Cor 5:17-21; Col 1:22), representation (Rom 4:25; 5:6-8), redemption (Rom 3:24; Eph 1:7; Heb 9:15), justification (Rom 3:24), blood sacrifice (Rom 3:25; 5:9; Eph 2:13; Heb 10:19; 1 Pet 1:2; 1 John 1:7; Rev 1:5; Acts 20:28), covenant sacrifice (Mark 14:24; 1 Cor 11:25; Heb 9:17-21; 13:20), Passover lamb (John 1:29, 36; 19:36; 1 Pet 1:19; Rev 5:6; 7:14; 12:11), cosmic reconciler (Col 1:20), destruction of the devil (Heb 2:14), forgiveness (Heb 9:22).

These many and diverse symbols have in common that at-one-ment (reconciliation) results from God's activity in the life and death of Jesus of Nazareth. From the human and historical point of view, Jesus' life and death may be viewed as a failure. Even in the hearts of Jesus' disciples (at least the male disciples), the shadow of death quenched hope and faith. They fled. But God did something new—something without analogy. By raising Jesus from the dead, God broke that ultimate threat of death and thereby established the ground for the confession that "nothing" can separate us anymore from God's love (Rom 8:38f.). This ground has two dimensions that must be kept in mind in any explanation of at-one-ment. The resurrection of Christ meant the defeat of death, what the apostle Paul celebrates as the death of death (1 Cor 15:54-57). At the same time, it meant that God has bound God's very being to the story of Jesus. No longer can Christian God-talk bypass Jesus' life, death, and resurrection.

The early Christian conviction that God has reconciled reality with God issued into a diverse variety of theories of at-one-ment that have evolved in the history of the church.[3] These theories are situational in the sense that they interrelate the soteriological dimension of the death and resurrection of Jesus with the available metaphors of their respective time and culture. In a feudal society, characterized by conquest, capture, imprisonment, ransom, and liberation, the death and resurrection of Christ was interpreted as a ransom to redeem prisoners (of sin). In societies where the honor and authority of the monarch or tribal chief needed to be carefully protected in order to provide a feeling of order, security, and welfare for the people, the death of Christ was interpreted as the offering or sacrifice needed to restore the honor of God. Where a religious cult with its sacrifices, rituals, representations, and atonements was determinative, Christ was seen as a sacrifice or a representative or atonement for our sins and the sins of the world. In other situations, juridical categories of covenant, law, transgression, guilt, sanction, repentance, and forgiveness were determinative and consequently Christ's death and resurrection were interpreted as establishing a new covenant, or as carrying the deserved sanction to fulfill the demands of the divine law. In modern times we tend to think more in personal categories of friendship, freedom, responsibility, community, betrayal, and restoration and consequently Christ can be seen as dying for his friends as the magnificent manifestation of the love of God that is prepared to give all in order to find the one lost sheep.

No theory says it all and therefore no theory is satisfactory. Human language and human thought always limp behind what they want to say. Each theory must be examined, whether it clearly spells out that our salvation is grounded in God's act of raising Jesus from the dead, and whether it becomes clear that Jesus was not an abstract Son of God, but that he lived a certain kind of life and that the opposition he experienced, his capture, trial, and crucifixion resulted from his vision of God and of life. Since, as we have seen in the previous chapter, Jesus' vision of life and of God has to do with what is right and just, the issue of justice must be at the heart of a satisfactory theory of at-one-ment.

It remains a challenge to discern the heartbeat behind the different metaphors and theories of atonement. Our theological task is not simply to repeat one or more of these approaches or to judge which approach is the most adequate one. We must try to detect the heart of the matter and then, ever again, try to say it in our own words.

When the early Christians confessed that "Christ died for our sins" (1 Cor 15:3) and thereby brought forgiveness, or that those "who were once estranged and hostile in mind, doing evil deeds, he has now reconciled in his fleshly body through death" (Col 1:21f.), they wanted to say that by raising Jesus from death, God "disarmed the rulers and authorities" that estrange people from God, and thereby "made a public example of them, triumphing over them" in the cross of Christ (Col 2:14f.). Viewed from the perspective of Easter and Pentecost, raising Jesus from death was understood as defeating the estranging powers of death and thus reconciling all things with God (2 Cor 5:17-21).

Any metaphor or theory that seeks to capture the soteriological thrust of the Christ-event must meet the following requirements:

- it must take seriously the estrangement and separation between God and humanity/creation;
- it needs to preserve carefully God's identity as life and love;
- it should clearly elaborate that humanity is incapable of undoing the separation by itself;
- it must spell out that at-one-ment happens when God identifies God's being with Jesus, especially in raising him from the dead;
- it must take seriously the life of Jesus and its interrelationship with his death;
- it must elaborate that at-one-ment is not only a past event but a continuing reality into which people are drawn by the Holy Spirit and their response in faith and baptism.

Atonement, then, is a relational reality. The event of reconciliation includes the ministry of reconciliation (2 Cor 5:19f.). Through faith, the divinely established reality flows over into the life of believers and begins to shape their existence: "... when you were dead in trespasses and the uncircumcision of your flesh, God made you alive together with him, when he forgave us all our trespasses, erasing the record that stood against us with its legal demands. He set this aside, nailing it to the cross" (Col 2:13f.).

On the basis of the death and resurrection of Christ, the author of Colossians can then ask the rhetorical question, "If with Christ you died to the elemental spirits of the universe, why do you live as if you still belonged to the world?" (Col 2:20). The exhortation follows naturally:

> So if you have been raised with Christ, seek the things that are above, where Christ is, seated at the right hand of God. Set your minds on things that are above, not on things that are on earth, for you have died, and your life is hidden with Christ in God. When Christ who is your life is revealed, then you also will be revealed with him in glory. (Col 3:1-4)

This conviction that in the resurrection of Christ, God has unmasked and defeated the powers of death and thereby established a new reality is of great relevance today. Humanity is engaged in a seemingly never-ending spiral of violence. That spiral of violence is interlocked with the struggle for justice. When poverty, ethnic hatred, struggle to find refuge or asylum, and religious intolerance spill over, the only way to harness the unleashed forces seems to be further violence. Violence meets violence and the spiral keeps turning. By raising Jesus from the dead, God identified with the nonviolent victim of injustice and thereby laid the foundation for justice and nonviolence.

When we read texts like Ephesians 6:12—". . . our struggle is not against enemies of blood and flesh, but against the rulers, against the authorities, against the cosmic powers of this present darkness, against the spiritual forces of evil in the heavenly places"—we underestimate the relevance of such texts when we talk of "spiritual warfare" in the sense of prayer wars against abstract spirits in the air or in another transcendent realm. What is meant is the daily human struggle against institution and structures that diminish human life. Structures and institutions like racism, child abuse, disrespect of refugees and asylum seekers, and the many injustices against indigenous peoples have a spiritual dimension. They not only affect our politics and our morality, but they affect our souls and they diminish the ethos of our societies. The forces of death come to us in human and historical structures and institutions. When corporations put profits before people, when governments lose the vision of a good society, when churches deny equal rights to women, then the forces of death spread their odor. Early Christians spoke of principalities and powers that dehumanize life. With that language, they were not thinking of abstract and disembodied spirits, but of agents of death that came to them in the shape of human and historical institutions that distort and diminish life. In recent years, research in this area and theologians such as Hendrikus Berkhof,[4] G. B. Caird,[5] and especially Walter Wink[6] have reminded us that the forces of death by whatever name—demons, rulers, principalities, powers, authorities—are not beings of another world who invite prayer battles that have nothing to do with the struggle for justice in our world. Such powers do not exist apart from their embodiment in political, social, economic, and religious structures and institutions and their functionaries who serve the estranging powers of death.

By raising Jesus from death, God exposed God's very being to death, and in that encounter God remained God. Since God the creator overcame the forces of death, *life* proved itself stronger than death. God did all that "for us," therefore God remained true to his covenantal promises, became the redeemer, and revealed himself as *love*. Not only life, but also love, as God's life for us, is stronger than death.

If with the resurrection of Christ we celebrate the death of death, then this has a number of consequences. The powerful and colorful work of the Spirit in raising Jesus from the dead creates an equally powerful and colorful rainbow of promise and hope in our life and in our world.

Hope for the Individual

There is hope and promise for the individual. People who like Abraham, Isaac, David, and Job died "in a good old age . . . and full of years" can claim the promise for themselves that Christ is "the resurrection and the life" (John 11:25). They, like all of us, are included in God's redemptive purposes (Rom 14:9; 1 Pet 3:18-20; 4:6). They died into the rich life of God. For them and for us, the words of the psalmist are fulfilled:

> . . . my heart is glad, and my soul rejoices;
> my body also rests secure.
> For you do not give me up to Sheol,
> or let your faithful one see the pit.
> You show me the path of life;
> in your presence there is fullness of joy,
> in your right hand there are pleasures forevermore. (Ps 16:9-11)

Believers know and anticipate that Christ's victory over death will have personal consequences: "Those who believe in me, even though they die, will live, and everyone who lives and believes in me will never die" (John 11:25f.; compare John 5:24). Faith in Christ brings to us the promise that God's being has been exposed to, but has not been conquered by, death. God has remained God in God's struggle with death. Therefore God's relationship to the believer will not be broken. That is what the promise that we "will never die" means. Faith in the risen Christ liberates believers from the strangling anxiety that death will mean a nihilistic end. On the basis of Christ's resurrection, the apostle Paul joyously confesses:

> I am convinced that neither death, nor life, nor angels, nor rulers, nor things present, nor things to come, nor powers, nor height, nor depth, nor anything else in all creation, will be able to separate us from the love of God in Christ Jesus our Lord." (Rom 8:38f.)

Hope for Unlived Lives

But then there is death as the untimely negation of life. We know of 12 million children under the age of five who die each year—35,000 each day—caused by lack of food, insufficient clean water, and inadequate medical care. Young people are blown up by land mines before they can reach the prime of their lives. Child soldiers learn to hate and kill rather than love and nurture from early days. War and ethnic hatred and torture chambers find their victims in young women and men who have had no chance to develop their potential. Children's bodies and souls are marred and broken by sexual abuse, child labor, and war.

In ancient Israel, such experiences gave rise to questions about God's faithfulness and God's justice: "Is your steadfast love declared in the grave . . . ?" (Ps 88:11). Can God's faithfulness and God's justice be limited or even annulled by the power of death? Will death and its messengers in the long run be able to laugh in the face of God?

> Not to us, O Lord, not to us,
> but to *your* name give glory,
> for the sake of *your* steadfast love
> and *your* faithfulness!
> Why should the nations say,
> "Where is their God?" (Ps 115:1f.)

In the context of this cruel reality, the promise of faith began to take shape that God is the God of life and justice, that "his steadfast love" and "the faithfulness of the LORD endures forever" (Pss 117:2; 118:1-4). This growing conviction[7] finds its fulfillment in the resurrection of Christ. The God who raised the crucified One from death promises justice and fulfillment to those whose lives have been marred or cut short here on earth.[8]

Hope in Face of Injustice

The problem is further intensified when death is the direct consequence of injustice. Death reigns in Afghanistan, Rwanda, Nigeria, Sudan, the Middle East, Indonesia, and Chechnya. Terror brings death and destruction to a nation. Innocent men, women, and children are maimed and killed in the power games of the world. If God is not only the creator of heaven and earth but also the sovereign master over history, how can it be that too often the righteous suffer and the wicked prosper (Jer 12:1; Ps 73:3-14)? If God is God, how can it be that those who engage themselves in upholding the divine law and who have no other passion than to do God's will are being persecuted, tortured, and killed without seeing the cause of justice succeed?

Again, the resurrection of the *crucified* Christ speaks to that situation. We have shown that Jesus' death was the end result of a life committed to God and to making human life human. With God raising that particular Jesus, the victim of injustice, from the dead, hope and promise is spelled to all people whose justice is denied here on earth. The meaning of life consists in being open and faithful to our vision of God. This God-orientation will outlast and outshine any lack of success and fulfillment that human and historical circumstances may withhold from us. Indeed, there is a sense that all human experience remains a fragile and incomplete longing for ultimate fulfillment in God.

Beyond the Shadow of Time

In all that I have said, I have emphasized the significance of the resurrection of Christ for the present. Too often has the relevance of the resurrection been spiritualized or transposed into some unknown future. Faith in the risen Christ makes a difference here and now. Nevertheless, there is cruelty and injustice for which it is difficult to see any redemption in time.

I was born in a country, Germany, that during my childhood years showed "disregard and contempt for human rights" that "have resulted in barbarous acts which have outraged the conscience of mankind."[9] Places like Auschwitz and concepts like genocide remind us of evil that transcends our imagination. Millions of people were brutalized, tortured, and murdered. Can those who have experienced such atrocities, can those who remember, ever forgive and forget?

I now live in a country, Australia, where in the recent past it was official government policy to breed Aboriginality out of the indigenous people. For that purpose, 50,000 to 100,000 children were forcibly removed from their parents, placed in children's homes, and brought up to be assimilated into the white Anglo-European culture.[10] Thousands of stories of horror have been uncovered. At best, the "stolen children," robbed of their parents and culture and not permitted to speak their language or contact their families, suffer a lifelong feeling of loss, separation, and crisis of identity: "Why me; why was I taken away? It's like a hole in your heart that can never heal."[11] At worst, they were beaten, sexually abused, and destroyed in body and soul. One girl, for instance, was taken away from her mother as a young child and placed in a home. When she became a teenager, she was sent into a white family for summer vacation. The man of the house sexually abused her. When she returned to the home and told the matron, her mouth was washed out with soap. Although she pleaded not to be sent back to that place, next summer she had to return. This time she was raped and became pregnant. When her child was delivered, it was immediately taken away from her and the young mother never saw it again.

There are hurts and pains and wounds so deep that they cannot be healed under the shadow of time and space. It is therefore important to emphasize that the healing power of the resurrection transcends the limitations of time and space. The reality of the resurrection of the crucified Christ opens up a future in which "the creation itself will be set free from its bondage to decay and will obtain the freedom of the glory of the children of God." This reality, grounded in the resurrection of Christ, entails the knowledge of hope that "not only the creation, but we ourselves, who have the first fruits of the Spirit, groan inwardly while we wait for adoption, the redemption of our bodies" (Rom 8:21-23).

"... In the Lord Your Labor is Not in Vain" —1 Corinthians 15:58

This brings us to the often-asked question: is it *worthwhile* at all to do what is right, if disadvantage, persecution, torture, and cruel death are often the consequence? Why not simply eat, drink, and be merry for the few years that are given to us on earth? One does not have to be religious to know that such an attitude is not only misleading, but it is false. It is negated by the universal human experience, which knows that there are things in life more important than life itself. People have always been willing to sacrifice their lives for what they considered to be an ultimate concern—their God, their country, their family.

In the Judeo-Christian tradition, faith in the God of life, love, and justice grew in the conviction that God will not allow God's relationship to God's people to be broken. God will not allow the wicked to triumph ultimately. God will make an ontological protest against the ultimate triumph of the torturer over his victim. The psalmist, for instance, after a long complaint against the prosperity of the wicked, comes to the conclusion that the relationship with God will prove stronger:

> When my soul was embittered,
> when I was pricked in heart,
> I was stupid and ignorant,
> I was like a beast toward you.
> Nevertheless I am continually with you;
> you hold my right hand.
> You guide me with your counsel,

and afterward you will receive me with honor. . . .
My flesh and my heart may fail,
but God is the strength of my heart
and my portion forever. (Ps 73:21-26)

God will be God. God will fulfill God's promises. God's faithfulness and God's steadfast love will ultimately triumph. This conviction led to an explicit resurrection faith in the post-exilic period—Isaiah 26:7-21; Daniel 12:1f.; 2 Maccabees 7—and in his great resurrection chapter (1 Cor 15), the apostle Paul concludes with an exhortation grounded in the resurrection of the crucified Christ: "Therefore, my beloved, be steadfast, immovable, always excelling in the work of the Lord, because you know that in the Lord your labor is not in vain" (1 Cor 15:58).

Summary and Conclusion

Therefore, recognizing the resurrection of Christ as it impinges on the estranging reality of death, we can make the following affirmations:

- Life is lived in a network of relationships: to God, to self, to each other, to the environment, to history.
- Death is the quenching, the distortion, the breaking down, and the denial of these relationships.
- Death, therefore, does not simply occur at the end of one's life. It reaches into life. Wherever relationships are distorted or broken or abused, there death is at work.
- God, however, is the God of *life*. Confronted with death and its powers, the Godhood of God is at stake.
- The dawning conviction in the Hebrew Bible that God's faithfulness and justice will outlast death, indeed the beginning of resurrection hope in pre-Christian Judaism, finds its ontological fulfillment in the resurrection of Christ.
- There God defeated the estranging powers of death and created a *new* reality, a reality that is in process, of which we are part, and that comes to its fulfillment when love will have its way and God will be all in all.
- Therefore, on the basis of the ultimate triumph of the crucified Christ, it is *worthwhile* to make God one's ultimate concern. "My flesh and my heart may fail, but God is the strength of my heart and my portion forever" (Ps 73:26).

The two pillars on which resurrection theology is built—the death of death and the fact that the risen Christ was the *crucified* One—have both shown that the resurrection cannot be frozen into the past, nor can its relevance be limited to the future. By raising the crucified One from the dead, God wants to change history in the direction of justice here and now. We shall now illustrate that point by discussing selective issues that in the New Testament were directly related to the new and history-changing reality of the resurrection (equality of gender, race, and class). Then we shall briefly address the issues of ecology and dialogue with other religions, both of which are also obvious implications of the resurrection of Christ.

Notes

[1] Kurt Marti, "leichenreden," in *rosa loui, republikanische gedichte, leichenreden* (zürich: buchclub ex libris, 1975), 153 (my translation).

[2] Gerhard von Rad, *The Theology of Israel's Historical Traditions*, vol. 1 of *Old Testament Theology*, trans. D. M. G. Stalker (Edinburgh and London: Oliver and Boyd, 1962), 387.

[3] I have briefly summarized some of them in "The Meaning of the Death of Jesus Christ," in *American Baptist Quarterly* 4 (March 1985), 3-34. Compare Gustaf Aulén, *Christus Victor: A historical study of the three main types of the idea of atonement*, trans. A. G. Hebert (New York: MacMillan, 1969 [1931]); Paul S. Fiddes, *Past and Present Salvation: The Christian Idea of Atonement* (London: Darton, Longman and Todd, 1989); Colin E. Gunton, *A Study of Metaphor, Rationality and the Christian Tradition* (Grand Rapids MI: Eerdmans, 1989); John McIntyre, *The Shape of Soteriology: Studies in the Doctrine of the Death of Christ* (Edinburgh: T&T Clark, 1992).

[4] *Christ and the Powers*, trans. John Howard Yoder (Scottdale PA: Herald Press, 1962).

[5] *Principalities and Powers: A Study in Pauline Theology* (Oxford: Clarendon Press, 1956); *The Language and Imagery of the Bible* (London: Duckworth, 1980).

[6] Foundational is *Naming the Powers: The Language of Power in the New Testament* (Philadelphia: Fortress Press, 1984). The other books build on *Naming the Powers* and show the ongoing relevance of Wink's thesis: *Unmasking the Powers: The Invisible Forces that Determine Human Existence* (Philadelphia: Fortress Press, 1986); *Engaging the Powers: Discernment and Resistance in a World of Domination* (Minneapolis: Fortress Press, 1992); *The Powers That Be: Theology for a New Millennium* (New York: Doubleday, 1998).

[7] This growing conviction is well portrayed by Hans Walter Wolff, *Anthropology of the Old Testament*, trans. Margaret Kohl (London: SCM, 1974), 107-10.

[8] Compare Jürgen Moltmann, *The Coming of God: Christian Eschatology*, trans. Margaret Kohl (London: SCM, 1996), 116-18.

[9] The quotation comes from the preamble of the *Universal Declaration of Human Rights*.

[10] For details, see *Bringing them home:Report of the National Inquiry into the Separation of Aboriginal and Torres Strait Islander Children from Their Families* (Commonwealth of Australia, 1997).

[11] Ibid., 177.

Chapter 5

Affirming the Risen Christ Today

"I am the resurrection and the life . . ."—John 11:25

Introduction

In this chapter I want to emphasize the history-changing significance of the resurrection. The resurrection keeps the "dangerous memory of Jesus"[1] alive. Too often in theological thinking and in church praxis, we have made the mistake of delegating the relevance and significance of the resurrection to the past, with the consequence that questions of historical verification have dictated and dominated the theological agenda. Or our emphasis has been primarily a focus on the future, so that the resurrection of Christ served mainly as the basis for our human hopes of resurrection beyond our life here on earth. Both past and future emphases are legitimate and important. But they must not overshadow the significance of the resurrection for the respective "here and now." Within a Trinitarian understanding of God, it is the Spirit, the same Spirit who raised Jesus from the dead, who wants to inspire and change things in the direction of God.

This is not the place to develop the social-ethical implications of the resurrection of the crucified Christ. However, I do want to indicate that when God acts, God wants to change things in the direction of justice. By raising Jesus from the dead, God did not legitimize the status quo but unmasked the injustice that brought Jesus to the cross. God confirmed Jesus' vision of reality, and God laid the foundation for a new reality of love, peace, and justice. We shall see that this life-changing reality of the resurrection was evident from the earliest days of the Christian faith.

At the same time, it can also be observed how the dynamic, history-changing reality of the resurrection was soon adapted to culturally and philosophically more acceptable patterns and replaced by debating whether it happened or not and what exactly took place. The river of faith threatened to become severed from its source. Intellectual discussions "about" an event can easily have a distancing effect. They tend to objectify and define and as such tease believers into becoming masters over rather than servants and interpreters of the event. Cultural accommodation has a leveling-out effect and tends to relativize the revolutionary nature of the resurrection. A voluntary, liberating, and obedient faith (discipleship) is easily replaced by convention, reason, and morality.

I want to illustrate the interesting dynamic of change and accommodation by briefly examining three different ways in which the resurrection transfigured social and cultural norms, and how at the same time such norms are persistent and constantly threaten to quench the yearning of faith for the implementation of justice. The examples I have chosen—racial, social, and gender equality; the ordination of women; and ecological responsibility—remain relevant to the present day.

A Community of Equals: Galatians 3:23-28

The history-creating revolution of the resurrection is captured in a text from the Pauline tradition, in Galatians 3:23-28:

> . . . before faith came, we were imprisoned and guarded under the law until faith would be revealed. Therefore the law was our disciplinarian until Christ came, so that we might be justified by faith. But now that faith has come, we are no longer subject to a disciplinarian, for in Christ Jesus you are all children of God through faith. As many of you as were baptized into Christ have clothed yourselves with Christ.
> There is *no longer Jew or Greek*,
> there is *no longer slave or free*,
> there is *no longer male and female*;
> for all of you are one in Christ Jesus.

Without going into details, the following remarks may summarize the message of this text.

Historical reality is divided into two periods. There is, first of all, the period "under the power of sin," which is the period "under the law." This period is negatively characterized as a period of imprisonment and restraint. The law is described as a παιδαγωγός "disciplinarian" (not διδάσκαλος, "teacher"). Παιδαγωγός is not a positive word. It does not refer to a schoolmaster who guides the pupil into positive human development. The "law" here is not understood as the positive teacher who leads Judaism toward Christianity. The παιδαγωγός refers to a slave who leads the child of his master to school and protects the child against molesters. He had the reputation of being rude and rough, limiting the freedom and development of the child.[2]

The period marked by sin and law comes to an end with the coming of Christ and the coming of faith. Christ is the fulfillment and the end of the law, as Paul says at another place (Rom 10:4). The restraint and the imprisonment under the law are replaced by the justification faith brings. The Christian therefore is no longer subject to the law. In Christ, a *new*, divine reality has broken into the history of estrangement, isolation, and death. Law and sin are replaced by gospel and faith (compare also Rom 3:21-26). Against the Jewish Christians in Galatia who maintained that respect and obedience to the Torah were still necessary for salvation, and with it insisted on the implied religious elitism of the Jewish people, Paul asserts a radical break, a discontinuity between law and gospel, sin and faith.

One is reminded of the important conference in Jerusalem narrated by the apostle Paul in Galatians 2:1-10. The issue was whether Gentiles could become Christians without first becoming Jews. Would a Gentile who wanted to turn to Christ by faith still have to be circumcised and still have to observe the instructions of the Torah? For Paul this issue was critical. His own calling, the credibility of the gospel, and therefore the nature of grace and of God were at stake at that point. Taking the uncircumcised Christian convert Titus with him, Paul and his entourage traveled from Antioch to meet the "pillars"—James, Peter, and John—in Jerusalem. Paul's very identity was related to the question of whether salvation was really by grace *alone* through faith *alone*. With it the truth and the freedom of the gospel hung in the balance. Paul therefore emphasizes, "we did not submit to them even for a moment, so that the truth of the gospel might always remain with you" (Gal 2:5). The Jerusalem conference can be described as a miracle of grace because the "pillars," James, Peter, and John, "recognized the *grace* that had been given to me" and "contributed *nothing* to me," except "that we remember the poor, which was actually what I was eager to do" (Gal 2:6-10).[3] We witness here the recognition that God's love is given unconditionally, but because it is *God's* love, therefore it entails the imperative to manifest justice for the disadvantaged.

The new reality of the resurrection of the crucified Christ arrives in the life of the believer and the believing community through faith and baptism. In faith and baptism, Christ becomes the determinative center of the life of the believer and the believing community.

By refusing to make faith and baptism dependent on religious or ethnic conditions or restrictions, the love of God and God's salvation are recognized as being universal. The title "children of God," traditionally used for Jews, through Christ and in the power of the Spirit, who universalizes the work of Christ, includes the Gentiles—"through faith" of course; and this faith is celebrated and publicly confessed in baptism.

The *newness* of the resurrection of Christ has arrived in the world and begins to shape history. The salvation that God has accomplished in the Christ-event undoes the estrangement and injustice of sin. "There can be no doubt that Paul's statements have social and political implications of even a revolutionary dimension."[4] Paul mentions three implications of the newness and the power of the resurrection when it arrives in the lives and communities of believers.

"There Is No Longer Jew or Greek"

Cultural barriers had separated Jews and Greeks for centuries, and from the Jewish point of view, it gave Jews a feeling of election, elitism, and superiority. "In Christ," any privileges based on nationality and culture and race are suspended. The "other" becomes interesting for her/his own sake, and "in Christ" we no longer need to see the "other" as a threat from which we must protect and separate ourselves. Indeed, we need the other to celebrate life and faith.

This message is of particular relevance today. Racism, ethnic and religious suspicion, and hatred are among the great problems of modern times. With the "two thirds" world not making much progress in escaping their abject poverty, with millions of refugees and asylum seekers looking for a space to live, the morality and sense of justice in the "one-third" world are challenged. Globalization is a fact of modern life. The question is not only whether it will serve economic and political interests of the rich and powerful, but whether it will also include responsibility for the millions of poor, oppressed, and uprooted people. Christians and the churches must be at the forefront in their engagement for finding ways of giving expression to the equality of all people, for encouraging a more equal distribution of the earth's resources, and for welcoming strangers into our midst.

"There Is No Longer Slave or Free"

Although it took the established churches 1800 years to hear or understand this implication of the resurrection of the crucified Christ, here "in Christ," where the gospel is heard, believed, and obeyed, the abolition of slavery must be realized and practiced. This probably caused major problems in the earliest churches because slavery was an important economic and social pillar of ancient society. The churches wanted to maintain good relations with the society around them in order to communicate the gospel. Indeed, the churches were so small and vulnerable that a social and political revolution was out of the question. When, for instance, the slave Onesimus was converted and sought the apostle Paul's advice, theoretically Paul could have counseled him to assert his newly found freedom "in Christ." Paul, however, had no power to suspend the institution of slavery. Paul sent Onesimus back to his master. But he did so with a letter in which he appealed to the owner Philemon to treat his slave as a brother. In Paul's situation, where the church was a vulnerable and fragile minority in an antagonistic world, this was understandable. To use Paul's understandable hesitation as a justification for an ongoing 1800 years of slavery is another of the tragic ironies of history and another of the terrible errors of the Christian church. Fortunately, today both the churches and the human community as a whole understand and agree that slavery is wrong. The abolition of slavery belongs to the core of human rights that have universal and absolute validity. Yet, reports from Sudan and Saudi Arabia speak of a lucrative slave trade, and many child laborers are fated to a life of slavery. But there is a worldwide movement with many governmental and nongovernmental organizations effectively opposing all forms of slavery.

"There Is No Longer Male and Female"

In whatever way we may look at this difficult statement, it clearly says "that in the Christian church the sex distinctions between man and woman have lost their significance."[5] This does not mean, of course, that there are no differences between men and women. Indeed the differences between men and women are important for the encounter of love, and they are essential for the survival of the human race. But "in Christ" the natural differences must no longer be used to determine theological roles.

Theologically it is significant that in Galatians 3:26-28 Paul picks up terminology from Genesis 1:27 when he asserts that in Christ Jesus "there is no longer male and female." The so-called "Priestly" creation story in Genesis 1:1–2:4a portrays the creation of the human being as being "in the image of God . . . male and female he created them" (Gen 1:27). Human beings are communal beings who seek communion with each other and practice the partnership of equals.

The same is true for the other creation story. The so-called "Jahwist" creation story in Genesis 2:4b–3:24 first portrays the creation of the male (humankind) (אדם—*adam*) "from the dust of the ground (אדמה—*adamah*), and (God) breathed into his nostrils the breath of life; and the man became a living being"

(2:7). But the male on his own is considered to be a deficient human being, so "... the LORD God said, 'It is not good that man should be alone'" (2:18). Humans are communal beings who become who they are in their togetherness: "... if they fall, one will lift up the other; but woe to the person who is alone when they fall and has not another to lift them up" (Eccl 4:10). So God made the human being *whole* ("at last," "one flesh") by creating "a helper as a *partner*" (2:18). This should be interpreted in the widest possible sense. It does not only mean that God created a sexual partner or a farm help for the man. "What is meant is the personal community of man and woman in the broadest sense—bodily and spiritual community, mutual help and understanding, joy and contentment in each other."[6] It would certainly go beyond the intention of the text to derive any subordination of woman to man from these Scriptures. This must be said despite the fact that 1 Timothy 2:13 uses this text to argue that a woman must "learn in silence with all submissiveness. I permit no woman to teach or to have authority over a man; she is to keep silent" (1 Tim 2:11f.). This grounding of ethics in creation (rather than in Christology) was widespread in early Christianity. It reflects the difficulties and problems of relating the *new* reality of faith in Christ to the traditional social orders and traditions. An ancient oriental way of thinking maintained that what is created *first* has greater value and dignity than what follows. Consequently, the fact that according to the Jahwist creation account in Genesis 2 "Adam" was created *first*, served as a validation for the subordination of the female to the male.[7] In contrast, the affirmation of the equality of male and female in Galatians 3:28 is based on a *christological* reflection according to which the salvation that has come with Jesus Christ undoes the subordination of the female to the male that, according to Genesis 3:16, was the consequence of sin.

Indeed, given the situation of patriarchy in which the biblical creation stories were formulated, these stories contain a social-critical thrust. Human beings can only become who they are in mutual partnership and assistance. The man therefore bursts forth in ecstatic joy when God gives him a partner: "'... this *at last* is bone of my bones and flesh of my flesh; this one shall be called Woman (אִשָּׁה) for out of Man (אִישׁ) this one was taken.' Therefore a man leaves his father and his mother and cleaves to his wife, and they *become one flesh*. And the man and his wife were both naked, and were not ashamed."(Gen 2:23-25)

Nevertheless, this state of unashamed bliss and partnership in creative relationship with God and nature is not how things are. Life as we know and experience it is different. We live in an estranged state where sin and self-will, rather than God's intention and will, rule. The human being wants to "have" and "define" and "rule." The consequences are estrangement from God, from each other, and from nature. An unbending self-will constantly frustrates the communal dimension of human existence. The striving for human autonomy presents a conflict with a life based on faith. Exploitation of nature for immediate and shortsighted human ends replaces a caring partnership with nature as creation. Creative partnerships on all levels issue into struggles for domination. This state of affairs, the way things are, the birth-pain and the subordination of women to men, as well as the hard work and the struggle with an unfriendly environment in order to make ends meet for the man, are interpreted as consequences of the human estrangement from God (Gen 3:16-19).

Since through her function as child-bearer and caring for the domestic family duties the woman was based in the home, while the man performed in public, this *functional* distinction was cemented into *structures of patriarchy* where a functional sharing of responsibilities became frozen into ontological structures of being in which the subordination of the woman to the man was cemented and then validated by philosophical and theological arguments.[8] The woman became the property of the man.

This result of estrangement and sin was undone by the death and resurrection of Christ. Through the ministry of Christ, God's original intention has been restored. Those who "hear" that and believe it, that is, those who are "in Christ," must allow this "new" humanity to take shape in their lives and in their midst. Christians can, therefore, no longer uncritically adopt social, cultural, political, religious, and economic customs and traditions. Their conscience is bound to Jesus Christ, and therefore they must seek to structure their life together to reflect their ultimate concern, which is Jesus Christ. This includes the affirmation and implication of the equality between male and female.

The Moral Basis for Equality

This causes us to raise the question about the moral basis for human rights in general and for the right of equality in particular. In our discussion of the equality of women and men, indeed the equal dignity of all human beings "without distinction of any kind, such as race, color, sex, language, religion, political or other opinion, national or social origin, property, birth or other status,"[9] we have touched on an important issue in the contemporary debate about the *basis* for human rights.

Human rights make ontological claims when they insist that "all human beings *are born* free and equal in dignity and rights" (§1, *Universal Declaration of Human Rights*). The *Virginia Declaration of Rights* (1776) says, "all men"—

whether in those days they included women, Native Americans, and slaves is doubtful—"are *by nature* equally free and independent, and have certain *inherent* rights" (§1, emphasis mine). The *French Declaration of the Rights of Man and of the Citizen* (1789) is introduced with the words, "Men *are born* free and equal in respect of rights" (§1, emphasis mine). The *Universal Declaration of Human Rights* tunes into those claims by asserting "the *inherent* dignity and . . . the equal and *inalienable* rights of all members of the human family" (preamble, my emphasis).

The intention of these formulations is clear. They underline the *universality* of human rights, and they assert that the dignity, freedom, and equality of human beings *transcends* the authority of human and historical institutions like the state, the law, the church, and human contracts. Historical institutions have neither invented nor granted human dignity; therefore they cannot take it away. Their noble function is to recognize, understand, and protect it.

The problem arises, however, when one tries to understand and explain the moral *foundation* for human rights. What does it mean that a person has certain "inherent" and "inalienable" rights; that people are "born" with certain rights that no one should take away from them; that human beings have these rights "by nature"? If people "are endowed with reason and conscience," who or what "endows" them with such?

Traditionally, Natural Law theories have been called upon to provide a universal basis for morality. But such theories have lost their power in the wake of having been used to justify slavery, racism, sexism, and nationalism. This loss of credibility poses a serious dilemma. A Swiss jurist, familiar with the human rights debate, says:

> From the legal point of view it must be insisted that some foundation is indispensable. Legal norms are usually respected not because they are backed by power and people fear the sanctions of power against transgressors; their validity rests primarily on belief in their legitimacy . . . . The question then inevitably arises of the source of this legitimacy. Legitimacy is necessarily meta-legal and meta-materialistic: as a rule and generally speaking it does not derive from such norms as self-evidence or from any inherent or "historical" necessity . . . .[10]

The most one can say at the present time is that there is an emerging consensus that human rights are grounded in the human person. Still, this does not solve the ontological challenge. It only raises new questions as to how the human person is to be understood and what content should be given to the *humanum*.

The problem and the challenge is clear: unless a universally valid moral foundation for human rights is discovered and agreed upon, human rights will be increasingly emptied of their validity and authority, and they will continue to be functionalized to serve national, economic, and other ideological interests.

At this point, the religions of the world as well as other ethical claims and systems must put their cards on the table. It is not only important what vision of life people have, but also where their vision of life comes from and how it is grounded in reality. Christians are clear and transparent at this point. Their ethical vision is grounded in God's raising the crucified One from death. We have tried to show that this foundational event implies a vision of reality in which the equality of all people is ontologically grounded.

The Special Contribution of the Christian Faith

Christians therefore have cause to rejoice that equality is deeply engrained in the human rights tradition:[11] "all human beings are born free and equal in dignity and rights" (§ 1); "Everyone is entitled to all the rights and freedoms set forth in this Declaration, without distinction of any kind, such as race, color, sex, language, religion, political or other opinion, national or social origin, property, birth or other status" (§ 2); "All are equal before the law and are entitled without any discrimination to equal protection of the law" (§ 7); "Everyone is entitled in full equality to a fair and public hearing . . ." (§ 10); "Everyone, without discrimination, has the right to equal pay for equal work" (§23:2).

Nevertheless, we have to recognize that the assertion that "all human beings are born free and equal in dignity and rights" is neither obvious nor apparent in our world. Aboriginal and Torres Strait Islander people in Australia, female children in India and China, poor black people in South Africa and African Americans in the USA, Christians in Muslim countries, women and Gypsies all over the world, do not enjoy equality in their respective situations. Indeed, by looking into the world as it is, there is more evidence for affirming inequality as a "natural" fact than equality. Even the historical situations in which equality rights were asserted are replete with ambiguity. When, for instance, the founding fathers in North America claimed equality with and independence from England, they did not think of giving the same equality and freedom to African slaves, to Native Americans, or to women. We have already noted that even in many churches women do not enjoy equality.

At the same time, I have tried to show that the foundational event for the Christian faith and the Christian church includes the suspension of patriarchy and the establishment of equality. Christians base their commitment to equality not on what human reason perceives in the nature of things, but on God's dealings with humanity as they become historically manifest in the story of Jesus. Christians assert the equality of all people because God has created all human beings to be equal in dignity. Individualism and selfishness, which has led to inequality, is seen as a result of turning away from grounding life in God. In Christ, God has dealt with the estranging power of sin and created a new reality, which includes equality for all people. This equality is affirmed, claimed, and implemented through faith in Christ. When the new reality that God has established in Christ becomes historically manifest, then a community is created in which "there is no longer Jew or Greek, there is no longer slave or free, there is no longer male and female; for all of you are one in Christ Jesus" (Gal 3:28).

Yet, there is a "more" that the Christian faith has to offer. For Christians, the affirmation of equality includes two dimensions that transcend an abstract affirmation of equality. On the one hand, Christians have the freedom voluntarily to suspend their equality rights, and on the other hand, Christians show a special partiality toward the marginalized and oppressed. Both affirmations should make churches especially sensitive to the denial of equality to women and should encourage men to exercise more justice and humility for the sake of the health and witness of the community of faith.

We may conclude, therefore, that the confession in Galatians 3:28 reminds us of the proclamation of "liberty, equality, and fraternity" during the French Revolution. Galatians 3:28 is a pre-Pauline deposit declaring the transfiguration of ontology through the resurrection of Jesus Christ. Here, the community of faith proclaims that with the resurrection of Jesus Christ the reality of God's *shalom* has broken into history in a new and intensive way. Racism and national elitism are replaced by the equal dignity "without distinction of any kind, such as race, color, sex, language, religion, political or other opinion, national or social origin, property, birth or other status."[12] Patriarchy and sexism are replaced by the equality of male and female. Slavery is abolished and the equal dignity of all human beings is affirmed. Ethnic superiority is suspended. This reality is true for all people and Christians can therefore rejoice that the human rights tradition affirms the equality of all people. What is true for all people becomes "duty" for the realm where Christ is believed and obeyed. The resurrection of Jesus has established a new understanding of reality. As such, it is a history-creating event. The difference between the church and the world is that the church is to live and practice what is true for all of God's creation.

The Ordination of Women

We shall now focus on one area in which equality is denied to half the human race purely on the basis of gender. It is certainly a matter of truth and justice when in a number of Christian denominations and churches, women are excluded from ordination to the ministry of word and sacrament on the grounds of gender. There are still Roman Catholic, Orthodox, Anglican, Baptist, and Lutheran churches that refuse to ordain women to the Christian ministry. That constitutes a major problem in a world where universal human rights affirm that "*all* human beings are born free and equal in dignity and rights" and that "*everyone* is entitled to all the rights and freedoms . . . without distinction of any kind, such as race, color, sex, language, religion."[13] Not that the church is necessarily bound to implement all human rights. But if the church refuses to do so, it must have good reasons—good *theological* reasons—for excluding human beings from the ordained ministry merely on the basis that they are female and not male.

The Roman Catholic church is up front in this matter, while other churches follow the same procedure, either in theory or practice or both—including a number of unions, conventions, and churches from the Baptist tradition in the context of which I minister. The Roman Pontiff has decreed that the ordination of women is a closed matter. It must not even be the subject of discussions within Roman Catholic circles: ". . . I declare that the church has no authority whatsoever to confer priestly ordination on women and that this judgment is to be *definitely held* by all the church's faithful."[14] The largest group of churches in the Baptist tradition, the Southern Baptist Convention in the USA, said in a recent doctrinal and confessional statement (adopted 14 June 2000): "While both men and women are gifted for service in the church, the office of pastor is limited to men as qualified by Scripture."[15]

Theological arguments for that theory and practice differ. While for Roman Catholics the maleness of Jesus and its representation by the priest at the Eucharist play a decisive role, Southern Baptists and other Protestant churches call upon the biblical passages in 1 Corinthians 14:34f. and 1 Timothy 2:11-15 and the New Testament household codes to justify their denial of ordination to women.[16]

Both ecclesiastical interests are served by the traditional exegesis of pivotal resurrection texts. The primary testimonies of the apostle Paul (1 Cor 9:1; 15:8) and the multiple attestations about Peter's Easter experience (1 Cor 15:5; Luke 24:34; John 21:1-17) suggest that the risen Christ appeared first to Peter and then later to Paul—both males. The long list of appearances in

1 Corinthians 15:5-8 does not mention women, although it is possible of course that some women were implied in the reference to "500 ἀδελφοί" ("brothers," but its usage could also include sisters). Nevertheless, in the list of appearances in 1 Corinthians 15 specific reference is made only to males: to Peter, the Twelve, James, all the apostles, and Paul. It can hardly be denied that both in Scripture and in tradition, the appearance to Mary of Magdala is either sidelined or suppressed.

Nevertheless, the question can no longer be silenced: what would it mean, what should it mean, for the status of women in the church, if the fragment in the later ending of Mark were correct that the first appearance of the risen Christ occurred not to Peter, but to Mary—a woman (Mark 16:9)?

The usual argument is that the first appearance of the risen Christ occurred to Peter in Galilee. The earliest formulas (1 Cor 15:5; Luke 24:34), the fact that the disciples fled to Galilee when Jesus was arrested and crucified, and the accumulation of Petrine resurrection narratives (John 21:1-14 [Luke 5:1-6, 8]; 21:15-17, 18-22; [compare Luke 22:31f.; Matt 16:17-19]) certainly point in that direction. Nevertheless, a healthy suspicion must also remind us that there was a tendency in the earliest churches to downplay the role of women and to highlight the witness of male apostles. We can observe that tendency in the way male witnesses began to be associated with major events like the crucifixion (Luke 23:49; John 19:26f.) and the discovery of the empty tomb (Luke 24:12; John 20:1-10).

It deserves therefore our special attention that the resurrection narratives in the Gospels also speak about an appearance of the risen Christ to a woman[17] (Matt 28:9f. and John 20:14-18). Indeed, in the later ending of Mark, this appearance to Mary of Magdala is described or interpreted as being the "first" one, preceding the other appearances (Mark 16:9).[18] The appearance to Mary is located in or outside Jerusalem at the empty tomb. In the Matthean version, the command of the angel to the women that they should go and tell the disciples their Lord had risen from the dead and that he would appear to them in Galilee (Mattt 28:7) is repeated before the encounter with the risen Christ is narrated. This is certainly a Matthean attempt to provide a link to the Galilean appearance stories. In contrast to the Matthean text, the Johannine version emphasizes that Mary should not "touch" or "hold" the risen Christ. John guards here against a possible misunderstanding that Jesus could have returned to an earthly existence. The pre-Johannine source was probably similar to the Matthean version where Mary "took hold of his feet and worshiped him" (Matt 28:9). But with his warning to Mary—"Do not hold me . . ."—the fourth evangelist resists an objectification of the resurrection. This emphasis is not contradicted by the Thomas episode (John 20:26-29). There the invitation to Thomas (John 20:27) to touch the risen Christ serves to underline the *reality* of the resurrection, while immediately following, the *objectification* of the risen Christ is rejected: "Blessed are those who have not seen and yet believe" (John 20:29).

While the differences between the Matthean and the Johannine versions can be explained, it is unlikely that the early church would have invented a tradition in which Jesus appeared to Mary. It is of course possible that such an appearance tradition was formed to underline that the tomb was indeed empty; and since Mary had discovered the empty tomb, while the disciples had fled to Galilee, it would follow the inherent logic of the tradition that Jesus must have appeared to Mary. But knowing the juridical stipulations that the testimony of women was, like that of children and imbeciles, not valid, and recognizing the hesitancy of early Christian authors to have women serve as the main witnesses to important events, while at the same time considerable liberty was exercised to place male disciples at important events (Luke 23:49; 24:12; John 19:26, 35; 20:1-10), it is more than likely that the first appearance of the risen Christ was indeed to a woman—to Mary, in or outside of Jerusalem.[19] Therefore Mark 16:9, although part of a later edition to the first Gospel, may in this case have preserved the accurate historical information. The fact that the pre-Pauline tradition in 1 Corinthians 15:5-7 does not include this testimony can have several reasons. We saw that the juridical situation discouraged the testimony of women. The pre-Pauline tradition in 1 Corinthians 15:3-7 has probably evolved over a period of years and in the process conflated traditions from Galilee (Peter) and Jerusalem (James). The fact that the appearance to Mary was left out may have to do with the fact that she did not have a leadership function in the early church, and in a patriarchal culture and a male-dominated church, there was little encouragement to highlight the importance of women.

We must therefore conclude that the process of failing to recognize, understand, and implement the equal dignity of women started early and has lasted in many ecclesiastical quarters to the present day. The revolutionary nature of the resurrection became accommodated to more acceptable cultural norms and practices. The new wine could not be tolerated by the old wineskins.

The Roman Catholic church continues to oppose the priesthood of women mainly[20] because for them the priest is a "sign" for Christ, which in their understanding calls for a natural and physical likeness. In their view, a woman cannot represent Christ at the Eucharist because she cannot act *in persona Christi*. In this argument, the humanity of Jesus is subordinated to his maleness. One may well ask, of course, whether the calling for a natural likeness would not also have to include the demand that all priests must not only be male, but must also be Jews, in order to reflect not only the maleness, but also the Jewishness of Jesus.

In Protestant churches, the opposition to the ordination and leadership of women in the church is based on what is perceived as biblical authority. Texts like 1 Corinthians 14:34f. and 1 Timothy 2:11-15 are absolutized without considering their relationship to the gospel and without evaluating why they differ from texts like Galatians 3:28. They can be better understood in terms of cultural and social adaptation from the suspension of patriarchy and the revolutionary proclamation of the equality of male and female—as witnessed in Galatians 3:28—to socially and culturally more acceptable norms and practices. First Corinthians 14:34f. is most likely a later addition to Paul's letter. It interrupts the literary flow, it stands in tension with the theological context in 1 Corinthians 12–14, it uses language similar to 1 Timothy 2:12 (ἐπιτρέπω—"allow," "permit") and the household codes (ὑποτάσσω—"subject," "subordinate," Col 3:18; Eph 5:21), and it is contradicted by 1 Corinthians 11:5 where the praying and preaching of women in the church is not questioned. The other text, 1 Timothy 2:11-15, was written long after Paul had died. To this we may add those texts that imply the subordination of the female to the male: Ephesians 5:22-24; Colossians 3:18; 1 Peter 3:1-5; Romans 7:3.

How can we explain the process from giving prominence to women and affirming the equal dignity of women in the resurrection event to a return to patriarchal patterns? Given the minority status of the churches at that time, which often had to survive under conditions of persecution, this emerging adaptation to the surrounding culture is understandable. We must also remember that the churches sought the respect by their social context,[21] not only for their survival, but also as a presupposition for making the communication of the Christian message easier.[22] Since the churches in the first three centuries met in houses, they adopted Greco-Roman household codes according to which the man was the head of the household. More conservative members of the house churches may have objected when women, and especially rich women (1 Tim 2:9f.), sought to assume roles of influence and leadership in the communities. At the same time, we hear of a female apostle ("Junia" in Romans 16:7) and of several women who were leaders of house churches.[23] But a subtle shift from affirming the full and equal dignity of women to culturally more acceptable norms cannot be overlooked and, given the minority situation in which the churches found themselves, can be explained.

To use such explanation of cultural adaptation 2000 years later, when the human family has recognized the equality of women and men in the Human

Rights Instruments, when the Christian church is well established and at least in the West is not opposed or interfered with by the state, but in many quarters continues to deny equality to women is another of the tragic ironies of history. It runs counter to the intention of the biblical message that wants to bring the liberating power of the gospel into particular situations and thereby change things in the direction of justice.

Those who build their theological position on "women in the church" and "women in ministry" on texts such as 1 Corinthians 14:34f. and 1 Timothy 2:11-15 have absolutized a situational element of the biblical message and have failed to hear the living and history-changing message of the Word of God. Christians and churches are always in danger of functionalizing texts to serve the status quo or not to rock the boat or to maintain traditional power structures. We need to learn ever again that biblical texts have their authority not in themselves but in witnessing to the one Word of God whom we are to hear, trust, and obey.

If the above observations are correct or at least probable, it would belong to the great and tragic ironies of the history of the Christian church that right from its beginning the church has struggled with trying to understand the revolutionary character of God's revelation through the resurrection of the crucified Christ. If in the resurrection appearances the foundational event for the Christian faith becomes manifest, then Jesus' first appearance to a woman would have suspended the patriarchal worldview and ushered in a new reality that no longer links roles and privileges with gender. It is a tremendous indictment on a church that has failed to recognize, understand, and implement this revolution and simply continued patriarchal patterns. That in many churches this failure to recognize the newness of the resurrection is still being continued must be considered either as a testimony to their theological poverty, or it must be seen as a direct and willful distortion of the very foundational event of the Christian church, the resurrection of the crucified Christ.

Ecological Responsibility

Finally, we mention the ecological responsibility implied[24] in affirming that God raised Jesus from the dead. There is no question that the striving for a sustainable biosphere is one of the great challenges of our time. "Ecocide is homicide."[25] The United Nations (Rio Earth Summit 1992,[26] Kyoto Conference 1997,[27] and The Hague Climate Conference 2000), the "Earth Charter Campaign," many governments,[28] several religions,[29] Christian churches,[30] and scientists[31] are intensely concerned and are working hard to achieve a change of consciousness and subsequent tangible results.

While most theologians base their ecological concerns in the doctrine of creation, I want to make the point that there is a christological imperative for constructive ecological justice.[32] The early Christians interpreted the resurrection as "ascension" and as "exaltation" to the "right hand of God".[33] On the basis of Christ's "ascension" and "exaltation," they confessed Christ as Κύριος ("Lord") of the universe.[34] They sang hymns to him and celebrated his presence in the preaching of the word, in the gathered community, and in the celebration of the Eucharist. But the point of this section is that such a cosmic understanding of Christ implies that salvation and healing includes *all* of reality, not only humanity, but also nature and the cosmos.[35]

For too long have we understood the consequences of the resurrection merely in historical and anthropological terms. We have related it to our human salvation and failed to include the healing of the environment that sustains us. We have limited the power of the resurrection to changing the human consciousness, to changing things in the historical process, to providing eschatological hope for a life in the beyond, for claiming eschatological verification for our present struggle for justice. The resurrection of Christ is all that—and yet, it is more inclusive. It also speaks to our growing awareness that we are not only historical beings, but that we are ontologically woven into a network of nature and the universe. This awareness implies that the protection of nature is fundamental for our survival. Every time in our daily life when we witness situations of conflict in which economic considerations are given priority over ecological concerns, we have a further illustration that we have not yet fully grasped the ecological dimensions of human existence. We realize today that it is not possible to separate nature and history. History and nature are essentially interrelated. Indeed the whole of nature and the cosmos is part of a continuing and ever-changing evolutionary process. We as human beings are, on the one hand, ontologically woven into this evolutionary process. Human life apart from nature and cosmos is not possible. On the other hand, we are also historical beings, and as such we can adopt an attitude toward nature and cosmos, and we can take a stand over against them. We can ignore or appreciate nature. We can destroy or restore nature. We are beginning to understand, however, that our historical consciousness in recent centuries has repressed our inherent dependence on nature, and the results of this repression come to the surface in the present ecology crisis.

Nature and the cosmos provide the context in which human life takes place. All talk about creation, sin, and salvation is therefore hanging in the air if it is not related to a theological appreciation of nature and the cosmos. Cosmic redemption is God's response to a cosmic estrangement. This estrangement becomes manifest in the ecological crisis today. On an even deeper level, it is also seen in the deep-seated unwillingness to recognize the seriousness of the problem and the subsequent laziness to take the necessary steps and accept the necessary conflicts to do something about it. Karl Barth summarizes this dimension of sin well:

> . . . sin has not merely the heroic form of pride but also, in complete antithesis yet profound correspondence, the quite unheroic and trivial form of sloth. In other words, it has the form, not only of evil action, but also of evil inaction; not only of the rash arrogance which is forbidden and reprehensible, but also of the tardiness and failure which are equally forbidden and reprehensible.[36]

Today, an active and concrete engagement in the struggle for a sustainable biosphere is imperative for Christians. "The earth is the LORD's and the fullness thereof, the world and those who dwell therein" (Ps 24:1). The ecological crisis is the result of human mismanagement, and this mismanagement is the consequence of a deep-seated self-will. For that reason, the healing process must also include a change of human consciousness and with it a modification of human action.

The resurrection of Christ is God's protest against the estranging forces of sin, and it is the revelation that in Christ, God has dealt with these forces and thereby freed believers to celebrate life. This celebration contains the affirmation of nature as creation with its own rights. We need to learn to be concerned not only with human rights, but also with environmental rights and with the rights of nature.[37] Apart from a functioning ecology, human survival is not possible. Faith in Christ therefore cannot only free us from our self-orientation and thus make a community of human brothers and sisters possible, but it can also be the foundation on which a partnership relation with nature can be restored. When the Priestly writer designated the human pair as the "image of God" and gave them "dominion" over nature (Gen 1:26-31), this was not meant in terms of domination, definition, control, and exploitation. Rather, humanity was entrusted with the privilege and responsibility of representing God on the earth and caring for the earth within the parameters that God had set. "Dominion" has to be understood in terms of responsible care and providing food, work, and shelter for the human population.[38]

By acknowledging the resurrection of the crucified Christ as the theological foundation in our struggle for a sustainable biosphere, we can, at least in theory, avoid the following pitfalls.

Firstly, by emphasizing the cosmic dimension of the resurrection of Christ, we resist a theological dualism. Allan D. Galloway says correctly:

> Unless one is prepared to accept the type of dualism which condemns the whole physical order as being not of God and interprets redemption simply as release from the physical order, then one is forced to raise the question of cosmic redemption not in contrast with, but as an implicate of the idea of personal redemption. Physical nature cannot be treated as an indifferent factor—as the mere stage and setting of the drama of personal redemption. It must either be condemned as in itself evil or else it must be brought within the scope of the redemptive act.[39]

Secondly, in response to ecologists who argue for the independent and inherent value of nature and cosmos, we claim that there is a ground, an ontology, both for the being of nature (God as creator) and for the restoration of nature (God as redeemer). As Christians, we confess that by raising Jesus from the dead and exalting him to "the right hand of God," God has laid the foundation in which the Christian imperative for ecological justice is grounded.[40]

We thirdly question the tendency to divinize nature.[41] This tendency is understandable as a reaction against the centuries-old focus of theology and philosophy on humanity and history. But it is not really helpful because it underestimates the radicality of evil and the subsequent need for help to come from "outside," from a God who is not separate from but different to nature and the universe.

As a fourth point we note that the emphasis on the crucified One makes us especially sensitive to the weaker links in nature and helps us affirm that God is concerned with everything God has created.[42] Since in the Christian understanding God is love, therefore the creator has a special tendency, indeed a partiality, to restore that which is broken, to heal that which is sick, to liberate that which is enslaved, and to save that which is lost. In contrast to a Darwinism that assigns privilege to the physically and naturally strong, an ontology focused on the resurrection of the *crucified* Christ gives us a heightened sensitivity so that when we are confronted with soil erosions, water shortages, carbon emissions, forest depletions, extension of deserts, and extinction of species, these are not presumed to be signs of a natural evolution, but of distortions, often created by human greed, that need to be rectified.

We need to be grateful to scientists, theologians, and philosophers—people like Albert Schweitzer,[43] Rupert Sheldrake,[44] Thomas Berry,[45] Paul Collins,[46] and Sallie McFague[47]—who have forcefully reminded us that our traditional emphasis on humanity, on personal sin, on human salvation, and on God's dealing with history has blinded us to our being bound into nature and the cosmos and to our ecological responsibility. The contemporary ecological crisis has shocked many of us into awareness.

At the same time, we do not find it helpful to divinize nature. Christ is God's mediator of salvation and this salvation includes all of reality. Therefore there are resources that are not part of the problem and as such can be the foundation for the answer we so urgently need.

Conclusion

In this chapter I have attempted to show that the resurrection of the crucified Christ makes a difference to history and to the cosmos. By raising Jesus from the dead, God the creator has revealed himself as God the redeemer and as such God has laid the foundation for the triumph of love, peace, and justice. The creator has taken the initiative to reconcile with God what had become estranged. This reconciliation is a fact and a process at the same time.

It is a fact in the sense that God in Christ has loved the world (John 3:16) and has reconciled the world with God (2 Cor 5:17-21). It is a process in the sense that the fact of reconciliation is being implemented through the ministry of the Holy Spirit. The work of the Spirit includes calling people to faith and empowering them to discipleship. Thereby they become agents of change, claiming the promises of God, anticipating the future when God will be "all in all" (1 Cor 15:28), and thereby changing history in the direction of justice.

I have illustrated this transformative nature of resurrection faith with reference to three social ethical challenges that call for urgent response in the church and in the world: a community of equals, the ordination of women, and ecological justice. Responding to these challenges as an integral part of our faith in Christ manifests our sensitivity to the Spirit of God and shows that faith in Christ has created within us "a living hope" for the "salvation ready to be revealed in the last time" (1 Pet 1:3-5). It is the promise of the risen Christ to be with his friends "always, to the end of the age" (Matt 28:20).

The question may be raised whether with the above emphases I have not limited the presence of Christ and thereby reduced the significance of the resurrection. That was not my intention. I am aware, of course, that Christians seek and find the presence of Christ in many different ways.

Christians yearn for the presence of Christ in their lives. Christians readily identify with the apostle's sentiment: "I want to know Christ and the power of his resurrection" (Phil 3:10). Indeed, Paul joyously confessed, "it is no longer I who live, but it is Christ who lives in me. And the life I now live in the flesh I live by faith in the Son of God, who loved me and gave himself for me" (Gal 2:20).

In the Orthodox churches, we can witness wonderful, awe-inspiring, and moving Easter liturgies, climaxing in the acclamation "Christ is risen," to which the gathered community joyfully responds, affirming the presence of Christ, "Christ is risen indeed!" There are quite a few churches in different parts of the world that are engaged in what they call liturgical renewal. It is from there, from carefully planned and enacted liturgies, that they expect the renewal of their churches to flow.

In the Protestant tradition, theologians tend to focus on Romans 10:17: "faith comes from what is heard, and what is heard comes through the word of Christ." "Word" (λόγος) in the New Testament not only symbolizes the incarnate word, but also the telling of the ongoing story of Jesus. This releases the hope and expectation for the risen Christ to be present in the sermon of a preacher who has acknowledged the authority of the biblical text and has faithfully prepared for the preaching event.

Baptists find encouragement in Jesus' promise that "where two or three are gathered in my name, I am there among them" (Matt 18:20). They see the Trinitarian κοινωνία ("fellowship," "community," "communion") reflected in the gathered community as they celebrate the presence of Christ in their midst. For them, the church happens when Christian believers "come together" (1 Cor 11:17f., 20, 33f.; 14:23) and thus "be together" (Acts 2:44) for worship, fellowship, learning, and ministry.

Anglicans, Episcopalians, and Roman Catholics claim the Lord's Supper tradition as they prefer to locate the presence of Christ primarily in the Eucharist. The church listens to the presence of the crucified One: "This is my body . . . . This cup is the new covenant in my blood" (1 Cor 11:24f.), and then confesses, "The cup of blessing that we bless, is it not a sharing in the blood of Christ? The bread that we break, is it not a sharing in the body of Christ?" (1 Cor 10:16).

And then, we are all aware of the conviction of the early churches who expected the risen Christ to encounter them in the children of the world ("Whoever welcomes one such child in my name welcomes me" [Mark 9:36f.]), and also in the poor and oppressed:

> I was hungry and you gave me food, I was thirsty and you gave me something to drink, I was a stranger and you welcomed me, I was naked and you gave me clothing, I was sick and you took care of me, I was in prison and you visited me. . . . As you did it to one of the least of these who are members of my family, you did it to me. (Matt 25:35-40)

In our awareness of these affirmations about the presence of Christ, we must be careful not to play one over against the other. I know of people who have discovered Christ in a worship service, in a lecture room, and in a refugee camp. Christian discipleship needs intellectual, biblical, and theological information. It cannot do without the inspiration of worship. It also needs the engagement of praxis.

But as we try to get an angle on the life of the risen Christ, it is not enough to say that it is all the same: worship, preaching, evangelism, mission, the struggle for justice. We may say, of course, that a healthy Christian life and a mature Christian community include all of those aspects. It is also possible that different groups within the church pursue different emphases. At the same time, I want to suggest that a wholesome Christology forces us to acknowledge and commit to certain emphases and priorities. We have tried to make the point that Jesus did not die of natural causes. He was opposed, captured, tried, tortured, and killed, not as a result of faithfully attending temple worship, not in consequence of diligently studying the Scriptures and of having fellowship with rabbis, scribes, Pharisees, and Sadducees. Whatever Christology we adopt, we must recognize that Jesus was opposed and killed because he engaged himself for justice. This intimate interrelationship between a life engaged for justice and the subsequent execution must be recognized by not denying that Christ can be found in many places, but by giving a procedural priority for the struggle for justice—so it was then, and so it should be now.

Notes

[1] This helpful concept is adopted from Johann Baptist Metz, *Faith in History and Society: Toward a Practical Fundamental Theology*, trans. David Smith (London: Burns and Oates, 1980) chs. 6 (e.g., 109f.), 11 (e.g., 184f.), and "Excursus: Dogma as a dangerous memory" (200-204).

[2] Hans Dieter Betz, *Galatians: A Commentary on Paul's Letter to the Churches in Galatia*, Hermeneia (Philadelphia: Fortress Press, 1979), 177.

[3] The cultic stipulations in Acts 15:20, 29 have to be interpreted in light of Paul's primary witness.

[4] Betz, *Galatians*, 190.

[5] Ibid. 195.

[6] Claus Westermann, *Genesis 1–11: A Commentary*, trans. John J. Scullion S.J. (London: SPCK, 1984 [1974]), 232.

[7] Compare Norbert Brox, *Die Pastoralbriefe*, Regensburger Neues Testament (Leipzig: St. Benno Verlag, 1975), 134f. The subordination of the female to the male is reflected in a number of New Testament texts, e.g., 1 Corinthians 14:35; Ephesians 5:22, 24; Colossians 3:18; 1 Peter 3:1, 5; Romans 7:3.

[8] Compare the description of this qualitative shift by Carol Meyers, "The Roots of Restriction: Women in Early Israel," *Biblical Archeologist* 41 (1978), 91-103.

[9] *Universal Declaration of Human Rights*, §2.

[10] Peter Saladin, "Christianity and Human Rights: A Jurist's Reflection," in Eckehart Lorenz, ed., *How Christian are Human Rights? An Interconfessional Study on the Theological Bases of Human Rights* (Geneva: Lutheran World Federation, 1981, 25-35), 30.

[11] Again, all references are to the *Universal Declaration of Human Rights*.

[12] *Universal Declaration of Human Rights*, § 2.

[13] *Universal Declaration of Human Rights*, §§ 1 and 2.

[14] John Paul II, "Apostolic Letter on Ordination and Women" (30 May 1994), in *Origins* 24/4 (9 June 1994): 49, 51f. (emphasis mine).

[15] "The Baptist Faith & Message" (2000), § VI (accessible on www.sbc.net).

[16] The so-called *household codes* in the early church are found in the following texts: Col 3:18–4:1; Eph 5:21–6:9; 1 Pet 2:13–3:7; 1 Tim 2:8-15; 3:4; 6:1f.; Titus 2:1-10; 3:1; Ignatius, Epistle to Polycarp 4:1–5:1; Polycarp, Epistle to Philippi 4:2–6:1. They describe the relationship of parents and children, masters and slaves, husbands and wives, often in terms that are close to the patriarchal non-Christian ethos of that time and culture. Yet, there is a change. In the Christian churches, those household codes are not only grounded in creation, tradition, or culture, but they begin also to be grounded in *Jesus Christ* ("you are slaves of the *Lord Christ*" [Col 3:24, compare Col 3:14]) and as such structures are being modified to create analogies to the gospel of Christ. The man must no longer subordinate the woman, but he must love her (Col 3:19; Eph 5:25), which in fact means that they must be subordinate *to each other*. "Be subject *to one another* out of reverence for *Christ*" (Eph 5:21).

[17] In Matthew, there are two Marys. But that is clearly an adaptation to Matthew's version of the "empty tomb" narrative (28:1-8, see v. 1).

[18] Luke may have discarded this appearance to Mary because for him the first appearance of Christ occurred to Peter (Luke 24:34).

[19] Elisabeth Schüssler Fiorenza therefore calls Mary Magdalene "the primary apostolic witness to the resurrection" (*In Memory of Her: A Feminist Theological Reconstruction of Christian Origins* [London: SCM, 1983], 332-33). Compare also the careful analysis of Martin Hengel, "Maria Magdalena und die Frauen als Zeugen," in Otto Betz, Martin Hengel, Peter Schmidt, eds., *Abraham unser Vater: Juden und Christen im Gespräch über die Bibel*, Festschrift für Otto Michel zum 60, Geburtstag (Leiden/Köln: Brill, 1963), 243-56, who argues that the prestige Mary Magdalene had in the early church can only be explained if the first appearance of the risen Christ occurred indeed to her (251, 256).

[20] In traditional Roman Catholic theology, another argument was related to what has been perceived as the natural inferiority of the female in comparison to the male.

[21] A bishop, for instance, "must be well thought of by outsiders" (1 Tim 3:7).

[22] Compare Margaret Y. MacDonald, *The Pauline Churches: A socio-historical study of institutionalization in the Pauline and Deutero-Pauline writings*, SNTSMS 60 (New York: Cambridge University Press, 1988), 223f., 235-38.

[23] Specific mention is made of Phoebe (Rom 16:1), Nympha (Col 4:15), Lydia (Acts 16:14f.40), Mary, the mother of John Mark (Acts 12:12), and Priscilla, who is often mentioned before Aquila (Rom 16:3.5a; Acts 18:18, 26; 2 Tim 4:19).

[24] In response to Neil Darragh ("Adjusting to the Newcomer: Theology and Ecotheology," *Pacifica* 13 [June 2000]: 160-80), I would argue that the ecological dimension of theology is not an intrusion into theology (166-68) but an implication of a Christ-centered approach to theology.

[25] Larry Rasmussen, "Human Environmental Rights and/or Biotic Rights," in Carrie Gustafson, Peter Juviler, eds., *Religion and Human Right—Competing Claims?* (Armonk NY: M. E. Sharpe, 1999, 36-52), 39. The ecological crisis is well-documented, for instance, in *State of the World 2000* (Worldwatch Institute, 2000; see www.worldwatch.org).

[26] Rio Conference, United Nations, *Agenda 21: The United Nations Programme of Action from Rio* (New York: United Nations Department of Public Information, 1992).

[27] The *Global Climate Change Treaty*, the so-called *Kyoto Protocol* was opened for signature on 16 March 1998 and enters into force when fifty-five nations have ratified it.

[28] For instance, *Global 2000—The Global 2000 Report to the President: Entering the twenty-first century*, report prepared by the Council of Environmental Quality and the Department of State, Gerald O. Barney, dir. (Washington, DC: US Government Printing Office, 1978), vols. 1-3.

[29] Kusumita P. Pedersen, "Environmental Ethics in Interreligious Perspective," in Sumner B. Twiss and Bruce Grelle, eds., *Explorations in Global Ethics: Comparative Religious Ethics and Interreligious Dialogue* (Boulder CO: Westview Press, 1998), 253-90 (lit.!); Hans Küng, ed., *Yes to a Global Ethic*, trans. John Bowden (London: SCM, 1996)—contains essays from various cultural and religious contexts.

[30] E.g., the World Council of Churches' Program on *Justice, Peace and the Integrity of Creation*.

[31] Following the Rio Earth Summit in the same year, 1600 scientists, including more than half of the Nobel Prize recipients, warned in an open letter that humanity and nature are on a collision course.

[32] In contemporary theology, Jürgen Moltmann has especially taken up this challenge and related the resources of Christian faith to the challenges of our time: *God in Creation: An Ecological Doctrine of Creation*, Gifford Lectures, 1984–1985, trans. Margaret Kohl (London: SCM, 1985); *The Way of Jesus Christ: Christology in Messianic Dimensions*, trans. Margaret Kohl (London: SCM, 1990). Sallie McFague's interesting and challenging *The Body of God: An Ecological Theology* (Minneapolis: Fortress Press, 1993) should also be mentioned here, although McFague does not ground her ecological concerns christologically.

[33] Explicit references to the interpretation of the resurrection as exaltation are found in Acts 2:32-35; 5:30-32; Rom 1:3f.; 8:34; and Eph 1:19-22. Other New Testament texts reflecting this interpretation are 1 Thess 1:10; Rom 14:9; Col 3:1; Eph 2:6; 4:8-10; 1 Pet 1:20f.; 3:18-22; Heb 1:3; 4:14; 5:5; 7:26; 8:1; 10:12; 12:2; 1 Tim 3:16; Mark 16:19; Matt 28:18b-20; Luke 9:51f.; 24:26; Acts 1:1f, 21f.; 3:19-21; 13:32f.; John 3:14; 12:32, 34.

[34] For instance, Phil 2:6-11; Col 1:15-20; 1 Tim 3:16; 1 Pet 3:22.

[35] Compare my *Resurrection and Discipleship: Interpretive Models, Biblical Reflections, Theological Consequences* (Maryknoll NY: Orbis Books, 1995), 284-95.

[36] *Church Dogmatics* 4/2, trans. G. W. Bromiley (1958): 403. He then notes that in "Protestantism, and perhaps in Western Christianity generally, there is a temptation to overlook this aspect of the matter and to underestimate its importance" (ibid.). The original German text is even more expressive when it interprets "Trägheit" ("sloth") with "Schläfrigkeit, Faulheit, Schwerfälligkeit, Rückständigkeit" ("sluggishness, indolence, slowness, inertia"): *Die Kirchliche Dogmatik* 4/2 (1955): 452; *Church Dogmatics* 4/2 (1958): 403. Compare also the essay by Sandra Postel on the various psychological attempts to "deny" the seriousness of the crisis. She alludes to a possible epitaph for humanity with the inscription, "they saw it coming but hadn't the wit to stop it happening" ("Denial in the Decisive Decade," in Lester R. Brown et al., *State of the World 1992*, A Worldwatch Institute Report on Progress Toward a Sustainable Society [New York/London: W. W. Norton 1992, 3-8], 8).

[37] Compare Larry Rasmussen, "Human Environmental Rights and/or Biotic Rights," in Gustafseon and Juviler, eds., *Religion and Human Rights*, 36-52.

[38] Compare also Gen 2:15 (Jahwist); Ps 104:14f., 23. Odil Hannes Steck comments on the creation narrative of the Priestly Code (Gen 1:1–2:4a): "The limitations laid down in Genesis 1 show that for P the possibility of an exploitation of the earth to the point of the exhaustion of its resources, or the contingency that autocratic man might poison and destroy living space on earth, is not remotely considered in this authorization. The subjection of the earth is only so that man may be supplied with useful plants [for food and nourishment]—and in addition the passage presupposes a permanent and completely sufficient supply of wild vegetation for the nourishment of wild animals, birds, and creeping things (1:30)"

(*World and Environment,* Biblical Encounter Series [Nashville: Abindgon, 1980], 107 [words in brackets added for clarification], compare further 102-108, 190-203).

[39] *The Cosmic Christ* (1951) 205; this text was also quoted by Joseph Sittler in his famous address at the WCC Assembly in New Delhi 1961: "Called to Unity," *SEAJT* 3 (1962, 6-15): 7.

[40] So also Brian F. Johnstone, CssR, "Transformation Ethics: The Moral Implication of Resurrection," in Stephen T. Davis, Daniel Kendall, Gerald O'Collins, eds., *The Resurrection: An Interdisciplinary Symposium on the Resurrection of Jesus* (New York: Oxford University Press, 1997, 339-360), 359. This would also be the Christian response for the matter raised by Larry Rasmussen: "The realization of human environmental rights and/or biotic rights will not happen apart from a cosmology (an overarching understanding of reality) or a narrative different from the one that gave us modernity" ("Human Environmental Rights and/or Biotic Rights," in Gustafson and Juviler, eds., *Religion and Human Rights,* 40).

[41] I detect that danger in the inspiring writings of Thomas Berry and Sallie McFague (see footnote 45 and 47 below).

[42] Jürgen Moltmann, *The Way of Jesus Christ,* pt. 6.

[43] Albert Schweitzer describes the moment in September 1915 when he discovered the principle that became central for his understanding and interpretation of reality: "Late on the third day, at the very moment when, at sunset, we were making our way through a herd of hippopotamuses, there flashed upon my mind, unforeseen and unsought, the phrase, 'Reverence for Life.' The iron door had yielded: the path in the thicket had become visible. Now I had found my way to the idea in which world- and life-affirmation and ethics are contained side by side! Now I knew that the world-view of ethical world- and life-affirmation, together with its ideals of civilization, is founded in thought" (*Out of my Life and Thought: An Autobiography,* postscript 1932–1949 by Everett Skillings, a Mentor Book, trans. C. T. Campion [New York: The New American Library of World Literature, 1953], 124, compare 125-28, 170-88). This discovery is unfolded in Schweitzer's *The Philosophy of Civilization* (New York: MacMillan, 1960 [1923]); further, *The Teaching of Reverence for Life,* trans. Richard and Clara Winston (London: Peter Owen, 1966).

[44] Compare *The Presence of the Past: Morphic Resonance and the Habits of Nature* (New York: Vintage Books, 1989); *The Rebirth of Nature: The Greening of Science and God* (New York: Doubleday/Bantam, 1991).

[45] Thomas Berry, "Creative Energy" (179-86), "The New Story: Comments on the Origin, Identification and Transmission of Values" (187-99), "The Dream of the Earth: Our Way into the Future" (200-15), "Twelve Principles for Reflecting on the Universe" (216f.), in *Cross Currents* (Summer/Fall 1987): 179-217; Thomas Berry, *The Dream of the Earth* (San Francisco: Sierra Club Books, 1988); Brian Swimme and Thomas Berry, *The Universe Story: From the Primordial Flaring forth to the Ecozoic Era—A celebration of the Unfolding of the Cosmos* (San Francisco: Harper, 1992).

[46] Paul Collins, *God's Earth: Religion as if matter really mattered* (Dove: North Blackburn, Vic. Australia, 1995).

[47] Sallie McFague, *The Body of God.*

Chapter 6

Christ and Other Religions

The true light, which enlightens everyone . . . —John 1:9

Introduction

We now turn to a sensitive but important and relevant issue: the relationship of Christ to other religions. Developing a theology of religions is one of the major challenges on the contemporary theological agenda.[1] If theology is to resource the Christian church for authentic and effective ministry in a pluralistic world, it must deal with the question of how Christians can and must relate to people of other faiths.

Despite claims to the contrary, too often and for too long has religion been part of the problem rather than the answer to the human predicament. Whether we look to Ireland, the Middle East, Indonesia, or Sudan; whether we reflect on the recent terror attacks on the symbols of the American way of life (11 September 2001), religion is always an issue. Some people feel deeply that they must protect the honor of their deity against infidels, heretics, and unbelievers. Others feel called to take their view of God and life to foreign shores. It is true that more often than not, religion is functionalized to serve other purposes, whether to deepen ethnic hatred or to fuel rebellion against injustice, poverty, and oppression. At the same time, every religion must examine its own religious substance and announce publicly whether and in what ways it is life-affirming or life-denying, whether it tends to build up or to tear down, whether it fuels hatred, intolerance, and violence, or whether it affirms tolerance, peace, freedom, and justice.

Some commentators suggest that future conflicts will be along the lines of religious and cultural identity rather than between nations. Religious leaders and religious people have to ask themselves seriously whether they want to further or to hinder the human community in its search for justice and peace. Hans Küng commences his important book *Global Responsibility: In Search for a World Ethic* with the following words: "No survival without a world ethic. No world peace without peace between the religions. No peace between the religions without dialogue between the religions."[2]

Our focus on the resurrection of Christ leads us to address this issue. There can be no doubt that the resurrection of the crucified One declares the central substance of our faith and at the same time affirms its universal and cosmic significance. By raising Jesus from death, God declares who God is and at the same time God establishes reconciliation with all of creation (2 Cor 5:17-21). This is the ground for the confession that *nothing* "will be able to separate us from the love of God in Christ Jesus our Lord" (Rom 8:39), and at the same time it gives rise to the imperative to "go . . . and make disciples of *all nations*" (Matt 28:19), indeed, to "proclaim the good news to the *whole creation*" (Mark 16:15). These are universal and cosmic assertions, but their intentions are not imperialistic. Their aim is not to impose by force a certain ideology upon others. It is therefore important to remind ourselves that with the resurrection of the crucified Christ, God has established an ontology of peace and justice. The declared intention of God's loving and liberating activity in Jesus Christ is to make human life human. This intention compels us to ask how the Christian understanding of the saving work of Christ relates to other claims of salvation.

Challenge

There is no virtue in denying or relativizing one's religious identity. Religion has to do with conscience and with ultimate concerns. It touches the very heart of our being. If dialogue means polite interchange of opinion and information, it can be interesting, but it may make no difference in a world that desperately needs to hear new words. A first step for every religion is therefore to ask itself how far and in what ways its own basis and substance affirms life, freedom, peace, and justice and leads its adherents to show respect toward others and, if possible, to cooperate with others for the common good. A Christian theology of religions must seek to shape the following affirmations and challenges into a coherent vision:

- God's triumph over the estranging forces of death has led to the conviction that God has not only created the world, but that God loves the *world* (John 3:16), that God has reconciled the *world* with himself (2 Cor 5:17-21), and that God "desires *everyone* to be saved and to come to the knowledge of the truth" (1 Tim 2:4).

- The fact that God raised *Jesus* from the dead has led to the confession that Jesus Christ is the "*one* mediator between God and humankind," that he *alone* is "the way and the truth and the life," that "no one comes to the Father except through" him, that in Jesus Christ "the whole fullness of deity dwells bodily," and that therefore "there is salvation in no one else, for there is no other name under heaven given among mortals by which we must be saved."[3] Christian theologians must try to hear, understand, and interpret the reality reflected in these biblical texts.

- For Christians, it is fundamental that the resurrection is a *liberating* event. Faith in Christ therefore entails what the New Testament refers to with words like παρρησία ("openness," "confidence," "courage"), ἐλευθερία ("freedom"), εἰρήνη ("peace"), and σωτηρία ("*shalom*," "salvation"). Faith brings freedom from the quenching threat and the oppressive reality of sin, fatedness, and death. It creates openness toward God, neighbor, and nature. It is therefore inadequate and would lead to a fundamental distortion of faith if Christ is seen merely as a good person, a pious man, a moral example, a courageous hero, or a committed revolutionary. To confess the liberating reality and energizing power of the gospel, Jesus Christ must be understood as savior, redeemer, reconciler, and mediator—lest faith changes into morality and liberty into legalism.

- The resurrection of Christ in the power of the Spirit implies a *trinitarian* understanding of God. God is the father of Jesus Christ and the creator of heaven and earth; the Spirit of God is the Spirit of life apart from whom nothing can exist or survive (Ps 104:29f.); Christ, who as the incarnate word is the mediator of creation "enlightens everyone" (John 1:3f. 9), is necessarily related to the story of Jesus.

- Although religions, including Christianity, claim to have answers to the human quest for meaning and salvation, not only do they have histories replete with war, torture, racism, nationalism, and other injustices, but they are still involved in most major conflicts in our world. Therefore the great challenge to all religions today is whether they are willing to serve *peace and justice* in our world and whether they are able to deal with their differences in a civilized, nonviolent, and constructive manner.

- Religious faith, rituals, doctrines, and practices do not necessarily help make human life human; they may in fact hinder the celebration of life. Religious faith can and does heal and liberate; but at the same time, religious faith can also enslave, oppress, and diminish. Religion can be divine or demonic; it can help or hinder in the quest for human fulfillment. It is therefore a challenge to all religions clearly to spell out the *ground* and the *criteria* by which they measure the authenticity of religious faith.

- Christians can no longer overlook the dignity and resources of other religions. Who would want to question the religious authenticity of a Mahatma Gandhi or of the Dalai Lama? Many Christians witness to the fact that they have been helped in understanding and practicing their *Christian* faith from encounters with members of other faiths. Respect and openness for the "other" is a basic ingredient of human life together.

- As Christians, we cannot and we must not forget that our history is replete with terrible aberrations of faith in Christ. In the name of the Prince of Peace, we have blessed weapons and fought wars. In the name of the one who came to heal people, we have broken the bodies and souls of opponents with sophisticated instruments of torture. In the name of the one whom we confess as the incarnation of love, we killed and damned those who departed from theological orthodoxy. In the name of the one who came to liberate the oppressed, we have failed to feed the poor and promise hope to the hungry. In many and various ways, Christians have been disobedient to the call of Christ. In light of the militarism, colonialism, and imperialism that have originated in countries where the Christian faith was dominant, we must also face the uncomfortable question whether our faith itself, and not only our failure to understand and implement it, was involved in shaping inhumane activities. One only has to think of what Christian societies did to Jews in Germany, to First Nations people in Canada, to Native Americans and to African Americans in the USA, and to Aboriginal people in Australia to realize that even with noble intentions we have erected barriers that make it difficult for such oppressed and disadvantaged and bruised people to come to a unprejudiced encounter with the gospel of Christ. Should they be punished for our insensitivities, callousness, and sins?

- The *post-modern paradigm* that influences or even dominates much of our thinking today suggests that most or even all things are situational and relative. The spiritual and moral authority of a grand narrative is being questioned. Our awareness of living in a global village seems to go hand in hand with the denial of a global ethic. How then are we to understand truth? Is there a common *humanum* that transcends religious differences? Can there be good and adequate reasons for making universal moral claims?

We must keep the above assertions and challenges in mind as we try to develop a constructive appreciation of and approach to other religious faiths.

Options

Although theologians are aware of the urgency for a Christian theology of religions, and the relevant literature is legion, it is somewhat daunting to realize that a convincing answer that brings the above challenges into a coherent vision has not yet evolved.

The "exclusivists," whether in the Evangelical or Roman Catholic camp, want to limit God's saving activity to those who have expressed an explicit faith in Christ and as such are members of the Christian church. But that option is difficult to sustain. It fails to respect other religions, and it fails to fully appreciate that in Christ, God has reconciled the *world* with God's self (John 3:16; 2 Cor 5:17-21).

The "inclusivists" rightly recognize God's universal intention and that, in Christ, God has provided salvation for all people. This salvation, so they claim, is real and effective for all people of good will who live according to the dictates of their conscience. The problem with this approach is that it assumes an "anonymous" presence of Christ in other religions and therefore it leaves itself open to the charge of religious imperialism.

The "pluralists" are painfully aware of the horrific consequences of Christian imperialism. They acknowledge the authenticity and saving efficacy of other religions and thereby give due recognition to the post-modern emphasis on the situational nature of truth claims. For them, all religions are equally true or false. At the same time, they seem to underestimate the demonic aspects of religions, and they underrate the importance of the human longing for universal truths. It is somewhat ironic that at a time when the major challenges facing humanity are global, calling for a global response, based on a global ethic and universal human rights, there is a tendency among ethicists to fall back into situationalism and relativism. It is true, of course, that many values are situational. Indeed, it would be a great pity if the diversity of human cultures were not encouraged. Nevertheless, the human rights tradition is a good reminder that within cultural diversity there are universal values. Torture, racism, child abuse, rape, genital mutilation, and slavery should not be acceptable in any culture, while religious tolerance should be affirmed against any cultural pressure to the contrary.

Dialogue

It is impossible to approach a solution apart from "looking people of other faiths in the eyes"—without, of course, forgetting one's own identity. True insight includes the heart. In ecumenical dialogues and in justice concerns involving indigenous people, refugees, and asylum seekers, I have often experienced how people's fears are allayed, their sensitivities heightened, and their reason facilitated when they actually open themselves to the situation at hand.

Dialogue therefore in no way implies that one surrenders or relativizes one's identity; quite the opposite. Christians, for instance, enter into a conversation with a trinitarian understanding of God. At the same time, dialogue requires a certain openness and anticipation in order to make a real encounter with the "other" possible.

The fear, often voiced by "pluralists," that the Christian claim of God being inherently linked with the story of Jesus implies elitism and superiority and therefore necessarily leads to imperialism is misplaced. It is as unrealistic to ask Christians to relativize the normativity of Christ as it is to expect Jews to suspend the normativity of the Torah, to expect Muslims to relativize the normativity of the Koran, and to require of Buddhists to relativize the normativity of Buddha's teachings and practices. Relativism contradicts the nature of religious faith as an ultimate concern. It would be an impossible position for a Christian. It would separate the Christian from the community of faith and from the content of their authoritative traditions. There is no virtue in denying or relativizing one's identity. That would lead to soteriological uncertainty and run counter to the very promises of a helpful religion. To engage in dialogue, one must have a position from which to speak. Everyone who can distinguish truth from lie, love from rape, selflessness from selfishness, and multiculturalism from racism, has a point of view. In religious matters, such a standpoint is generally firm, because we are dealing with questions of ultimacy and therefore with matters of life and death.

On the other hand, a Christian theology of religions does not exclude the expectation and even presumption that there may be truth and grace in other religions. How can we affirm the cosmic significance of the resurrection of Christ and then in principle exclude certain areas of reality from his influence? Indeed, arguing from a certain point of view and at the same time presuming that there may be truth and grace in other faiths makes dialogue possible and it can make such a dialogue an interesting, rewarding, and enriching experience.

Similarity and Difference

Occupying one's own standpoint—and not denying but affirming one's own identity and expecting others to do the same—makes dialogue possible and promising. What method can we adopt that makes it possible to affirm our own identities and at the same time to keep an open mind and an open heart toward "others," indeed to expect the encounter with others to deepen or modify our own ultimate concern?

I suggest the approach of similarity and difference.[4] "Similarity" because Christian faith shares with all or with most religions the longing for and the experience of "more" than what human and historical immanence can supply. All major religions address the human quest for meaning and suggest ways to structure human relationship to the divine. They also have basic moral convictions in common, like reverence for life, commitment to tolerance, truth, and nonviolence, just distribution of the earth's resources, and partnership between women and men.[5] At the same time, we also have to ask for "difference," because a dialogue would become uninteresting if the differences were not named. In today's world, given the aberrations of religious faith on the one hand and the moral challenges in our global village on the other, all religions must allow themselves to be measured by whether they are a help or a hindrance to making human life human.

Christian identity is grounded in the resurrection of the crucified Christ. Since God raised Jesus in the power of the Spirit, our focus on the resurrection as the foundational event for Christian faith and for the Christian church implies a trinitarian understanding of God. Relating such an understanding to the challenge for a theology of religions, keeping in mind the approach of similarity and difference, suggests the following reflections.

God as Creator—the Ground of Being

The Christian believer *experiences* God as savior, redeemer, reconciler, and liberator. When such experience asks for its ground, it finds it in God, who is also the "creator of heaven and earth." God is the all-encompassing reality, the ground of being. Christians therefore do not believe that there are many gods. They affirm that there is one God who holds all things together, who accompanies creation with saving grace, who provides ever-new possibilities in the ongoing process of history, and who gives meaning to reality. Early Christians therefore confessed that God is the God of Jews *and* Gentiles (Rom 3:29). They believed that *all* people are responsible to God, because "ever since the creation of the world his eternal power and divine nature, invisible though they are, have been understood and seen through the things he has made" (Rom 1:20). The evangelist Luke in a portrayal of a Pauline sermon explicitly claims that the unnamed deity worshiped at the Areopagus in Athens is none other than the Christian God (Acts 17:22-28). It is not surprising therefore that Christians affirm that the God who in Israel's history makes covenant after covenant to show his passion for his creation "has sent his Son as the Savior of the world" (1 John 4:14).

If God is God, then Christians must entertain the possibility that everyone who reaches beyond their human limitations and finds wholeness and meaning in this existential search is in touch, in however broken manner, with the same divine reality that Christians call "God." This is widely accepted with reference to Judaism and Islam where the controversy is not God as such, but the way God has been made known: in the Torah, in the Koran, or in Jesus Christ; but this presumption needs to be extended to all authentic and humane religious claims.

Together with most religions, Christians claim that "God," however "God" is understood, is necessary to explain the world and to live meaningfully within it. With other religions, Christians agree that relationship to "God" is a necessary aspect of the *humanum*. For Christians as well as for people of other religions, being fully human includes relationship to other humans, to nature, to history, and to the divine.

Differences emerge with those religions for whom the deity or the divine does not have a personal character, where the difference and "over-againstness" of the deity is played down, and where therefore prayer becomes a monologue rather than a dialogue. For Christians it is also of supreme importance that God is not only a personal but also a liberating reality. The symbols of the "exodus" in the Hebrew Bible and of the "resurrection" in the Christian Bible signify God as a lover of life and of freedom. It is obvious that Christians would also differ with those visions of reality, like atheism, Marxism, and some forms of humanism, that see religious faith as infantile regression, as compensation for personality deficiencies, or as projection of one's own needs and interests and who therefore want to explain reality without reference to the divine.

For Christians, God is not merely a divine principle that permeates everything; nor is God a deity who lives in splendid isolation, untouched by the human struggle for meaning and survival; nor is God a deity that in the long distant past has put a process of creation into motion and then left the process to itself; nor is God merely the immanent force that gives meaning and direction to the process of nature and history. For Christians, God is ontologically different from God's creation: God is "over against" creation. But this over-againstness is not one of separation. It is an over-againstness of *relationship*. God is therefore spoken of in personal terms. God is active as creator, redeemer and fulfiller. God can be addressed in prayer and worship; God does not impose a heteronomous claim upon the human conscience, but God liberates the human conscience from forces and structures that estrange it from its true being. With these observations, we have already entered the discussion of what is meant by the word "God" or "divine" or "deity." The Christian answer to this is clear and distinct.

God as Reconciler—the Ground of Salvation and the Norm for Life

The question of truth and content cannot be avoided when we speak of an ultimate concern, which religious faith by definition is. It is simply not true to say that "all roads lead to God"; it is simply not true that all religious experiences have liberating, saving, and humanizing dignity. Religious experiences can be life-denying and demonic—also within the Christian religion, of course. Every religion must therefore address the question of truth and content. Who is the all-encompassing reality that human beings call "God," "Allah," or the "divine"?

The Ground of Salvation

Christians claim that an authentic religious experience must have a ground, and it must be life-affirming and life-enhancing. It must address the fundamental challenges of human life: Where do I come from? Why am I here? Why do the righteous suffer? Is freedom real or is it an illusion? How do I confront sin, fate, and death? Is there life in the beyond?

Christians believe that faith is grounded *extra nos* ("outside of us"). The Christian assertion that all human beings are sinners is not a moral condemnation; it is a religious claim resulting from the perceived need for God and the experienced reality of estrangement and forgiveness. Christian faith includes the discovery and subsequent admission that the human attempt to ground ultimate reality in ourselves has failed. At the same time, Christians affirm that there is no need to ground human life in ourselves, because God has done for us what we could not do for ourselves. Christian faith is not only a system of doctrine, nor is it an institution. It is grounded in Jesus Christ who is and remains external but at the same time related to the believer. Faith, though ontologically bound to Christ, confesses that Christ is not dissolved into faith. There is yet more truth to be expected! But the truth implied in the experience of faith relates God to the story of Jesus and consequently to the experience of freedom, love, joy, courage, and hope.

For dialogues with other religions, it is important that faith is aware of its noetic limitations. The intellect is only partially able to grasp and formulate the rich content of faith. Faith grants soteriological certainty, which finds expressions in such texts as 1 Timothy 2:5, John 14:6, Colossians 2:9, and Acts 4:12. At the same time, faith is aware of a qualitative difference between God and the believer: ". . . now we see in a mirror, dimly, but then we will see face to face. Now I know only in part; then I will know fully, even as I have been fully known" (1 Cor 13:12). Christians therefore distinguish between *certitudo* ("certainty"), which is an essential part of faith, and *securitas* ("security"), whereby God would be verified on rational or experiential terms. Although we confess by faith that Jesus Christ is God for us, the understanding and implications of that faith remain an ongoing process.

The ground for the Christian experience of salvation is God's saving and liberating act in Jesus Christ—his life, death, and resurrection. For Christians, Jesus Christ is not only a good person, a pious believer, or a courageous hero, but he is a risen savior, reconciler, and redeemer. He is our peace with God. He is our salvation. In Jesus, God has made God's very being vulnerable to the onslaught of human selfishness, betrayal, and violence. God has exposed God's very being to the estranging forces of death and in that struggle—how else, given the poverty of human language and human understanding, shall we describe it?—in that struggle between God and death, God has remained God. When this victory of the divine struggle with the estranging forces of death became historically manifest in the appearances of the risen Christ to believers, the church confessed, "'Death has been swallowed up in victory.' . . . thanks be to God, who gives us the victory through our Lord Jesus Christ" (1 Cor 15:54-57).

The biblical witness asserts that what God has done in Christ, God has done for all people, indeed for all of creation. In Christ, God "loved" the world (John 3:16) and "reconciled" (2 Cor 5:17-21) the world with God's self in order to fulfill the divine aim for "everyone to be saved and to come to the knowledge of the truth" (1 Tim 2:3f.). The reality of salvation that God has provided for all in Christ becomes actual in the event of faith and obedience. The *event* of reconciliation therefore includes the *ministry* of reconciliation, by which people, all people, are "entreated" ("requested")[6] to "be reconciled to God" (2 Cor 5:20).

We are not surprised therefore that in the early church salvation was also promised to those who did not know or explicitly name "Christ" as the basis of their life. Salvation was pronounced on the poor, the hungry, the despised, and those who shared their lives with them (Luke 6:20-23; Matt 25:31-40). Their lives were interpreted as belonging to the kingdom of God: "Blessed are you . . . !" (Luke 6:20-22); "Come, O blessed of my Father, inherit the kingdom prepared for you from the foundation of the world" (Matt 25:34). They participated in the promise of God's unconditional love that became event in Jesus Christ. What Christians know to be true through their faith in Christ is implied for these people who seem to have no explicit knowledge of Christ. This will become clearer in our comments on the Holy Spirit. In a trinitarian understanding of God, the Spirit witnesses to Christ (John 14–16) and as such will not contradict what God has done in Christ. Nevertheless, by confessing that the Spirit has her own identity within the trinity, the church wanted to say that the Spirit's work includes a "more" to the person and work of Christ. This "more" includes the ministry of the Spirit outside the realm of an explicit confession of the name of Jesus as the Christ.

The early Christians therefore confessed that what has come to expression in Jesus Christ was in the being of God from the beginning. The Johannine prologue is a classic expression of that view (John 1:1-18):

> In the beginning was the Word, and the Word was with God, and the Word was God. *He* was in the beginning with God. *All things came into being through him*, and without him not one thing came into being. What has come into being *in him was life*, and the life was the light of *all* people. The light shines in the darkness, and the darkness did not overcome it. . . .
>
> The true light, which enlightens *everyone*, was coming into the world. . . .
>
> And the Word became flesh and lived among us, and we have seen his glory, the glory as of a father's only son, full of grace and truth. . . .
>
> No one has ever seen God. It is God the only Son, who is close to the Father's heart, who has made him known.

We may therefore conclude that for Christians, Jesus Christ is the ground of salvation. This implies two important assertions. It provides the basis for confessing that "God *is* love," and it underlines that salvation includes *all* people, indeed *everything* that God has created. The difference between Christians and non-Christians is that Christians know and confess Jesus Christ as the ground of their salvation, while non-Christians do not. At the same time, the Spirit of God, who is the Spirit of life and of salvation, is at work everywhere trying to draw people into God's unconditional love. Christian faith includes the realization and the humility that we "know only in part" and therefore, given the universal passion of God, we may well presume that the God of Jesus can be known in unexpected places.[7]

The Norm of Life

The promise of salvation is associated with a certain response, disposition, and action on the side of human beings. Human beings strive to live in harmony with their ultimate concerns. As Christians, we therefore claim that Jesus Christ is not only the *ground* of salvation, but he is also the *norm* of the experience of salvation and indeed for the journey of life. Experience and tradition teach us that the divine Spirit can and must be distinguished from the human spirit. An unbending human self will and the subsequent human estrangement from God is of such depth that even religious faith is in danger of being functionalized to serve gods that are not God, and therefore will lead the human conscience astray. Religious faith must therefore name a norm to evaluate experience. In the early church, it was one of the gifts of the Spirit "to distinguish the spirits" (1 Cor 12:10; 1 John 4:1). And the measure was not just the name "Christ," but the reality and content for which that name stands, the "humanity" of Christ which, as we saw in chapter 3, stands for his liberating solidarity with "late comers," "unbelievers," and "outsiders" (1 Cor 11–14). The fact that these texts are spoken to churches and church leaders, and that the apostle even entertains the impossible possibility that the church can cease being the church in spite of all religious experiences and rituals (1 Cor 11:20-22), makes it abundantly clear that people who don't have an explicit knowledge of Jesus can be closer to the reality that Christ fleshed out than people who confess Jesus as Lord.

Given that we are saved by grace alone and not by our works, and given that this grace can be found in unexpected places, it would be a denial of the very foundation and content of Christian faith if we were to limit God's grace to our explicit doctrinal confession of Christ and to being a member of a Christian church. Wherever a genuine need for God is felt, wherever people reach out for salvation, wherever there is a sincere yearning for or experience of freedom, wherever there is an expression of selfless love and engagement for freedom, justice, and peace, wherever the "other" becomes interesting and important for one's own quest for life, there we may presume that the God whom Jesus called "abba" and in whose name Jesus brought "good news to the poor" and proclaimed "release to the captives and recovery of sight to the blind, to let the oppressed go free" is at work.

This in no way makes mission superfluous. It is a great pity that mission is often seen as imperialism and imposition. Love is in sharing and therefore every genuine faith has the impulse to mission. That is the very reason why not only Christian but also Muslim and Hindu countries agree to freedom of religion as a universal human right. Freedom of religion includes the telling of one's story and also the right to change one's religion.[8] As far as Christians are concerned, the universal significance of the resurrection of Christ calls for the gospel to be preached so that all people may know and celebrate that God is a good God. The name of Jesus guarantees the goodness of God and therefore adds a dimension of intimacy and liberation that clarifies and enhances the experience of salvation.

God as Spirit of Life and Salvation—Presence and Experience

All or most religions make universal claims, and therefore, by implication, they are missionary religions. Christians speak of the work of God's Spirit when they refer to the universal *missio dei*.

The confessions that refer to Christ as the way, the truth, and the life arise from the *experience* of ultimacy. This experience is not the result of rational deduction, moral striving, or religious instruction. It results from the coming of faith in the story of Jesus, which has an inherent, liberating, and integrating claim upon the human conscience. This claim is not a heteronomous authority imposed upon the human conscience. It is a "saving" reality that frees the human conscience from heteronomous and penultimate claims. It frees the human conscience from being caught in the accusing role of morality, and thereby it restores the conscience as the integrating center of the human person and as the guide for an ethos of responsible freedom.

This "coming" of faith in Christ includes the recognition that human attempts to provide their own answers to the problems of sin, meaning, fate, and death have been a massive failure. Faith includes the grateful admission that what humanity failed to do, God has done in the life, death, and resurrection of Jesus Christ. In the event of faith, humankind becomes liberated from the need to create its own ultimate meaning, and it finds in Christ a reality that provides a meaningful vision of life.

This faith experience is ultimate. It is not one experience among others. It is the experience that can only be described in terms of *creatio ex nihilo* ("creation out of nothing"; Rom 4:5 and 17), life out of death, salvation from lostness, being found after being lost, reconciled after being estranged.

This experience of faith therefore calls for an ontology, and it has universal implications. If God is creator and if therefore all people and indeed all of nature are creature and creation, then what is true for Christian experience must be possible for all people. The Judeo-Christian tradition therefore confesses God's Spirit as the necessary ground of being: "When you hide your face, they are dismayed; when you take away their breath, they die and return to their dust. When you send forth your spirit, they are created; and you renew the face of the ground" (Ps 104:29f.).

At the same time, the experience of ultimacy does not remove the qualitative difference between God and the believer. God is God, while the believer remains human. It was the crucified Christ, not the believer, who was raised from the dead, while the believer walks "in newness of life" (Rom 6:4).[9] This ontological distinction (not separation!) between God and humanity becomes manifest in the fact that our knowledge of faith limps behind our experience of faith: ". . . now we see in a mirror, dimly, but then we will see face to face. Now I know only in part; then I will know fully, even as I have been fully known" (1 Cor 13:12). God's "yes" is unconditional and eschatological ("as I have been fully known"); the knowledge of that "yes" grants certainty in the conscience, but for our understanding, it is a process that constantly reminds us of the difference between the human and the divine. Tolerance and humility are therefore correlates to the Christian experience of faith.

The Spirit of God is not only the Spirit of life. The Spirit is also the effective activity of God, which seeks to apply the salvation that God has accomplished in Christ to all people. By shaping its understanding of the trinity, the church wants to express that while the ministry of the Spirit is related to what God has done in Christ, it is not identical with it.[10] This means that the saving and liberating activity of the Spirit draws on the ontological depth of the death of Christ and includes the passion for all that is lost.

This does not mean, however, that the Spirit's work is necessarily tied to the cognitive confession of Jesus as Christ. With the Logos-Christology, with the affirmation of the preexistence of Christ, with the confession that Christ was mediator of creation, and with the insistence that the saving work of Christ covers the living and the dead of all times (1 Pet 3:18-22; 4:6), the theologians of the early church wanted to say that what God has done in Christ is grounded in the depth of God's being and therefore changes the reality for all people at all times. Just as the Spirit as the Spirit of God, the father of Jesus Christ, was active before Jesus came, so the Spirit is active alongside the explicit acknowledgment of Jesus. Wherever the reality that has come to expression in Jesus Christ is found, wherever there is a true search for truth, wherever there is a selfless openness for "God," wherever there is a true engagement for justice, wherever peace is waged, there we may presume the Spirit of God to be at work.

This appreciation of the "wide" work and "broad" significance of the Spirit of God should in no way play down the importance of knowing the name of Jesus. It simply wants to recognize that God as redeemer is the same whom we confess as creator and sustainer of heaven and earth. In the trinitarian being of God, the Spirit is intimately related to the story of Jesus and it belongs to the Spirit's activity to make the possibility of explicit faith in Christ an actual event.

The claim that the Spirit is part of the trinitarian reality of God and as such necessary to explain life and salvation may be seen as presumptuous by those who deny God (Atheism; Marxism; certain forms of humanism) and those for whom God is not "one" and "personal" and "over against" (New Age? Buddhism?). Such different interpretations of reality cannot be avoided and the Christian must not be hesitant to enter into dialogue about the nature of being and reality. Such a dialogue should certainly be dictated by respect and tolerance and, need one say it, nonviolence. In such a dialogue, all who listen can be enriched.

Conclusion—By Their Fruits You Shall Know Them!

Christian theology is aware of the danger of moralizing faith, of making faith dependent on human performance, and thereby losing its liberating power. At the same time, Christianity along with all other religions must spell out and submit itself to the norms of truth, peace, and justice.

The fact that Christian faith makes an ultimate claim upon the believer implies a truth claim. This truth claim is accompanied by a noetic humility arising from a qualitative difference between the believer and God. Since it is fundamental for Christians that the redeemer God is the creator of heaven and earth, and since God has revealed God's will to save God's creation, therefore the Christian may presume that the God who has established the event of salvation in Jesus Christ seeks and finds many ways in which the content of the story of Jesus can free the human conscience. Whether it actually is the Spirit who proceeds from the Father of the Son can only be known by the fruits of the Spirit. We recall the important passage from the Gospel of Matthew:

> When John heard in prison what the Messiah was doing, he sent word by his disciples and said to him, "Are you the one who is to come, or are we to wait for

another?" Jesus answered them, "Go and tell John what you hear and see: the blind receive their sight, the lame walk, the lepers are cleansed, the deaf hear, the dead are raised, and the poor have good news brought to them. And blessed is anyone who takes no offense at me." (Matt 11:2-6).

In a world where we daily hear of torture and genocide, where terrorists unsettle the human soul with the use of terrible and uncontrollable means and methods, where the threat of the use of nuclear bombs is not diminishing but increasing, where the rich become richer and the poor become poorer, where ecological dignity is powerless against economic interests, religions must declare, explain, and make manifest that they are on the side of truth, peace, and justice.

Christians enter into dialogue with other religions in the awareness that God's concern is for all people, that God's salvation in Christ is offered unconditionally, that this grace is accessible in whatever broken manner to all people, that its only limitation is given by the nature of God as love that cannot coerce, but that longs to become manifest in hope, justice, liberation, and *shalom*.

Notes

[1] This chapter is a modified version of my article "Towards a Christian Theology of Religions: Christianity in Dialogue with other Faiths," in *Interface: A Forum for Theology in the World* 2/1 (May 1999), 39-55.

[2] Hans Küng, *Global Responsibility: In Search for a World Ethic*, trans. John Bowden (London: SCM, 1991), xv. See also Hans Küng's series *The Religious Situation of our Time: Judaism*, trans. John Bowden (London: SCM, 1992); *Christianity— Its Essence and History*, trans. John Bowden (London: SCM, 1995). Further, see Hans Küng and Jürgen Moltmann, eds., English language ed. Marcus Lebébure, *Christianity among World Religions: Concilium* 183 (Edinburgh: T. & T. Clark, 1986); Hans Küng, Josef von Ess, Heinrich von Stietencron, Heinz Bechert, *Christianity and the World Religions: Paths of Dialogue with Islam, Hinduism, and Buddhism*, trans. Peter Heinegg (London: Collins, 1987); Hans Küng and Jürgen Moltmann, eds., *Islam: A Challenge for Christianity: Concilium* 1994/3 (London: SCM; Maryknoll: Orbis, 1994).

[3] These quotations are taken from 1 Tim 2:5, John 14:6, Col 2:9, and Acts 4:12.

[4] This is a rough analogy to Karl Barth's thesis that phenomena in the world can become reflections of the kingdom of God, but at the same time they need to be measured by Christian revelation to determine whether they are such ("The Christian Community and the Civil Community" [1946], in Karl Barth, *Community, State, and Church: Three Essays* [Gloucester MA: Peter Smith, 1968], 149-89, especially § 14).

[5] For details, see Hans Küng, *Global Responsibility: In Search for a World Ethic*, trans. John Bowden (London: SCM, 1991); Hans Küng, ed., *Yes to a Global Ethic*, trans. John Bowden (London: SCM, 1996); Hans Küng and Jürgen Moltmann, eds., *The Ethics of World Religions and Human Rights: Concilium* 1990/2 (London: SCM, 1990).

[6] Paul's use of δεόμεθα ("beg," entreat," "request") has the intention of saying that the way of communication must cohere with the content of what is being communicated.

⁷ In reading the Gospel of Mark, for instance, one is struck by the motif that the ὄχλοι ("crowds"), Gentiles, women, blind people, and other outsiders see and understand what the disciples (believers, church) fail to see and understand.

⁸ For details, see my *Freedom of Religion as a Human Right,* Baptist Human Rights Booklet 3/1999 (McLean VA: Baptist World Alliance, 1999).

⁹ The author of Colossians fails to recognize or appreciate this important theological distinction when he locates the resurrection of the believer in baptism: ". . . you were buried with him in baptism, you were also raised with him through faith in the power of God, who raised him from the dead" (Col 2:12).

¹⁰ Traditional Christology, especially in the Reformed tradition, has often tended to identify the ministry of the risen Christ with the ministry of the Spirit. Trinitarian thinking attempts to recognize the Holy Spirit as having her own identity and at the same time insists that that identity is essentially interrelated with the identity of the second person, the story of Jesus the Christ.

Chapter 7

Discipleship

Walking in the resurrection of Jesus Christ —The Schleitheim Confession[1]

Prelude

Finally, we need to acknowledge the importance of the believer in God's economy. We saw that the resurrection of Christ includes the creation of faith and the call to mission. Christians are called to be "God's fellow workers" (συνεργοί θεοῦ, 1 Cor 3:9). God's grace does not bypass human faith and obedience. On the contrary, it inspires and empowers believers for the celebration of life and the mission of love. We face the sad fact, however, that many believers, many churches, and indeed whole theological traditions understand faith primarily in private, personal, and individual terms, and therefore consider the struggle for justice as secondary to the experience of faith. This prompts us to consider the interlocking of the resurrection of the crucified One with the believer.

In the previous chapters, I have argued that the resurrection of Christ is a *real* event and that as such it is the foundation and the wellspring for faith and for the community of faith, the church. At the same time, I have tried to take seriously that resurrection texts of the New Testament narrate the resurrection as an event that established a *new* reality. Together with the life and the death of Jesus, it established what the Apostle Paul called "reconciliation" and what theologians tend to call "atonement" (at-one-ment). In and through the Christ-event, God has defeated the isolating and estranging forces of sin and death and thereby provided the basis for the promise of faith and justice.

The new reality, established by the life, death, and resurrection of Christ, is narrated in the New Testament as a *relational* reality. The resurrection of Christ is not simply "there" to be affirmed or denied. It is an "open" event. The risen Christ is "the *firstborn* within a large family" (Rom 8:29), the "*first fruits* of those who have fallen asleep," and the "*first-born* from the dead" (1 Cor 15:20, 23; Col 1:18; Rev 1:5; compare Matt 27:52f.). The resurrection is a history-creating and history-shaping event. As a trinitarian event, God the Father acting in the power of the Spirit, the resurrection carries within itself the energy and promise of fulfillment.

We saw that the resurrection of Christ therefore includes the following dimensions:

- As an integral part of the Christ-event, it establishes reconciliation with God.

- This is what the apostle Paul called the death of death. The powers that separate humanity from the source of its being have been defeated by an act of God. The ultimate threat of nihilism has been removed. The resurrection of Christ entails the promise of eternal life.

- The same Spirit who raised Jesus from the dead reveals God as being for and with others and as such creates faith and obedience.

- The content of resurrection faith must be discerned by taking seriously that Jesus, as the consequence of a certain vision of God and a particular lifestyle, was opposed and killed, and then was raised from the dead.

- Since human beings are social beings, with the creation of faith there comes the formation of the community of faith.

- With the creation of faith also comes the call to mission, drawing the believer into God's passion to redeem what God has created.

- By raising Jesus from the dead, God established an ontology of peace and nonviolence.

- Since the resurrection is an act of God, it carries within itself the promise for the ultimate triumph of love, grace, and justice.

I hope to have made it clear that both the historical positivists—who tend to freeze the resurrection into the past and who tend to be primarily interested in questions of what happened 2000 years ago—and the existentialists—whose interest is focused on the experience of believers and the communities of faith but who show little interest in what happened to the dead Jesus—fail to give sufficient attention to the life-transforming power of the resurrection.

Conservative evangelicals fail to realize that an affirmation of the resurrection of Christ should not lead to an apologetic defense of the resurrection as a historical event but should motivate them to be vitally interested in what is happening in our world here and now. A proper understanding of the resurrection of the crucified Christ would lead them to a holistic concept of mission as participating in God's passion to actualize the reconciliation God has established in Christ.

Liberal theologians, on the other hand, seem to underestimate the power of human selfishness, violence, sin, and consequently the need for the event of reconciliation in which God did for us and the world what we could not and what we cannot do for ourselves. Unexpected resources can fuel a vision for peace and justice that we need so urgently in our world today. Christians believe that God in Christ has broken the power of sin and death. By claiming God's gift, the Christian community can make a significant contribution to peace and justice in our world.

We need to ask, however, how the God who in the power of the Spirit raised Jesus from the dead, how the Jesus who has been raised from the dead, and how the empowering πνεῦμα ἁγιωσύνης ("spirit of holiness," Rom 1:3f.) can be known. How can we respond to the resurrection of Jesus Christ in terms worthy of the event itself—not merely serving our needs and interests?

In the course of this chapter, I want to elaborate on the following thesis: the foundational event of the Christian faith, the resurrection of the crucified Christ, calls for Christian discipleship so that the identity and relevance of Christian faith is preserved. On the other hand, Christian discipleship needs the foundational reality of the resurrection so that its liberating manifestation of the gospel is not reduced to a sterile moralism.

Options

What are the options for knowing the Christ whom God raised from the dead? How do Christians best respond to the resurrection of Christ? I am not concerned to limit the options. The mysterious and colorful reality of an act of God deserves to be acknowledged, received, and appreciated with all facilities of knowing that are available to us. It is more a matter of priority. What is the way of knowing that is most appropriate to the nature and dignity of the resurrection of the crucified Jesus?

Reason

Do we respond most adequately with our reason? Given the modern understanding of reason that acknowledges something as real if it can be empirically verified, we would then try to prove or at least demonstrate that Jesus after his death appeared to the disciples and that the tomb into which his corpse was placed was empty. Consequently, if it could be shown that the appearances were not subjective visions and that the body was not stolen from the tomb or that the women went to the wrong tomb, God must have raised Jesus from the dead. This is the way Carl F. H. Henry,[2] William Lane Craig,[3] and many conservative theologians argue. They lament the cognitive vacuum in modern theology and they want to make the Christian faith, with the resurrection at its center, an option for the modern intellectual.

There seems to be an insatiable longing in many Christians to have their faith confirmed by reason. Certain theological circles seem to have gotten stuck in the age of reason. They seem to have forgotten that reason is part of "fallen" humanity and participates in the uncertainty and ambiguity of all human achievements. There is no question, of course, that reason can do much and that, in fact, reason has done much. It has brought us the scientific and technological revolution. It has made more comfortable and longer lives possible. It has given us computers and CD players and television sets and medicines and airplanes and motorcars. It has provided valuable philosophical interpretations, insights, and critiques. At the same time, we all know that reason is no guarantee for virtue, morality, and justice. The most horrific crimes against humanity have been conceived and implemented by rational means. It must therefore be clear on what terms reason operates. Does it receive reality and then think about it? Or does it produce reality and thus arrogate divinity to itself? Does it acknowledge given criteria of evaluation or does it produce its own criteria? For Christians, reason that fails to acknowledge the possibility of the divine or that tries to replace God has overstepped its mark and become an idol with clay feet.

I am not denying, of course, that there is a cognitive dimension to our faith in Christ. Indeed, by writing and reading these lines we exercise such reason. But given the above-mentioned possibilities and temptations of reason, our general understanding of reason must be judged as inadequate to capture what God has given us with the resurrection of Christ. Reason is not holistic. It distances the object of inquiry. Modern reason will speak of the resurrection as some kind of super-miracle, but it cannot capture the fact that it is a relational and "open" event, aiming at our holistic response of faith and obedience. Modern reason can understand that Jesus did not die of an illness or as the result of a judicial error, but that he was captured, tortured, sentenced, and killed in response to a certain kind of life. But reason cannot go beyond that. It cannot meaningfully affirm that the death of Jesus was transfigured into an event of salvation by a special activity of God. Reason therefore tends either to "jump" from the historical Jesus and his death to the faith experience of the early believers—all events that reason can understand and affirm—or it makes claims about the resurrection that stretch reason beyond its modern usage. Reason is not able to receive the risen life of Christ in such a way that it satisfies the human longing for meaning and then determines the believer's conscience and shapes the believer's existence. Reason can speak of resuscitations, but it cannot appreciate the insistence of the biblical narratives that the *crucified* Jesus was raised from the dead; that this Jesus was not resuscitated, but that he was taken out of the realm of death altogether and will therefore "never die again" (Rom 6:9).

Reason must not disappear from the theological stage, but it must take a backward step. It must think what faith in Christ is all about, but it must not try to replace faith. Our admiration for theologians such as Dietrich Bonhoeffer, Gustavo Gutiérrez, and Desmond Tutu is due to the fact that they have been willing to live their theological insights. Reason can interpret and at times even illuminate the praxis of faith; if it tries to replace it, the identity and integrity of faith in Christ become seriously distorted.

Worship

What about worship as a way of responding to the resurrection of Christ? Peter Carnley has argued that worship is the most adequate response to the resurrection and that it belongs perhaps to "*the* glory of Anglicanism" with its "preference for liturgy as a way of expressing truth over the Latin proclivity for defining doctrines and dogmas" to have understood and preserved this.[4]

Worship is certainly a more adequate and more holistic response to God as God than reason, especially if we understand worship in the tradition of the Hebrew prophets, the apostle Paul, and the author of the Epistle to the Hebrews as the holistic response to the gospel.[5] Real worship then does not happen in the sacred space, at the altar on Sunday morning, but "outside the gate" for the rest of the week in the marketplaces of life.

But the word "worship" is misleading. It no longer gathers up the prophetic criticism against the cult, Jesus' relativization of law and cult, Paul's insistence that worship happens with our "bodies" in the everyday affairs of life, and the dimension of suffering that is so clearly part of worshiping Christ. Indeed, Carnley's reference to "liturgy" and his comment that the Anglican Church rightly spends "more time in the production of our Prayer Books than in definitions of dogma"[6] suggests such a reduction in the understanding of worship.[7] In church-centered worship, the poverty of Jesus is too easily dissolved into the riches of our altars, vestments, and liturgies. Whatever our worship is, we must try to bring to expression that it was really *Jesus* who was raised from the dead—the same Jesus who shared his life with the wretched of the earth. The social and political conservatism of many Christian worshipers and the hesitancy of many church leaders to identify clearly with the marginal people in their society make me wonder whether worship is the right word to shape our response to the resurrection of the crucified Christ.

I want to proceed by retrieving a forgotten tradition, bringing it into correlation with the biblical-theological motif of "witness," and then engaging with the hermeneutical insights of Paul Ricoeur and Francis Schüssler Fiorenza.

Retrieving a Forgotten Tradition

Mainline theology has overlooked the contribution the nonviolent Anabaptists of the sixteenth century Reformation in Central Europe have made to the Christian story.[8] One of their insights was that only those willing to follow Jesus can really know him. They suspected a distortion of faith and a reduction of the gospel when the magisterial Reformers (e.g., Martin Luther, Huldrych Zwingli, Jean Calvin) made a distinction between justification and sanctification and when they focused on locating the presence of Christ in the preaching of the word and in the (proper) administration of the sacraments. Since preaching the word and administering the sacraments were essentially limited to the ordained clergy, this in fact led to an institutionalizing of the gospel. It also overlooked or relativized the prominent biblical promise that Christ is not only present in word and sacrament, but also in the gathering of God's people (Matt 18:20) and in the wretched of the earth (Matt 25:31-46). The nonviolent Anabaptists agreed with the magisterial Reformers in their insistence on *sola gratia* (by grace alone), *sola fide* (through faith alone), and *sola scriptura* (the Scriptures alone), but their reading of the New Testament convinced them that faith means more than the individual and personal appropriation of salvation. It means "following Jesus" in the context of an intentional Christian community and taking seriously what the Sermon on the Mount teaches. They criticized the Reformers' understanding of faith as being superficial and shallow. From their perspective, the Reformers preached "a sinful sweet Christ" who does not lead to a "betterment of life."[9]

The first article in the oldest Anabaptist communal statement, the *Schleitheim Confession* (1527), spells out the following requirement for candidates of baptism:

> Baptism shall be given to all those who have been taught repentance and the amendment of life and (who) believe truly that their sins are taken away through Christ, and to all those who desire to walk in the resurrection of Jesus Christ and be buried with Him in death, so that they might rise with Him; to all those who with such an understanding themselves desire and request it from us...."[10]

A central biblical text that shaped the Anabaptists' understanding of the resurrection of Christ and its effect on Christian existence is Romans 6:4: "... we have been buried with him by baptism into death, so that, just as Christ was raised from the dead by the glory of the Father, so we too might walk in newness of life."

Then and now, Baptist theology has been accused of being moralistic, legalistic, and biblicistic. That was not and is not the intention. The intention was and is the recognition that sin includes sleepiness and sloth, longing for the "fleshpots of Egypt." The nonviolent Anabaptists felt to be close to the intention of the gospel when they understood faith as obedience to the liberating claims of Christ. Applied to our topic, belief in the resurrection must include "life with the living Christ now."[11]

Here are some Anabaptist voices coming to us from the Reformation struggles in the first half of the sixteenth century.[12] Balthasar Hubmaier writes, "Faith alone makes us holy before God.... Such faith can not remain passive but must break out to God in thanksgiving and to mankind in all kinds of works of brotherly love."[13] Conrad Grebel writes to Thomas Müntzer: "... today ... every man wants to be saved by superficial faith, without fruits of faith, without baptism of trial and probation, without love and hope, without right Christian practices, and wants to persist in all the old manner of personal vices...."[14] Jakob Kautz challenged the Protestant clergy of the city of Worms on 13 June 1527 by insisting, "Jesus Christ of Nazareth did not suffer for us and has not satisfied (for our sins) in any other way but this: that we have to stand in his footsteps and have to walk the way which he has blazed for us first, and that we obey the commandments of the Father and the Son, everyone according to his measure. He who speaks differently of Christ makes an idol of Christ."[15] And Hans (John) Denck summarizes the Anabaptist ethos of Christian discipleship: "... none may truly know (Christ) unless he follow after him with his life. And no one can follow after him except in so far as one previously knows him."[16]

In our time, this understanding of faith is found in the theologies of Dietrich Bonhoeffer, Karl Barth, Jürgen Moltmann, and in the various branches of Liberation Theology. Bonhoeffer's distinction between "cheap" and "costly" grace echoes the Anabaptist distinction between a "sweet" and a "bitter" Jesus:

> Cheap Grace is the deadly enemy of our Church. We are fighting today for costly grace. Cheap grace means . . . Grace without price; grace without cost! . . . Cheap grace means grace as a doctrine, a principle, a system. It means forgiveness of sins proclaimed as a general truth, the love of God taught as the Christian "conception" of God. An intellectual assent to that idea is held to be of itself sufficient to secure remission of sins. . . . Cheap grace therefore amounts to a denial of the living Word of God, in fact, a denial of the Incarnation of the Word of God. . . . Cheap grace is the grace we bestow on ourselves. Cheap grace is the preaching of forgiveness without requiring repentance, baptism without church discipline, communion without confession, absolution without personal confession. Cheap grace is grace without discipleship, grace without the cross, grace without Jesus Christ, living and incarnate . . . . The word of cheap grace has been the ruin of more Christians than any commandment of works.[17]

The emphasis of this "forgotten tradition" is that knowledge implies involvement and responsibility, what liberation theologians call "praxis." The object of our knowledge becomes determinative for the way we know. We intentionally, with our lives, participate in the process of knowing. We become involved with what we know. True knowledge of this sort makes a claim upon us. This insistence on knowledge as involvement coheres with biblical emphases, it is emphasized in modern hermeneutics, and it is conducive to a theology of the resurrection.

"Witness"

The biblical traditions are replete with an emphasis on knowledge as involvement. The Hebrew prophets, for instance, emphasize that knowing God means to do justice (explicit in Jer 22:13-19). When Jesus was asked concerning his messianic identity, he pointed to his activities: ". . . the blind receive their sight, the lame walk, the lepers are cleansed, the deaf hear, the dead are raised, and the poor have good news brought to them" (Matt 11:2-6). The post-Easter communities found their identity in the crucified and risen Christ and they knew this implied an inward journey to word and sacrament and an outward journey seeking Christ in the poor and oppressed (Matt 25:31-46). The author of the Letter of James summarizes, "Anyone, then, who knows the right thing to do and fails to do it, commits sin" (Jas 4:17).

I want to draw attention to a biblical motif that has been downplayed in theological discussions, while at the same time it has received a great deal of interest in recent hermeneutical reflections. It is the category of "witness."

The Protestant emphasis on *sola* gratia and *sola* fide and the fear of *synergism*[18] have numbed our theological sensitivity toward an understanding of reality that surfaces in texts like 1 Corinthians 3:9, Matthew 5:13-16, 11:2-6, 25:31-46 and James 2:14-26, all of which emphasize that grace does not bypass human faith and obedience but becomes manifest and changes things, and that it can be discovered in unexpected places—Matthew 25:31-46!

In addition, both the Roman Catholic and the Protestant traditions have primarily located the presence of Christ in word and sacrament, church and church office, and consequently have given inadequate attention to the witness motif. Theologians of all traditions therefore need to take note that the witness motif features prominently in the Hebrew and in the Christian Bible. Indeed there are a number of distinctive theologies of witness in the Bible.[19]

It is not surprising therefore that New Testament resurrection texts interrelate the resurrection of Christ with believers who become witnesses of the event. In the Gospel of Luke, the risen Christ commissions his disciples, "You are witnesses of these things" (Luke 24:48); the apostle Paul distinguishes between true and false witnesses (1 Cor 15:15); the Book of Revelation links the witness to Christ with Christian martyrdom (6:9); and in the Gospel of John, Christians believe in Jesus because he bears "witness to the truth" (18:37). This leads us to ask what theological function the witness motif has for the event of the resurrection.

Is Wolfhart Pannenberg right when he interprets Paul's listing of witnesses in 1 Corinthians 15:5-8 as giving "proof . . . for the facticity of Jesus' resurrection"?[20] This would mean that the witnesses stand in the service of affirming the resurrection of Christ as an objective historical fact. Indeed, there is a tendency to interpret the biblical theology of witness in such apologetic terms. The witness would then have the function in our post-modern secular age to give rational credibility to the historical foundation of the Christian faith, and as such make faith in the resurrection an acceptable option for the modern intellectual. But there is more to the biblical understanding of "witness."

Witnesses testify to the givenness of an event, and by doing so they become part of the event itself. They keep the event alive. If there were no witnesses, an event would have no ongoing history (what Germans call *Wirkungsgeschichte*). It would be forgotten. It would disappear in the abyss of history. Through the appearances of Christ and their obedience of faith, the witnesses are drawn into the resurrection event. Christ is the "first fruits" of the divine process leading to God being "all in all." The witnesses are important links in the historical process. They receive and pass on in word and deed the good news that God raised Jesus from the dead and that God is thereby in the process of reclaiming what has become estranged or separated from God.

This "receiving" and "passing on" is more than the communication of theoretical information. The nature of the event requires not only the juridical dimension that God raised Jesus from the dead, but also the existential dimension that with raising Jesus from the dead, our being and the being of the world has been *changed*. This new being can only be understood, demonstrated, and communicated in a holistic way.

The truth of the testimony, therefore, is not only related to the "that" but also to the "how." The very existence of the witness has kerygmatic significance. The apostle Paul, for instance, interprets his Christian existence in light of the cross and resurrection of Christ (2 Cor 4:8-10):

> We are afflicted in every way, *but not crushed;*
> perplexed, *but not driven to despair;*
> persecuted, *but not forsaken;*
> struck down, *but not destroyed;*
> always carrying in the body the death of Jesus, *so that the life of Jesus may also be made visible in our bodies.*

The witness is not a neutral and objective observer. Through faith and baptism, the crucified and risen Christ flows over into the existence of the witnesses and shapes their existence.

These biblical insights have been taken up in recent hermeneutical studies. Let me briefly mention two such studies, one by Paul Ricoeur and the other by Francis Schüssler Fiorenza.

Paul Ricoeur

In the essay "The Hermeneutics of Testimony" (1972),[21] the French American philosopher and theologian Paul Ricoeur warns that when we deal with questions of ultimacy, we must be sensitive in selecting our categories of understanding.

He says, for instance, that the category of "example," where Jesus might be understood in terms of a heroic example, does not really fit the claims and promises of the Christian faith. An example cannot justify; it cannot deal with sin and estrangement and death. An example has significance when we are strong and need moral exhortation, but it is powerless and even burdensome when we are weak, lost, and in need of a savior.

Ricoeur also considers the category of "symbol" inadequate to spell out who Christ is for us. A symbol can give rise to what Ricoeur calls "productive imagination" (122), but it cannot grasp the "historic density" (122) for which the Christian faith stands.

Our question is still how can we best respond to the resurrection of the crucified Christ? Ricoeur invites us to take the biblical categories of witness and testimony more seriously in our theological reflections.

The witness mediates the narrative of an event to a potential listener. The listener responds to the narrative on the basis of that testimony. Such testimony obviously includes information (124). But information alone is not enough to maintain the dignity of the narrative. Part of the persuasive truth of the argument is what difference the narrative has made to the orator, and by implication, can make to the listener. The "character of the orator" (127) and the "quality of the witness" (128) become part of the event of communication.

This is crucial. A witness is more than "an exact even scrupulous narrator" (129). Witnesses stake their lives on their testimony. "The witness is capable of suffering and dying for what he believes" (129). The difference between the false and the true witness is engagement, "the engagement of a pure heart and an engagement to the death" (130). A witness who has succumbed to the "tragic destiny of truth" (130) is called a martyr (μάρτυς is the Greek word for "witness").

We continue this reflection, always keeping in mind our own question as to how we can most appropriately respond to the resurrection of Jesus. Witnesses do not live out of their own resources. "It is not possible to testify *for* a meaning without testifying *that* something has happened which signifies this meaning" (133). Therefore, witnesses include in their act of witnessing the "fact" or the "narrative kernel," but at the same time, that "fact" or "narrative kernel" has become existentially significant for the witness. Indeed, it has become a matter of life and death for the witness.

Theologically speaking, if the narrative becomes separated from the event that God raised Jesus from the dead, then we end up in Gnosticism, Docetism, or existentialism (139). If on the other hand, the witness becomes separated from the narrative, then we end up in existential subjectivism as far as the believer is concerned and historical objectivism as far as the event is concerned. The theological challenge is therefore to think of the event, the narrative, and the witness together.

Francis Schüssler Fiorenza

We find a similar emphasis in the work of the Roman Catholic theologian Francis Schüssler Fiorenza. He sees the hermeneutics of testimony as an alternative to traditional Roman Catholic fundamental theology.[22] Traditional Roman Catholic fundamental theology sought to identify a foundation that was "independent of faith"[23] and open to reason on which the theological building could be erected. Such a foundation was to provide an objective rational foundation for theology.[24]

This tendency to provide an independent and objective foundation for theological thinking is often explained in terms of needed apologetics. It is felt that in a secular and scientific age the church must give an intelligible account for what it believes. But there is more to it. Behind this felt need there lurks the human longing for security, indicating a subtle shift from the certainty inherent to faith to an empirical security demanded by reason. It is interesting that the longing for such security is found in all quarters of the Christian church and their theologies. Conservative Protestants postulate an infallible Bible, although every first-year theology student learns that the biblical texts themselves do not allow for such conclusions. Roman Catholic theologians have to obey an infallible church, whose "Congregation for the Doctrine of the Faith" declares what can and what cannot be, even though, as in the case of the ordination of women, there may be a solid theological opinion against the ruling of the magisterium. Charismatic, liberal, and existential theologians flee from the frailty of history and its institutions to trusting their own experience, although history is replete with stories that portray the ambiguity and fallenness not only of reason, but also of experience.

Back to Francis Schüssler Fiorenza. Having discussed some ways in which modern Roman Catholic theology has tried to deal with the problem of foundationalism, Francis Schüssler Fiorenza returns to the biblical texts and asks for the hermeneutical thrust, the "rhetorical power," of the earliest testimonies to the resurrection.[25]

The earliest Christian confession, "God raised Jesus from the dead," has its place in worship and baptismal instruction and has therefore a hymnic, liturgical thrust. The emphasis is on the present reality of the risen Christ in faith and worship.

The same is true for the appearance narratives. Their main intention is not to provide an objective historical foundation for faith. They start with the presence of the risen Christ who has commissioned the believer and the believing community to mission. The appearance narratives are used to show that the present experience of Jesus after his death is in continuity with the Jesus in and before his death.[26] The combination of the motifs of commissioning and identity show that the basic goal of the appearance stories is not to prove the resurrection of Jesus but to show the link between the Church's mission and the historical Jesus. The identity of the Risen Lord with the historical Jesus is the key to the appearance stories.[27]

It is no accident then, that many of the resurrection narratives are linked with the motifs of mission and Eucharist. The hermeneutical starting point is the present experience of the risen Christ. This then is bound to the story of Jesus and lived in the world.

Francis Schüssler Fiorenza therefore reminds us that Christ cannot be frozen into the past. He is a living reality in the event of faith, but the identity and authenticity of Christ's presence demands continuity with Jesus.

Beyond the "Objective–Subjective" Dilemma

The concept of "witness" found, as we saw, in biblical theology and in modern hermeneutical discussions promises to help us transcend the "objective-subjective" dilemma and formulate a more adequate way of responding to the resurrection of the crucified Christ.

The objectifying danger is that we view the resurrection of Christ as an event that has occurred and is completed in the past and as such is open for rational inquiry. The claim and expectation is that if one would approach the relevant texts without scientific or philosophical pre-commitments—for instance, that a resurrection cannot happen—then the impartial investigator would have to come to the conclusion that Jesus must have been raised from the dead.

There are major problems with this approach. It is not able to respect the intentions of the New Testament texts that emphasize the newness and the uniqueness of the event. We saw that the New Testament speaks of the resurrection of Christ as an open event and that this new, unique, and open event includes humanity by creating faith. The New Testament therefore knows of no uninvolved spectators to the resurrection. Through the appearances of the risen Christ, the earliest witnesses are drawn into the reality of the resurrection. It is at that point, not with the historical Jesus, where the birth of Christianity needs to be located. Objectifying the event distances it from us rather than relating it to us. It encourages separation rather than involvement.

The other danger consists in dissolving the resurrection into the subjective experience of believers. That should be resisted because, given our human estrangement, we need to hear a word from beyond, and the New Testament texts do not only speak about new life and empowerment, but they also emphasize that Christ has been raised from the dead, not the believers, and that such new life and empowerment is grounded in the story of Jesus.

I therefore agree with Francis Schüssler Fiorenza when he says that the New Testament testimonies to the resurrection of Christ "are not simply symbolic interpretations of liberation from bondage, but affirm God's act on behalf of Jesus and the post-Easter reality of Jesus."[28] He says that ". . . testimony is not simply a report about what happened; rather, testimony brings to expression the meaning of what happened. The meaning and significance of an event do not exist independently and isolated from the testimony about the event. Instead, the meaning and significance of the event emerge in the testimony about the event."[29] The witness, therefore, who hears the testimony and passes it on is part of the event and its history, but in this togetherness it must not be forgotten that procedural priority must be given to what God has done in raising Jesus from death.

While Francis Schüssler Fiorenza suggests "that the foundation of our Christian faith in the resurrection is the faith of the early Christian community,"[30] I am more comfortable with his distinction between an ontological and an epistemological ground of faith.[31] The ontological ground of faith is God's act of raising Jesus from the dead, while the epistemological ground of faith is the early Christian testimonies to the resurrection, preserved in the New Testament.

We conclude, therefore, that the ontological foundation for faith and for the community of faith is God's act in raising Jesus from the dead. This event *is for others*. Its *telos* is to reach out and include us, creation, the cosmos. The Spirit who raised Jesus from the dead is the Spirit of the creator God whose mission is to save that which is lost, to reconcile that which has become estranged, and to restore what has been broken. Through the appearances of Christ, the Spirit created faith in the earliest believers and as such began and fueled the process of God's claiming back God's creation.

Faith as Discipleship

With the event of faith, the Holy Spirit brings Christ into the life of the believer. The human conscience is freed by Christ from penultimate concerns and becomes focused on Christ. He is the one story that Christians are to hear, trust, and obey. The apostle confesses, "I have been crucified with Christ; . . . it is no longer I who live, but it is Christ who lives in me. And the life I now live in the flesh I live by faith in the Son of God, who loved me and gave himself for me" (Gal 2:19f.).

The shaping content of faith is Jesus Christ. Jesus Christ lived a certain kind of life and as a consequence he was persecuted, captured, sentenced, tortured, and killed. This interlocking of faith in Christ with the particular story of Jesus has too often been discarded. Culture and self-interest has shaped Christian faith more than the story of Jesus. Faith in Christ has too often been understood in terms of a personal and private religious experience. In addition, Christian faith has too often been transformed into a civil religion where Christ is used to validate national, economic, military, and political interests. It can therefore not be emphasized enough that faith in Christ receives its essential content from the life, death, and resurrection of Christ—and from nowhere else!

Having in mind our discussion on "witness," we seek to preserve the orientation of faith on the crucified One by understanding faith in terms of "following Jesus." With the symbol of discipleship, we seek to preserve the *sola gratia* dimension of faith without forgetting that it is the *crucified* Christ who is the *content* of our faith.

When we designate "discipleship" as the most appropriate way of responding to the resurrection of the crucified Christ, we do not want to depart from the assertion that God through the appearances of Christ created *faith* in the earliest witnesses. Nevertheless, faith has become a concept that is widely misunderstood. Paul Tillich said in his wonderful little book *Dynamics of Faith* (1957):

> There is hardly a word in the religious language . . . which is subject to more misunderstandings, distortions and questionable definitions than the word "faith." It belongs to those terms which need healing before they can be used for the healing of men. Today the term "faith" is more productive of disease than of health. It confuses, misleads, creates alternately skepticism and fanaticism, intellectual resistance and emotional surrender, rejection of genuine religion and subjection to substitutes.[32]

Being aware of the many misunderstandings and distortions of faith,[33] we need to interpret "faith" with a concept that maintains the divine initiative in the journey of faith and at the same time remains aware that the togetherness of God with the believer and the community of faith is shaped by the cross of the risen Christ. The concept of "discipleship" commends itself for the following reasons:

- Discipleship is a biblical concept deeply engraved in the Gospel narratives where Jesus called people to follow him and share his vision of God and of life (for instance, Mark 1:16-20; 2:14; 8:27–9:1; 10:17-31; Matt 8:19-22 = Luke 9:57-60 [Q]).

- Discipleship maintains the divine initiative and the christological content because it is *Jesus* who calls people, and he calls them to follow *him* as friends on a journey of personal allegiance.

- Faith as discipleship features highly in those great theologians of modern times who have emphasized the prophetic and transforming power of faith, for instance, Dietrich Bonhoeffer, Karl Barth, Jürgen Moltmann, Elisabeth Schüssler Fiorenza, Dorothee Sölle, Gustavo Gutiérrez, Jon Sobrino, and Robert McAfee Brown.

- Discipleship is relevant in that it insists that faith must display creative solidarity with the wretched of the earth and become involved with their struggle for justice.

- Discipleship gathers up a central emphasis of the Baptist tradition out of which I am writing.

- Discipleship is kept alive today by committed and prophetic Christian groups inside and outside the established churches.

The Content of Discipleship

There has been much writing on discipleship, especially in the three decades after World War II. In the wake of Dietrich Bonhoeffer's courage, and being confronted with the sad failure of most churches to speak and incarnate the word of the Lord in challenging times, theologians have retrieved this important biblical motif. Let me try to summarize the content of discipleship.[34]

1. Discipleship maintains the Reformation emphasis on *sola gratia* ("by grace alone") and *sola fide* ("through faith alone) that God, through Christ and in the power of the Spirit, is the sole author of faith. The discipleship stories in the Gospels are windows into the being of God. They emphasize that it was Jesus who took the initiative in electing ("seeing") and calling his disciples.

2. The Reformation emphasis on *sola scriptura* (by the Scriptures alone), affirming the content of the Holy Scriptures of the Christian church, Jesus Christ, as the only authority and content for faith (*solus Christus*—"Christ alone"), is maintained in that the disciples are called to follow *Jesus*. The call to discipleship is an ultimate concern that relativizes reasonable but penultimate obligations like burying one's father (Matt 8:21f. = Luke 9:59f.). Miroslav Volf comments appropriately:

> At the very core of Christian identity lies an all-encompassing change of loyalty, from a given culture with its gods to the God of all cultures. A response to a call from that God entails rearrangement of a whole network of allegiances. As the call of Jesus' first disciples illustrates, "the nets" (economy) and "the father" (family) must be left behind (Mark 1:16-20). Departure is part and parcel of Christian identity. Since Abraham is our ancestor, our faith is "at odds with place" . . . .[35]

3. The call to discipleship is addressed to the human conscience—not to enslave the conscience as Ludwig Feuerbach, Karl Marx, Sigmund Freud, Friedrich Nietzsche, and their followers have suggested, but to liberate the conscience from penultimate concerns. When the apostle Paul confessed that he experienced life under the "law" as restrictive "until Christ came" and "until faith would be revealed" (Gal 3:23-29), he meant that his conscience, the center of his personality, was reconciled with God by the gracious work of God's Spirit. When the apostle asserted that he had "been crucified with Christ; and it is no longer I who live, but it is Christ who lives in me" and "the life I now live in the flesh I live by faith in the Son of God, who loved me and gave himself for me" (Gal 2:19f.), he did not mean his ego was enslaved, that his identity was replaced, and that his personality became dominated by heteronomous claims. Quite the contrary. He celebrated that the coming of Christ into his life restored him to the life-giving and life-sustaining relational network that is necessary for true self-discovery. True self-discovery does not happen by withdrawal or by turning in upon oneself, but by living in relation to God (faith, prayer, and worship), to one's fellow human beings (love, service), to oneself (seeing our dignity not in

what we can achieve, but in who we are), to nature (work, culture, art), and to history (responsible citizenship).

4. For the life of discipleship, it is determinative that the call to follow Jesus is a call to freedom. The challenge and the hardship of discipleship cannot be sustained by command, duty, and will. The Christian view of reality is therefore characterized by words like "freedom," "love," "joy," and παρρησία ("openness," "courage," "boldness," "confidence," "fearlessness"). Since Jesus is the ground and the content of freedom, therefore freedom should not be understood in imperialistic or individualistic categories, and joy is certainly more than fun.[36] The freedom, love, joy, and παρρησία that undergird and inspire the Christian life come from the awareness of Christ as the determining center of our conscience. The Epistle to the Hebrews says it well:

> ... since we are surrounded by so great a cloud of witnesses, let us also lay aside every weight and the sin that clings so closely, and let us run with perseverance the race that is set before us, looking to Jesus the pioneer and perfecter of our faith, who for the sake of the joy that was set before him endured the cross, disregarding its shame, and has taken his seat at the right hand of the throne of God. (Heb 12:1f.)

5. The life of discipleship is not only initiated by God's grace, but it remains totally dependent on God. It is gathered up in the prayer: "Come, Holy Spirit and renew us!" The Christian disciple seeks a way and lifestyle beyond the ideologizing of *sola gratia* (it is God's job to save me!) on the one hand and Christian work ethics (I can, and therefore I must earn my identity and acceptance by God) on the other. In the tradition of Pauline theology, the Reformation churches have renewed the emphasis on justification by faith. This means our identity is not in what we can achieve, but our identity is a gift of God that we have the privilege to receive. It is therefore of utmost importance to develop a spirituality of discipleship in which our continuing dependence on God's grace becomes transparent.

6. Discipleship is lived and exercised in community. Although faith comes to each individual, and therefore each individual is called to discipleship, faith in Christ does not individualize people. It creates a community. In our individualistic West this deserves special attention. The great dangers we need to avoid are sectarianism, the withdrawal from accepting responsibility for the society and the world in which we live, and individualism, the refusal to see the sister and brother as necessary for our spiritual survival. The practices of baptism, where

faith goes public, and church membership, where believers intentionally commit themselves to the community of faith, are integral parts of discipleship.

7. We have emphasized the *sola gratia* and *sola fide* aspects of discipleship. We have said our identity is not in what we do, but in allowing God to be for us. Those emphases must not tempt us to overlook that grace aims to transform us, that faith has content, and that with God's gift of salvation comes the task of being God's people. What Paul says in 1 Corinthians 3:9 deserves more attention than it generally receives. Paul interprets his work and the work of his fellow laborers as being "God's fellow workers." This in no way diminishes the sole work of God for our salvation. Referring to his and Apollos's ministry, Paul says, ". . . neither he who plants nor he who waters is anything, but only God who gives the growth" (1 Cor 3:7). It is God who as part of God's saving and reconciling work (*sola gratia*) calls people into the divine partnership. The resurrection of Jesus Christ does not exclude, but it includes human response and human activity. This is what the concept of partnership brings to expression. Within their ontological dependence upon God, human beings maintain a relative independence. This relative independence is the presupposition and the ground for human responsibility, for human obedience and for human creativity. People accept their responsibility and thereby participate intentionally in shaping their lives and futures. In and through this responsible participation, possibilities of grace become actualized in human history. God provides the possibilities; their actualizations include the partnership of the human person. The refusal to enter this partnership means closing oneself to the active grace of God, and as such it is sin.[37]

8. Discipleship knows that it is better to give than to receive, that one can gain the whole world but forfeit one's soul. When Jesus called people to follow him, he called them to participate in his mission to heal the sick, to comfort the sad, and to liberate the oppressed. We saw that the call to mission is an essential part of the resurrection narratives. The Lukan overture to the story of Jesus (4:16-30) and the Matthean summary (28:16-20) make it abundantly clear that attachment to Jesus, though voluntary and liberating, includes the call to share his story with all people.

9. This call to mission includes a special leaning to participate in Jesus' preferential option for the poor. The Christian disciple endeavors to reflect the being of God by being with and for others. Karl Barth elaborates that Jesus "exists analogously to the mode of existence of God." He therefore "shares . . . the strange destiny which falls on God . . . —to be the One who is ignored and forgotten and despised and discounted by men." Jesus manifested the partiality of God in

that "He ignored all those who are high and mighty and wealthy in the world in favor of the weak and meek and lowly."[38] It is that special tendency that the disciple is invited to echo and to share.

10. The general content of Christian discipleship is given with the story of Jesus as that story shines through from the various New Testament traditions. That general content must be applied to interpret and modify particular situations. Christians in Nicaragua, Germany, Australia, the USA, or Afghanistan have different understandings of their common faith in Christ. In each situation, they must correlate their faith with the situation in which they find themselves. Disciples of Jesus must learn to read the signs of the times. The "Barmen Theological Declaration" of 1934 in Germany,[39] the *Kairos Document: Challenge to the Churches* (1985)[40] that addressed South Africa's struggle against apartheid, and *The Road to Damascus Document: Kairos and Conversion* (1989),[41] are modern illustrations of how the gospel must prophetically challenge church and state in situations of crisis. Christians who feel challenged to oppose ecological disaster or militarism or global imperialism must adopt different strategies. It is therefore an important task of Christian social ethics to develop social ethical guidelines to apply the general Christian vision of reality to particular situations.[42]

11. Christian discipleship feeds on the promise that "in the Lord your labor is not in vain" (1 Cor 15:58). This promise is grounded in the resurrection of the crucified Christ and it finds its fulfillment in the triumph of the lamb that was slain (Rev 5), when God will be [τὰ] πάντα ἐν πᾶσιν ("all in all," 1 Cor 15:28). In light of the ultimate triumph of the crucified Christ, the Christian can practice patience, endure hardship, and manifest solidarity with those who have truth and justice on their side, even though the principalities and powers of this world have failed to recognize their just cause. People like Mohandes Ghandi, Dietrich Bonhoeffer, Oscar Romero, Martin Luther King Jr., Steve Biko, Nelson Mandela, Xanana Gusmao, and Aung San Suu Kyi come to mind. Then there are the countless anonymous women and men whom this world has stamped as irrelevant and insignificant, but whose passion for truth and justice will not be forgotten by the one who shared his life with the poor and oppressed and who will be the final judge of all things. The cross of the risen Christ may be sought and may be echoed in unexpected places. The apostolic exhortation remains relevant:

> For since, in the wisdom of God, the world did not know God through wisdom, God decided, through the foolishness of our proclamation, to save those who believe. For Jews demand signs and Greeks desire wisdom, but we proclaim Christ crucified, a stumbling block to Jews and foolish-

ness to Gentiles, but to those who are the called, both Jews and Greeks, Christ the power of God and the wisdom of God. For God's foolishness is wiser than human wisdom, and God's weakness is stronger than human strength. Consider your own call, brothers and sisters: not many of you were wise by human standards, not many were powerful, not many were of noble birth. But God chose what is foolish in the world to shame the wise; God chose what is weak in the world to shame the strong; God chose what is low and despised in the world, things that are not, to reduce to nothing things that are, so that no one might boast in the presence of God. (1 Cor 1:21-29)

12. Since discipleship does not withdraw from involvement in and responsibility for the world, it becomes vulnerable to guilt and shame. The sinlessness of Jesus, Jesus' deity, did not mean withdrawal from the ambiguities of life, but it meant the solidarity of love, the fellowship with tax collectors and other sinners in which grace became an event. Dietrich Bonhoeffer suggests that love implies the willingness to share in the guilt of others.[43]

13. Since discipleship has to do with following Jesus, the willingness to suffer is part of the journey. There is no virtue in suffering as such and Christian faith must be carefully distinguished from a martyr's complex. Yet the Christian must be mindful that Jesus' messianic journey was from its beginning met by opposition and within a reasonably short time ended in capture and crucifixion. Whatever Christology we adopt, we cannot overlook the fact that Jesus did not die of natural causes, but that he was "executed as a political subversive and crucified between two social bandits. It appears that Jerusalem elites collaborating with their Roman overlords executed Jesus because he was a threat to their economic and political interests."[44] There is no doubt that if Christians resist the racism, violence, militarism, ethnic hatred, and ecological exploitation of our time, the willingness to suffer must be part of being friends of Jesus.

Conclusion

I have attempted to show that the resurrection of Jesus Christ is an act of God that aims to include us in its reality. Through the appearances of Christ, God in the power of the Spirit reaches for our faith and obedience. Those who have heard and believed become *witnesses,* who in and through their existence keep the reality of the resurrection alive. The resurrection is therefore on the one hand essentially linked to the life and death of Jesus, and on the other hand to the life of the witnesses and the witnessing community, and, through the witness and the community, to the life and future of the world.

We recognize and affirm the unity of the Christ-event when we realize that our faith in the risen Christ cannot bypass the fact that during his life Jesus ministered to and showed solidarity with the outcast, the poor, the oppressed, and the sick. With them he shared the colorful grace of God. It is therefore in our concrete engagement with the needs of the world in our time that we show whether we believe in the Jesus who lived a certain life, who was killed because of it, and who was raised from the dead to demonstrate that his vision of reality is true. This partiality of God for those who are lost and broken must become evident in the witness to the resurrection. Otherwise the event is distorted.

At the same time it must be emphasized that, although the reality of the resurrection of Christ flows over into the existence of the believer and constitutes the believer as a witness, the resurrection is not dissolved into the existence of the believer. The difference and the distance between Christ and the believer remain. Christ has been raised from the dead, while the witnesses walk in newness of life (Rom 6:4). There is a clear distinction between Christ and the believer. He is risen, not the believer. He manifests the power of the resurrection by empowering the believer to a newness of life. This newness of life cannot mean withdrawal from responsibility for the world because it must become evident that it was the crucified Christ who was raised from the dead.

With the resurrection of the crucified Christ, God has spoken a concrete and life-giving word into history. This word aims to be heard, and being heard, it creates the concrete obedience of faith that we call discipleship. Not individual piety or doctrinal orthodoxy but the concrete following of Jesus in our everyday life is the most adequate response to the resurrection of Jesus Christ.

What the nonviolent Anabaptists meant when they differentiated between the "sweet" and "bitter" Jesus, what Dietrich Bonhoeffer referred to when he spoke of "cheap" and "costly" grace, what the biblical motif of "witness" and the modern hermeneutical appropriation of that motif implied may help us to ask and to answer—each in our situation and together as the body of Christ—what it means to confess the crucified Christ as risen.

Allow me to repeat the thesis I have tried to substantiate in this chapter: the foundational event of the Christian faith, the resurrection of the crucified Christ, calls for Christian discipleship so that the identity of Christian faith is preserved. On the other hand, Christian discipleship needs the foundational reality of the resurrection so that its liberating manifestation of the gospel is not reduced to sterile moralism.

Notes

[1] The *Schleitheim Confession* is the earliest Anabaptist statement expressing in seven articles the identity of the nonviolent Anabaptists in the 1520s in Southesn Germany and Switzerland. Quoted from *The Schleitheim Confession* (1527), trans. and ed. John Howard Yoder (Scottdale PA: Herald Press, 1973, 1977), 10.

[2] *God, Revelation and Authority* (WacoTX: Word Books, 1976–1983), e.g., 3:147-63.

[3] Paul Copan, ed., *Will the Real Jesus Please Stand Up? A Debate between William Lane Craig and John Dominic Crossan*, moderated by William F. Buckley, Jr. (Grand Rapids: Baker Books, 1998), 25-32, 40-44, 48-70, 156-79.

[4] *The Structure of Resurrection Belief* (Oxford: Clarendon Press, 1987), 358; compare 368.

[5] The reference is, of course, to such well-known texts as Jer 6–8; Isa 1:11-16; Amos 5:21-24; Hos 6:6; Mic 6:6-8; Rom 12:1f.; and Heb 13:12f.

[6] *Structure of Resurrection Belief*, 358.

[7] This in no way reflects on Bishop Carnley's ministry. In Australia, Bishop Carnley belongs to those all-too-few church leaders who are passionately committed to justice as the social outworking of the gospel of Christ.

[8] I emphasize "nonviolent" Anabaptists to counteract the widespread tendency to view and evaluate the Anabaptist movement through the prism of *Müntzer* and *Münster*. Neither Thomas Müntzer, nor the city of Münster where excesses of violence occurred, are representative of the Anabaptist movement. I refer to Anabaptist traditions in Switzerland, in Southern Germany, and in the Netherlands. Their commitment to discipleship, intentional community, and nonviolence continues to influence and inspire Christian peace churches and Christian peace movements to the present day.

[9] Conrad Grebel and friends, "Letters to Thomas Müntzer" (5 September 1524), trans. Walter Rauschenbusch (revised) in George Huntston Williams and Angel M. Mergal, eds., *Spiritual and Anabaptist Writers*, Library of Christian Classics 25 (Philadelphia: Westminster, 1957, 73-85), 74, 78f.

[10] *Schleitheim Confession*, 10.

[11] Harold S. Bender, "'Walking in the Resurrection'—the Anabaptist Doctrine of Regeneration and Discipleship," *MennQR* 35 (1961, 96-110), 96. The whole article is informative for our investigation. See also John C. Wenger, "Grace and Discipleship in Anabaptism," *MennQR* 35 (1961), 50-69.

[12] Further literature discussing the Anabaptist view of discipleship includes J. Lawrence Burkholder, "The Anabaptist Vision of Discipleship," in Guy F. Hershberger, ed., *The Recovery of the Anabaptist Vision* (Scottdale PA: Herald Press, 1957), 135-51; John Driver, *Community and Commitment* (Scottdale PA: Herald Press, 1976); Walter Klaassen, ed., *Anabaptism in Outline: Selected Primary Sources* (Kitchener Ont: Herald Press, 1981), 85-100; Philip LeMasters, *Discipleship for all Believers: Christian Ethics and the Kingdom of God* (Scottdale PA: Herald Press, 1992); Franklin H. Littell, "The Discipline of Discipleship in the Free Church Tradition," *MennQR* 35 (1961), 111-19; John C. Wenger, "Grace and Discipleship in Anabaptism," *MennQR* 35 (1961), 50-69.

[13] "Eighteen Theses" (1524), in W. R. Estep, ed., *Anabaptist Beginnings (1523–1533), A Source Book* (Nieuwkoop: B. De Graaf, 1976, 23-26), 24.

[14] Grebel and friends, "Letters," in *Spiritual and Anabaptist Writers*, 74.

[15] Cited from R. Friedmann, *The Theology of Anabaptism: An Interpretation* (Scottdale PA: Herald Press, 1973), 85.

[16] "Whether God Is the Cause of Evil" (1526), trans. George Huntston Williams, in *Spiritual and Anabaptist Writers* (88-111), 108.

[17] Dietrich Bonhoeffer, *The Cost of Discipleship*, trans. R. H. Fuller and Irmgard Booth (New York: MacMillan, 1963 [1937]), 45-47 and 59.

[18] Synergism (from the Greek συνεργεῖν; Latin "cooperatio") is the theological heresy that the human person may "co-operate" with God in the work of salvation or justification.

[19] See the brief survey in my *Resurrection and Discipleship: Interpretive Models, Biblical Reflections, Theological Consequences* (Maryknoll NY: Orbis Books, 1995), 209-22.

[20] Wolfhart Pannenberg, *Jesus—God and Man*, trans. Lewis L. Wilkins and Duane A. Priebe (Philadelphia: Westminster, 1968), 89.

[21] Paul Ricoeur, "The Hermeneutics of Testimony" (1972), in *Essays on Biblical Interpretation*, ed. with introduction by Lewis S. Mudge, trans. David Stewart and Charles E. Reagan (Philadelphia: Fortress, 1980), 119-54. All references are to this article.

[22] Francis Schüssler Fiorenza, *Foundational Theology: Jesus and the Church* (New York: Crossroad, 1986); "The Resurrection of Jesus and Roman Catholic Fundamental Theology," in Stephen T. Davis, Daniel Kendall, SJ, Gerald O'Collins, eds., *The Resurrection: An Interdisciplinary Symposium on the Resurrection of Jesus* (New York: Oxford University Press, 1997), 213-48. References are to *Book* and *Essay*.

[23] *Essay*, 214.

[24] For a description and critique of fundamental theology, see *Book*, ch. 1, 5-28.

[25] *Essay*, 223.

[26] *Essay*, 229f.; *Book*, 37f.

[27] *Book*, 38.

[28] *Essay*, 240.

[29] *Book*, 31.

[30] *Essay*, 243.

[31] Ibid., 245.

[32] *Dynamics of Faith* (New York: Harper & Row, 1957), ix; also found in Carl Heinz Ratschow, ed., *Paul Tillich: Main Works/Hauptwerke*, vol. 5 (Berlin/New York: De Gruyter, 1988, 231-290), 231.

[33] I have listed some of these distortions in *Resurrection and Discipleship*, 195-97.

[34] The literature on discipleship is legion. This topic is decisive for understanding the resurrection. At the same time, its rediscovery is important if the church is to retrieve its identity and relevance. I therefore depart from my general procedure of not having long footnotes and list those sources that have been important for my own understanding of faith as discipleship: Karl Barth, "The Command as the Claim of God," in vol. 2, pt. 2 of *Church Dogmatics*, trans. G. W. Bromiley, J. C. Campbell, Iain Wilson, J. Strathearn McNab, Harold Knight, R. A. Stewart, ed. G. W. Bromiley, T. F. Torrance (Edinburgh: T. & T. Clark, 1957), §37, e.g., 569-71 and 613-30; "The Doctrine of Creation," vol. 3, pt. 4 of *Church Dogmatics*, trans. A. T. Mackay, T. H. L. Parker, Harold Knight, Henry A. Kennedy, John Marks, ed. G. W. Bromiley, T. F. Torrance (Edinburgh: T. & T. Clark, 1961); especially "The Call to Discipleship," in vol. 4, pt. 2 of *Church Dogmatics*, trans. G. W. Bromiley, ed. G. W. Bromiley, T. F. Torrance (Edinburgh: T. & T. Clark, 1956), § 66, 3:533-53; "The Royal Man," ibid., § 64, 3:154-264; Harold S. Bender, "'Walking in the Resurrection'—the Anabaptist Doctrine of Regeneration and Discipleship," *MQR* 35 (1961), 96-110; Dietrich Bonhoeffer, *The Cost of Discipleship* (New York: MacMillan, 1963 [1937]), especially §§ 1/1-5; J. Lawrence Burkholder, "The Anabaptist Vision of Discipleship," in *The Recovery of the Anabaptist Vision* (Scottdale PA: Herald Press, 1957), 135-51; John Driver, *Community and Commitment* (Scottdale PA: Herald Press, 1976); Segundo Galilea, *Following Jesus*, trans. Sr. Helen Phillips (Maryknoll: Orbis, 1981); Athol Gill, *Life on the Road: The Gospel Basis for a Messianic Lifestyle* (Scottdale PA: Herald Press, 1992); *The Fringes of Freedom: Following Jesus, Living Together, Working for Justice* (Homebush West: Lancer, 1990); Ferdinand Hahn, "Pre-Easter Discipleship," in *The Beginnings of the Church*, trans. Iain and Ute Nicol (Edinburgh: Saint Andrews Press, 1970 [1969]), 9-39; Martin Hengel, *The Charismatic Leader and His Followers*, ed. John Riches, trans. James C. G. Greig (Edinburgh: Clark, 1981); Joachim Jeremias, *New Testament Theology: The Proclamation of Jesus*, trans. John Bowden

(New York: Scribner's, 1971), § 5/19; Ernst Käsemann, *Jesus means Freedom: A polemical survey of the New Testament*, trans. Frank Clarke (London: SCM, 1969); *Kirchliche Konflikte*, Band 1 (Göttingen: Vandenhoeck and Ruprecht, 1982); Walter Klaassen, ed., *Anabaptism in Outline: Selected Primary Sources* (Kitchener Ont: Herald Press, 1981), 85-100; Jürgen Moltmann, *The Way of Jesus Christ: Christology in Messianic Dimensions*, trans. Margaret Kohl (London: SCM, 1990 [1989]), 116-19; "Nachfolge Christi im Zeitalter der Massenvernichtungsmittel," in *Politische Theologie—Politische Ethik* (München: Kaiser, Mainz: Grünewald, 1984), 180-92; *Following Jesus Christ in the world today: Responsibility for the world and Christian discipleship* (Elkhart IN: Institute of Mennonite Studies, 1983); "Responsibility for the World and Christian Discipleship," in Jürgen Moltmann, *On Human Dignity: Political Theology and Ethics*, trans. M. Douglas Meeks (London: SCM, 1984), 59-131; *The Open Church: Invitation to a Messianic Lifestyle*, trans. M. Douglas Meeks (London: SCM, 1978); Eduard Schweizer, *Lordship and Discipleship*, trans. Frank Clarke, SBT (London: SCM, 1960); "Discipleship and Church," in *The Beginnings of the Church*, trans. Iain and Ute Nicol (Edinburgh: Saint Andrews Press, 1970 [1969]), 85-104; August Strobel, "Discipleship in Light of the Easter-event," in *Beginnings of the Church*, 40-84; John C. Wenger, "Grace and Discipleship in Anabaptism," *MQR* 35 (1961), 50-69; Ched Myers, *Who Will Roll Away the Stone: Discipleship Queries for First World Christians* (Maryknoll: Orbis, 1994).

[35] Miroslav Volf, *Exclusion and Embrace: A Theological Exploration of Identity, Otherness, and Reconciliation* (Nashville: Abingdon, 1996), 40.

[36] Gustavo Gutiérrez, "Joy in the midst of suffering," in Hilary D. Regan, Alan J. Torrance, Antony Wood, eds., *Christ and Context: The Confrontation between Gospel and Culture* (Edinburgh: T&T Clark, 1993), 78-87.

[37] Karl Barth's understanding of sin as "sloth" ("*Trägheit*") is helpful at this point. Sin is described as the refusal, the laziness, the slowness, the sluggishness, the sleepiness, the disobedience, and the ungratefulness to join the passion God has displayed in Jesus Christ for the world and its needs; compare "The Sloth and Misery of Man," vol. 4, pt. 2 of *Church Dogmatics* (1958), 403-83, especially 403-409; similarly, Jürgen Moltmann, *Theology of Hope*, trans. James W. Leitch (London: SCM, 1967), 22-26.

[38] "The Royal Man," vol. 4, pt. 2 of *Church Dogmatics* (1958, §64,3), 166-68; see the whole section, 154-264.

[39] The *Barmen Theological Declaration* (1934) is reproduced in many books and liturgical resources, for instance, in Robert McAfee Brown, ed., *Kairos: Three Prophetic Challenges to the Church* (Grand Rapids: Eerdmans, 1990), 156-58; J. H. Leith, ed., *Creeds of the Churches* (Richmond: Knox, rev. ed. 1973), 517-22; see a more recent translation in *JTSA* 47 (June 1984), 78-81.

[40] *The Kairos Document: Challenge to the Churches; A Theological Comment on the Political Crisis in South Africa* (2d ed. 1986), in Brown, ed., *Kairos*, 15-66.

[41] *The Road to Damascus: Kairos and Conversion: A document signed by Third World Christians from El Salvador, Guatemala, Korea, Namibia, Nicaragua, Philippines, South Africa* (1989), in Brown, ed., *Kairos*, 109-38.

[42] This would be the task of a Social Ethic from a Christian perspective. The following are attempts in that direction: Paul Tillich, "The Method and Structure of Systematic Theology," vol. 1 of *Systematic Theology* (Chicago: Chicago University Press, 1951), 53-66; "Independence and Interdependence of Existential Questions and Theological Answers," vol. 2 of *Systematic Theology* (Chicago: Chicago University Press, 1957), 13-16; Dietrich Bonhoeffer, *Ethics*, ed. Eberhard Bethge, trans. Neville Horton Smith (London: SCM, 1955), 79-100; John C. Bennett, *Christian Ethics and Social Policy* (1946) 58-88; John C. Bennett, "Principles and the Context: Can ethical principles guide action?" in John C. Bennett et al., *Storm over Ethics* (Philadelphia: United Church Press, 1967), 1-25; J. Philip Wogaman, *Christian Moral Judgment* (Louisville: Westminster/John Knox, 1989); Arthur Rich, *Wirtschaftsethik: Grundfragen in Theologischer Perspektive* (Gütersloh: Mohn, 1987), 2/7 and 8 (173-243).

[43] *Ethics* (1964), 240f.

[44] William R. Herzog II, *Parables as Subversive Speech: Jesus as Pedagogue of the Oppressed* (Louisville: Westminster/John Knox Press, 1994), 9.

Chapter 8

Summary and Conclusion

Affirming Life

My main concern in this book has been to take seriously the ancient and ever modern Christian confession that the resurrection of Christ, in the context of Jesus' life and death, is the foundational event for the Christian faith, the Christian church, and the Christian life. If Jesus had not been raised from the dead, there would be no Christian faith and no Christian church. The resurrection of Christ is the ontological basis for confessing and celebrating that life is stronger than death. The life-denying and estranging powers of death will not have the last and final word. Life is not fated and nihilism is not its destiny. Life is grounded in the very being of God.

The resurrection of the crucified One is the basis on which we can patiently and confidently join the struggle against injustice and violence. The resurrection of Christ intensified a divine process that offers the promise of the triumph of love, when God will be all in all. This promise can be frustrated, slowed down, and diverted, but it cannot be undone or invalidated by human disobedience, selfishness, sloth, and injustice.

Our joyful affirmation of life, despite the intimidating reality of terror, torture, and destruction; our patient but confident struggle for justice, despite the overwhelming invasion of hatred and injustice; our waging of peace and nonviolence amid the clamor of war and violence; our determination to keep going despite the ever-encroaching temptation of sloth—all of that is grounded in the deep-seated conviction that God has exposed God's very being to violence, injustice, and death and in that encounter has remained God. While the opposition to Jesus and the resulting execution on the cross exposed a world ruled by intrigue, self-interest, injustice, and violence, God established and revealed another reality. By raising Jesus from the dead, God established an ontology of peace, justice, and nonviolence.

God revealed this new reality with the appearances of the risen Christ to the first believers. These appearances created faith, which found its verbal deposit in the Christian confession that "God is love" (1 John 4), that "nothing" can separate us from God's love (Rom 8), and that the Christian faith entails the promise of the triumph of grace (1 Cor 15). By identifying with the victim, without ceasing to be God, God laid the foundation for the apostolic empowerment that "in the Lord your labor is not in vain" (1 Cor 15:58).

It would be good for all Christians and all churches to remember and retrieve this empowering confidence in the resurrection as the wellspring for our faith. On the basis of the resurrection, we can affirm that "where sin increased, grace abounded all the more" (Rom 5:20). Indeed, it is the same "Spirit of him who raised Jesus from the dead," who "dwells in you," and who "will give life to your mortal bodies" (Rom 8:11). The resurrection of Jesus Christ and our participation in this life-giving event belong together.

Nevertheless, the celebration of this togetherness is not alive and well in our hearts and in our churches. It is the noble task of theology to reflect on this deficiency and try to remind Christians and churches of their rich resources.

Beyond "Liberal" and "Conservative"

An increasing number of Christians and theologians are inclined to follow the "liberal" persuasion that questions the event character of the resurrection and argues that we are on safer ground by relying on the historical Jesus or by depending on our human experience. In recent decades, there has been an explosion of historical Jesus research. The interest has not merely been historical. There is the often hidden but sometimes revealed claim that the historical Jesus is the basis and object of faith. With that claim, Jesus research acquires immediate theological relevance. In recent theological discussions, we can therefore note a shift from the soteriological and eschatological significance of cross and resurrection to the historical Jesus.

I do not want to deny the importance of the quest for the historical Jesus. Christian faith is linked to Jesus and cannot survive apart from knowledge about the historical Jesus. But to make the historical Jesus the ground and the object of our faith would change the saving and liberating power of faith. Historical information aimed at reason and morality would replace the gospel aimed at freeing the conscience. Jesus would be seen mainly in terms of a heroic human being and moral example rather than a liberating savior. Heroes and moral examples are important. Who can fail being impressed and empowered by the courage, intellect, and discipline of Nelson Mandela and Aung San Suu Kyi? They and countless others are inspirational examples of the human spirit. But they cannot meet our need for knowing God and they would of course make no claim in that direction. In situations of ultimacy, only God can speak an integrating word carrying a message of eternal hope into our lives.

God's word comes to us in the encounter of faith. Faith "comes" (Gal 3:23-25), and it "comes from what is heard" (Rom 10:17). What is heard is not a history lesson about what Jesus said and did 2000 years ago. It is the living word of the gospel in which the "story of Jesus" uncovers our need for God and interlocks with our existential quest for meaning and relevance. In that event of word and faith, the Spirit of God makes us attentive and assures us of God's unconditional love.

Of course, the "story of Jesus" as the story of God's unconditional love contains historical elements. If there were no Jesus, there would be no story of Jesus. If Jesus did not imply a passion for freedom and justice, then the story of Jesus would not be liberating good news ("gospel"). Historical Jesus research can make a significant contribution enriching and defining the correlation of word and faith. Our faith is clarified and deepened as historical research informs us how in many different life situations Jesus stands for the affirmation of life, for freedom, for peace, for justice. Such input will safeguard against using our faith for causes that are not in harmony with the vision of God for which Jesus lived and died. Nevertheless, the theological focus is not on the historical facts. They are given, and as such they need to be investigated, analyzed, and made known. The theological emphasis is on the message that addresses the human conscience and invites it into a relationship with God. This is what the fourth evangelist means when he hears Jesus saying—after Easter!—"Very truly, I tell you, anyone who hears my word and believes him who sent me has eternal life, and does not come under judgment, but has passed from death to life" (John 5:24). When the word of the gospel finds faith and obedience, time thickens into the moment of knowing God.

What then is the importance of research into the words and deeds of the historical Jesus? Although there are good reasons to be skeptical whether we shall ever discover much detail about the historical Jesus, we need that research in order to demonstrate *continuity* between our faith in Christ and Jesus the Christ. This continuity cannot be one in form, but it needs to be one in content. We do not need to copy what Jesus did or repeat what Jesus said. But when we claim for ourselves and proclaim to others that God says "Yes" to sinners, when we base our praxis on God's preferential option for the poor, when in our lifestyle we try to create analogies to the cross and resurrection, when we welcome the stranger in our midst, when we accept the joy and pain of Christian discipleship, then this vision of life must be in continuity with what Jesus lived and died for. This orientation toward Jesus safeguards our faith from merely serving our own immediate needs and interests. Faith is our participation in the God who shared his being with Jesus and raised Jesus from the dead. In contrast to the "liberal" option, I would therefore maintain that the explosion of language at Easter, confessing not only God but also Jesus as the object of faith, is not a mythological statement. We are invited to believe "in Jesus" because God raised Jesus from the dead.

I have also been somewhat dissatisfied with the conservative evangelical approach that debates the resurrection primarily in apologetic terms, trying to prove that it actually happened. Here expertise and energy are not invested in historical Jesus research but in forming arguments that would support and verify the historicity of the resurrection. This approach is often linked with a simplistic and uncritical understanding of the Scriptures. It is therefore intellectually unconvincing. But what is more important, it does not echo the heartbeat of the biblical message. The conservative evangelical approach tends to reduce the lifegiving mystery of the resurrection to the straitjacket of the poverty of human reason. Historical inquiry tends to leave the resurrection in the past and limit its significance to the intellect. The power of the risen Christ as a present and life-changing reality is easily forgotten.

I have wanted to find a way of understanding the resurrection of Christ on its own terms. I feel that with a close reading of the relevant texts and by entering the dynamics of these texts, we see the resurrection of Christ portrayed as a dynamic, new, ongoing, and history-changing event inviting believers into the adventure of affirming and celebrating life where the estranging powers of death are determinative.

The Argument

In the first two chapters, I entered into a dialogue with the "liberal" and the "conservative evangelical" positions, reaching the conclusion that the resurrection of Christ is a real, an "open," a relational event; an event that embraces the future of creation. Its effect on human history came with the appearances of the risen Christ to the first believers. They were drawn into God's passion to reconcile humanity and creation with God. To celebrate and share their faith, the first believers found themselves in a community where Christ in the power of the Spirit was the determining and liberating presence.

In my conversation with the liberal and the conservative approaches, I had a twofold interest. I did not want to evade the question of ontology, but at the same time I wanted to tune in to the heartbeat of what I perceived to be the resurrection reality that lies behind the biblical texts. The answer I propose is that we must overcome the subject-object dichotomy and develop a relational understanding of reality.

At the same time, the resurrection of the crucified victim Jesus reveals that the reality established by the resurrection is one of peace, justice, and nonviolence—that is, those values for which Jesus lived and died. By tuning into God through faith, the believer and the community of faith are voluntarily and therefore joyfully committed to justice, peace, and nonviolence. It is this ontology of faith that keeps us going and makes the cost of discipleship possible and worthwhile.

Although the Christian life is made up of many dimensions reflecting the colorful grace of God, I have argued on christological grounds that a commitment to justice deserves a certain priority. I have tried to argue that point not so much on narrow biblical grounds (Matt 25!) or on grounds of relevance given by the terrible state of the world around us, but by recognizing the two basic pillars that determine the reality of the resurrection: the defeat of the estranging powers of death (chapter 4), and the fact that it was the crucified Christ who was raised from the dead (chapter 3). The defeat of death liberates believers from the ultimate threat of nihilism and death and empowers them to become servants of life. And by retrieving the life of Jesus in its interlocking with his passion and death, we do not only recognize that faith is related to Jesus, but we discern that Jesus was opposed, captured, tortured, tried, and killed because he engaged himself for justice. This living and dangerous memory must inform faith and as such protect faith against many alluring distortions.

These emphases have implications for our individual lives in providing hope, meaning, and content. But beyond that, they compel the believer to resist the estranging forces of death and enhance the reconciling forces of life. This can be a difficult and costly undertaking, but it is our holistic worship in response to what God has done for us.

In chapter 5, I then illustrated the history-changing nature of the resurrection by discussing its effect on the social structures of its day. Taking a text like Galatians 3:28 as one of the first verbal deposits of what God has done by raising Jesus from the dead, I showed that affirming the resurrection implies creating a community in which race, gender, or class can no longer serve as a justification for privilege, but that in God's economy all people are equal. Since the equal dignity of women was a problem then and continues to be a challenge now, I intensified the discussion, having in mind many churches' denial of ordination to women merely on the point that they are female. I have suggested that that is not merely a moral but a theological issue in that it denies the power of the resurrection. As a third example, I chose an issue that is implied in affirming the resurrection but that was not yet in the consciousness of the early Christians. It is the ecological crisis, perhaps the greatest challenge that humanity faces today. I have tried to show that the Christian response can be grounded not only in a doctrine of creation but in the identity-shaping understanding of the presence of the risen Christ.

In chapter 6, I took up the difficult but urgent problem of the relationship between the Christian faith and other religions. Since Christ was raised "to the right hand of God," which is the symbol for God's universal authority, therefore the question of Christ's universal reign and its relationship to other claims of salvation must be on the Christian agenda. This is urgent and relevant. An increasing number of analysts and commentators see religion as part of the problem rather than part of the answer to the many challenges humanity faces today.

Without wanting to adopt the imperialism that seems to be implied in the "inclusivist" option, I have proposed that we as Christian theologians cannot retreat from the assertion that "God *is* love" and that therefore God loves the world, that God has reconciled the world with God, and that it is not God's will that human dignity and human fulfillment be denied to anyone. What God has shown us in Jesus Christ must be true for all of creation. Yet humility and respect for others demand that we do not reduce God's revelation to our understanding and appropriation of it. There is always more light to break forth from the healing and liberating mystery of God's love. Amid remaining uncertainty as to how the truth and universality of Christ can be thought in relation to other religions, it is nevertheless clear that faith in the risen Christ implies the imperative of responsibility for making human life human in a global context.

Finally, in chapter 7, I acknowledged that the resurrection narratives affirm the continuity between the crucified Jesus and the Christ of faith. They insist that it was the *crucified* Christ whom God raised from the dead and who in the power of the Spirit began to shape the lives of believers and the life of the community of faith. This raised the question as to how we can most appropriately respond to the resurrection of the crucified Christ. How can the dignity and the integrity of the event be preserved in our way of knowing and being? I have argued that neither individual piety nor worship liturgies nor doctrinal orthodoxy, but the concrete following of Jesus in our everyday lives, is the most adequate way of responding to the resurrection of the crucified Christ. By retrieving some theological emphases from the nonviolent Anabaptists of the sixteenth century and by acknowledging modern hermeneutical discussions on a theology of witness, I have suggested that the believer and the believing community are part of the resurrection reality—without removing the procedural priority of Christ. The resurrection of the crucified Christ calls for a life of faith in which Jesus' passion for God and therefore for justice is echoed.

Author and Subject Index

A

"Abba" ....70f.
Anabaptists 9, 142–44, 158, 159n8
Anglican church ....114, 141f.
Apologetics ....3f.
Apostles' Creed 63n12
Athanasian Creed 63n12
Atonement 11, 80, 84–89
Aulén, Gustaf 94n3
Auschwitz 91
Avis, Paul 39n24

B

Bach, J. S. 66
Baptist church 114
Baptist theology 142–44
Baptist Theological Seminary at Richmond 9
Barmen Theological Declaration 156, 161n39
Barney, Gerald O. 117n28
Barth, Karl 22, 40ns36, 41, 111, 117n36, 134n4, 144, 152, 155, 160f.n34, 161n37
Barton, Stephen 39n24
Bechert, Heinz 134n2
Bender, Harold S. 159n11, 160f.n34
Bennett, John C. 161n42
Berkhof, Hendrikus 88
Berry, Thomas 112, 118n41, 118n45
Bethge, Eberhard 161n42

Betz, Hans Dieter 115ns2, 4
Betz, Otto 116n19
Biko, Steve 156
Blasphemy 77–79
Blass, F. 62n3
"Body" 49f., 52, 56–60
Bommarius, Alexander 39n24, 41n53
Bonhoeffer, Dietrich 141, 144, 152, 156–58, 159n17, 160f.n34, 161n42
Booth, Irmgard 159n17
Bowden, John 39n30, 41n53, 81n9, 82n21, 117n29, 134ns2, 5; 160f.n34
Braaten, Carl E. 81n5
Bromiley, G. W. 117n36, 160f.n34
Brown, Lester R. 117n36
Brown, Robert McAfee 152, 161n39
Brox, Norbert 115n7
Buckley Jr., William F. 39n33, 159n3
Bultmann, Rudolf 4, 9n1, 13, 68, 81n5
Burkholder, J. Lawrence ..159n12 160f.n34

C

Caird, G. B. 88
Campbell, J. C. 160f.n34
Campion, C. T. 118n43
Canberra Baptist Church 9

Carey, Merilyn 9
Carnley, Peter 18, 39n28, 63n13, 141f., 159ns4, 6, 7
Children . . . . .91f.
Church 3f., 25, 51, 58–60, 80f., 154, 167
Clarke, Frank 160f.n34
Collins, John J. 52, 63n11
Collins, Paul 112, 118n46
Conscience 120, 132, 153
Copan, Paul 39n33, 40n38, 42n74, 159n3
Craig, William Lane 7, 20f., 34–36, 39n33, 40n38, 42n74, 140f., 159n3
Creation 125–27
Crossan, John Dominic 4, 7, 12, 20f., 23–28, 29, 31f., 34f., 38n1, 39n33, 40ns38, 40, 42; 44–51, 48f., 54, 71, 81ns3, 10, 11; 159n3
Crucifixion 68–79
Cult 77–79
Cupitt, Don 39n24

D

Darragh, Neil 116n24
Darwinism 112
Davis, Stephen T. 39ns24, 25, 28, 31; 118n40, 160n22
D'Costa, Gavin 39n24, 62n5
Death 5, 8, 47, 83
Death Penalty 78
Debrunner, A. 62n3
Denck, Hans (John) 143
De Laplace, Pierre Simon 37
Dialogue . . . . .124f.

Discipleship . . .8f., 55, 62, 76, 79f., 115, 137–61, 166
Docetism 147
Driver, John 159n12, 160f.n34
Dualism 26, 112

E

Ebeling, Gerhard . .39n9, 68, 81n6
Eck, Wolfgang 40n36
Ecology crisis, 5f. . . .8, 61, 109–15
Ecumenism . . . . .6f.
"Empty" tomb 4f., 29, 34, 48–53, 61
Epistemology 18, 150
Equality 96–104
Estep, W. R. 159n13
Ethics, 6, 18f. . .95–118, 125, 133f.
Ethnic hatred 98
"Evangelical" theology 4, 7, 9, 13–17, 20, 34–38, 51, 54, 61, 123, 138f., 140f., 149f., 164–66
Exclusivism 123
"Existential" theology . .13–17, 20, 36–38, 138f., 147, 149f., 164–66
Experience 130–34
Expiation 80, 85

F

Faith, 5, 22f. . . . . . .38, 44–47, 51, 60–62, 68, 121, 131f., 137–61, 165f.
  Ground/foundation 11f., 27, 33, 43–63, 127–34, 138
  Content 65–82, 138
Feuerbach, Ludwig 153
Fiddes, Paul 94n3

Flew, Anthony G. N. 15–17, 39n10
Forgiving sins 76
Foundationalism 18, 148
Freedom of religion 131
French Declaration of the Rights of Man 102
Freud, Sigmund 153
Friedmann, R. 159n15
Friedrich, Gerhard 40n41
Fuchs, Ernst 13–15, 21, 38n2, 55
Fuller, Reginald H. 63n13, 159n17
Fuller, Ilse 63n13
Fundamental theology 18, 148
Fundamentalism 21

G

Galilea, Segundo 160f.n34
Galloway, Allan D. 112
Garrett, Graeme 9
Ghandi 156
Gill, Athol 160f.n34
Gnosticism 147
Grebel, Conrad 143, 159n9
Greig, James C. G. 160f.n34
Grelle, Bruce 117n29
Guilt 157
Gunton, Colin E. 94n3
Gusmao, Xanana 156
Gustafson, Carrie 116n25, 117n37, 118n40
Gutiérrez, Gustavo 141, 152, 161n36

H

Habermas, Gary R. 15–17, 39ns10, 16, 23
Hahn, Ferdinand 160f.n34
Handel, G. F. 66
Harrisville, Roy A. 81n5
Hartshorne, Charles 15
Hebert, A. G. 94n3
Heinegg, Peter 134n2
Hengel, Martin . . .82n21, 116n19, 160f.n34
Hennecke, Edgar 42n83
Henry, Carl F. H. . . . . .140f.
Hershberger, Guy F. 159n12
Herzog, William R. 81n3, 82ns13, 15, 16, 17, 20; 161n44
Hick, John 17
Hirsch, Emanuel 32
Historical critical method 22
Holy Spirit . . .7f., 18, 30, 53f., 68, 121, 129, 130–34, 139, 154
Hope 89–92
Hoskyns, Edwin C. 40n36
Household codes 105, 116n16
House churches 108
Hubmaier, Balthasar 143
Human rights 5f., 8, 101–104, 111, 123, 134
Humanum 99–101, 126

I

Idolatry . . . . .43f., 65f.
Inclusivism 123

J

James 46

Jeremias, Joachim 81n9, 160f.n34
Jesus Christ
    appearances .... 7f., 16, 17–19, 28–34, 44–47, 51–54, 60–62, 105–109, 149, 166f.
    ascension 19, 61
    body of 58–60
    cross 65–82
    death ...11, 25, 65–82, 84–89
    example 27, 121, 147, 164–66
    "first born of the dead," 12
    ground of salvation 127–31
    "historical Jesus" ...4, 11, 14f., 25–28, 58, 61, 65–82, 164–66
    incarnation 11, 44
    life 65–82
    mediator 121
    norm of life .... 130f.
    pre-existence 19
    savior 27, 121, 127–31, 164–66
    symbol 147
    unity of Jesus' life, death, and resurrection ......4, 157f.
    virgin birth 19
Jesus Seminar 20, 27
Jewish anthropology 52
John Paul II 116n14
John the Baptist 77
Johnson, Luke Timothy 40n38, 1n3
Johnstone, Brian V. 18f., 118n40
Joseph of Arimathea 34
Jüngel, Eberhard 62n1

Junia 108
Justice 5, 65–82, 83, 86, 88–94, 95–118
Justification 85, 142–44, 154
Juviler, Peter 116n25, 117n37, 118n40

K

Käsemann, Ernst .63n19, 68, 81n5, 160f.n34
"Kairos Document" 156, 161n40
Kautz, Jakob 143
Kelber, Werner H. ...40n38, 81n3
Kendall, Daniel ...39n24, 118n40, 160n22
Kennedy, Henry A. 160f.n34
King Jr., Martin Luther 156
Kingdom of God 81n8
Klaassen, Walter 159n12, 160f.n34
Klappert, Berthold 40n41
Knight, Harold 160f.n34
Kohl, Margaret 40n41, 63ns13, 19; 81n2, 94ns7, 8; 117n32, 160f.n34
Krause, Helmut 40n36
Küng, Hans 117n29, 119f., 134ns2, 5
Künneth, Walter 13–15, 21, 38n2
Kyoto Protocol 117n27

L

Laity ....6f.
Lazarus 52
Lebébure, Marcus 134n2

Leith, J. H. 161n39
Leitch, James W. 161n37
LeMasters, Philip 159n12, 160f.n34
"Liberal" Theology . . . 4, 7, 9, 20f., 23–34, 36–38, 41n71, 61f., 139, 164–66
Liberation Theology 144
Littell, Franklin H. 159n12, 160f.n34
Lord's Supper . . . . 58, 67, 81, 148f.
Lorenz, Eckehart 116n10
Lorenzen, Thorwald 9, 9n5, 40n34, 41ns 52, 70, 71, 42n84, 62ns4, 10, 63n11, 94n3, 117n35, 134n1, 135n8, 159n19
Love 77–79
Lüdemann, Gerd . . . 7, 12, 17, 20f., 28–34, 39n24, 41n53–69, 48f., 54

M

MacDonald, Margaret Y. . . 116n22
Mackay, A. T. 160f.n34
Mandela, Nelson 156, 165
Marginal people, 71, 77, 152
Marks, John 160f.n34
Marquardt, Friedrich-Wilhelm 40n36
Marti, Kurt 83f., 94n1
Marx, Karl 153
Marxsen, Willy 23, 40n41
Mary 36, 53, 106–109, 116n19
McFague, Sallie . . 17, 112, 117n32, 118ns41, 47
McIntyre, John 94n3
McNab, J. Strathearn 160f.n34

Meeks, M. Douglas 160f.n34
Meier, John P. 81ns1, 4, 7; 82ns12, 19
Mergal, Angel M. 159n9
Metaphor 12, 23–28, 37f., 54, 60–62
Metz, Johann Baptist 115n1
Meyers, Carol 115n8
Michel, Otto 116n19
Miethe, Terry L. 39n10
Ministry 3
Miracles . . . . 71f.
Mission 45–47, 51, 60, 62, 130f., 148f., 155
Modernism 4
Moltmann, Jürgen 39n30, 63ns13, 14, 81n2, 94n8, 117n32, 118n42, 134ns2, 5, 144, 152, 160f.n34, 161n37
Montague, W. J. 81n5
Moule, C. F. D. 39n24, 40n41
Mudge, Lewis S. 160n21
Müntzer, Thomas 143, 159ns8, 9
Myers, Ched 160f.n34

N

Napoleon 37
Natural law . . . . 102f.
New Birth 80
Niceno-Constantinopolitan Creed 63n12
Nicol, Iain 160f.n34
Nicol, Ute 160f.n34
Nietzsche, Friedrich 153
Nonviolence . . . 18f., 79–81, 159n8
Novum 20, 31, 33, 41n71

O

Objective . . . . 11–38, 31, 38, 149f.
O'Collins . . . . .Gerald, 18, 39n24, 39n28, 118n40, 160n22
Oepke, Albrecht 40n43
Özen, Alf 41n53
Onesimus 99
Ontology . . . . . .12, 13, 14, 25–28, 31f., 43–63, 67, 79–81, 95f., 112, 120, 122f., 127–31, 150, 163f.
Ordination 105–109
Orthodox church 114

P

Packer, James I. 15–17, 39n22
Pannenberg, Wolfhart 15f., 21, 39n19, 48f., 52, 62n5, 145, 159n20
Parables . . . . .75f.
Parker, T. H. L. 160f.n34
Partiality 104, 155, 158
Patriarchy 99–101, 104
Paul the apostle 12, 29f., 46, 105–109
Peace . . . . .18f.
Pedersen, Kusumita P. 117n29
Peter 29f., 50, 105–109
Pfändler, Marcel 40n36
Philemon 99
Phillips, Sr. Helen 160f.n34
Pluralism . . . . .6, 123f.
Politics . . . . .74f.
Post-modernism .4, 17–19, 20, 122
Postel, Sandra 117n36
Powers . . . . .88f.
Praxis 77–79, 144

Priebe, Duane A. 159n20
Priesthood 105–109

Q

Q-tradition 61

R

Racism 98, 104
Ransom . . . . .80, 85f.
Rasmussen, Larry 116n25, 117n37, 118n40
Ratschow, Carl Heinz 160n32
Rauschenbusch, Walter 159n9
Reagan, Charles E. 160n21
Reason, 4f. 14, 15–17, 19f., 28f., 48–53, 140f., 145
Reconciliation . . . .44, 80, 84, 85f.
Redemption . . . . .80, 85f.
Reformation 142–44
Regan, Hilary D. 161n36
"Reign of God" 70–79, 82n20
Relational ontology . . . . . .5, 7, 14, 43–63, 95f., 126f., 127–31, 137f., 150, 166f.
Religions 119–35
Representation 80
Rich, Arthur 161n42
Riches, John 160f.n34
Ricoeur, Paul 9, 142, 146–148, 160n21
Rights of nature 111
"Road to Damascus Document" 156, 161n41
Roman Catholic theology . . . . . .17–19, 39n25, 105, 107f., 114, 116n20, 123, 148f.

Romero, Oscar 156

S

Sabbath . . . . .73f.
Sacrifice 80
Saladin, Peter 116n10
Salvation 7, 12, 33, 86, 127–31
Sanctification 142–44, 147
Sawicki, Marianne 12, 54
Schleitheim Confession . .137, 143, 158n1
Schmidt, Peter 116n19
Schneemelcher, Wilhelm . . .42n83
Schüssler Fiorenza, Elisabeth 116n19, 152
Schüssler Fiorenza, Francis 9, 18, 26, 142, 146, 148–50, 160n22
Schweitzer, Albert 112, 118n43
Schweizer, Eduard 63ns13, 19, 20, 160f.n34
Scullion, John J. 115n6
Septuagint 63n15
Sheldrake, Rupert 112, 118n44
Simon the Zealot 82n18
Sin 85, 87, 100f., 110f., 113, 122f., 127
Sittler, Joseph 118n39
Skillings, Everett 118n43
Slavery, 98f. 104
Smith, Neville Horton 161n42
Sobrino, Jon 152
Social ethics 95–118
Sölle, Dorothee 152
Southern Baptist Convention 105, 108
Spiritual warfare . . . . .88f.
Spong, John Selby 4

Stalker, D. M. G. 94n2
Stanton, Graham 39n24
Steck, Odil Hannes 117f.n38
Stewart, David 160n21
Stewart, R. A. 160f.n34
Strauss, David Friedrich . . .4, 9n2f., 12, 41n52
Strobel, August 160f.n34
Subjective . . . . . . .11–38, 31, 149f.
Subjective vision 28–34, 41n52
Substitution, ...80
Suffering 157
Suu Kyi, Aung San 156, 165
Swimme, Brian 118n45
Synergism 145, 159n18

T

Temple 72f., 74, 77–79
Testimony 144–49
Theology, method . . . . .43, 51, 53, 60, 68f., 86, 95f., 155f.
Theology of religions . . .6, 119–35
Thiselton, Anthony C. 40n35
Thomas . . . . .36, 106f.
Tillich, Paul 38f.n8, 151, 160n32, 161n42
Torah 72f., 77–79, 96–98
Torrance . . . . .Alan J., 161n36
Torrance . . . . .T. F., 160f.n34
Trinity 53–56, 95f., 121, 125–34
Troeltsch, Ernst 9n4
Truth . . . . .127–31, 133f.
Tutu, Desmond 141
Twiss, Sumner B. 117n29
Tyndale, William 85

U

United Nations 117n26
Universal Declaration of Human Rights 101–103, 116ns9, 11–13

V

Virginia Declaration of
    Rights 101
Violence 18f., 79–81
Volf, Miroslav 153, 161n35
von Ess, Josef 134n2
von Rad, Gerhard 84, 94n2
von Stietencron, Heinrich . . .134n2

W

Wagner, Günter 9
Wealth 73
Welker, Michael 45, 62n2
Wenger, John C. 159ns11, 12; 160f.n34
Westermann, Claus 115n6
Wilkins, Lewis L. 159n20
Williams, George
    Huntston 159ns9, 16
Wilson, Iain 160f.n34
Wilson, R. A. 39n30
Wilson, R. McL. 42n83
Wink, Walter 88
Wirkungsgeschichte 25, 146
Witness 144–49
Wogaman, J. Philip 161n42
Wolff, Hans Walter 94n7
Women, ordination 105–109
Wood, Antony 161n36
World Council of Churches 117n30
World Watch Institute 116n25, 117n36
Worship . . . . .18, 78f., 141f.

Y

Yoder, John Howard . .94n4, 158n1

Z

Zealots 74f., 82n18

Scripture Index

Genesis
1:1–2:4a 99, 117n38
1:26-31 111
1:27 99
2 100
2:4b–3:24 99
2:15 . . . . .117n38
3:16-19 101
3:16 100
9:6 72
15:1-6 22

Exodus
3:7f. 55
3:14 55
3:17 55
20:2f. 63n16, 70
21:23-25 72

Leviticus
24:16 78
24:20f. 73

Deuteronomy
5:6f. 63n16
13 78
17 78
19:21 73

Psalms
16:9-11 89
24:1 111
73:3-14 91
73:21-26 . . . . .92f.
73:26 94
88:11 90
104:14f. 117n38
104:23 . . . . .117n38
104:29f. 121, 132
115:1f. 90
117:2 90
118:1-4 90

Ecclesiastes
4:10 100

Isaiah
1:11-16 . . . . .159n5
7:3-9 22
26:7-21 93
28:14-22 22

Jeremiah
6–8 1 . . . . .59n5
12:1 91
22:13-19 144

Daniel
12:1f. 93

Hosea
6:6 . . . . 159n5
13:4 . . . . .63n16

Amos
5:21-24 . . . . 159n5

Micah
6:6-8 . . . . .159n5

2 Maccabees
7 93

Jubilees
2:25 .74
50:8 .74

Matthew
5:13-16 145
5:38-48 73
8:10 .76
8:19-21 152
8:21f. 72, 153
11:2-6 . . . . .71, 133f., 144f.
11:5 .72
11:19 71
12:1-8 . . . . 82n14
12:9-14 . . . . 82n14
13:53-58 . . . . 82n14
16:17-19 106
17:24-27 74
18:6 . . . . .40n37
18:20 . . . . .114, 142
22:15-22 74
23:3 .72
23:23 72
25 . . . . .8, 167
25:31-46 145
25:31-40 . . . . 128, 142
25:34 129
25:35-40 114
27:52f. 45, 137
27:62-66 . . . . 42n83
28:1-8 . . . . 116n17
28:7 106
28:9f. 106
28:9 106
28:16-20 155
28:17 32
28:18b-20 . . . . 117n33
28:19f. 46
28:19 120
28:20 113

Mark
1:16-20 . . . . 152f.
1:16 .71
1:21-28 . . . . 82n14
2:1-12 76
2:14 152
2:23-28 . . . . 82n14
2:7 76
3:1-6 . . . . 82n14
3:4 74
3:6 74
3:18 . . . . 82n18

Reference	Page
3:31-35	72
5:21-24a	24
5:35-43	24
5:34	76
6:1-6	82n14
7:15	73
8:27–9:1	67, 152
8:31	26
9:31	26
9:36f.	114
9:42	40n37
10:17-31	152
10:17-22	73
10:33f.	26
10:45	85
10:52	76
11:15-19	74
11:18	74
12:13-17	74
12:17	75
12:25	56
14:3-9	26
14:24	85
15:39	36, 69
16:1-8	50
16:4-6	62n8
16:9	106f.
16:14	32
16:15	46, 120
16:19	117n33

Luke

Reference	Page
2:41-52	69
4:16-30	82n14, 155
4:18f.	70
4:31-37	82n14
5:1-6	106
5:8	106
6:1-5	82n14
6:6-11	82n14
6:15	82n18
6:20-23	128
6:20-22	128f.
7:9	76
7:11-15	24
7:34	71
8:1-3	71
9:51f.	117n33, 153
9:57-60	152
9:59f.	72
11:20	71
11:42	72
13:10-17	82n14
14:1-6	82n14
17:19	76
20:20-26	74
22:31f.	106
23:2	74
23:49	106f.
24:12	42n83, 48, 106f.
24:13f.	11
24:25	42n83
24:26	117n33
24:34	62n8, 105f., 116n18
24:40	65
24:41	32
24:46-49	46
24:48	145

John

Reference	Page
1:1-18	129
1:1-14	79
1:3f.	121
1:9	121

1:12f. 80
1:29 85
1:36 85
3:14 ....117n33
3:16 ....44, 113, 120, 123, 128
5:24 ....51, 89, 165
11:25f. 89
11:25 ....84, 89, 95
11:38-44 24
11:50 19
12:23 69
12:32 ....117n33
12:34 ....117n33
14–16 129
14:6 ....128, 134n3
17:1 69
18:37 145
19:26 ....106f.
19:35 107
19:36 85
20 36
20:1-10 ....106f.
20:2-10 ....42n83, 48
20:8 50
20:14-18 106
20:21 46
20:26-29 107
20:27 107
20:29 ....36, 107
21:1-17 105
21:1-14 106
21:15-17 106
21:18-22 106

Acts
1:1f. 117n33
1:8 46

1:13 ....82n18
1:21f. 117n33
2 30
2:32-35 ....117n33
2:44 114
3:19-21 ....117n33
4:12 ....128, 134n3
5:30-32 ....117n33
9:17 ....62n8
12:12 ....116n23
13:31 ....62n8
13:32f. 117n33
15:20 ....115n3
15:29 ....115n3
16:14f. 116n23
16:40 ....116n23
17:22-28 126
18:18 ....116n23
18:26 ....116n23
20:28 85
26:16 ....62n8

Romans
1:3f. 117n33, 139
1:3b-4 53
1:5f. 53
1:5 68
1:20 126
3:21-26 97
3:24 85
3:25 85
3:29 125
4:5 ....21, 131
4:17 ....21, 131
4:24f. 28
4:25 ....37, 85
5:6-8 85

5:9	85
5:10f.	85
5:20	164
6:4	132, 143, 158
6:9	24, 34, 38, 84, 141
7:3	108, 115n7
7:4	58
8	164
8:3	85
8:11	164
8:21-23	92
8:29	45, 137
8:34	117n33
8:38f.	45, 59, 60, 85, 89f.
8:39	120
10:4	97
10:17	51, 68, 114, 165
12:1f.	159
12:1	79
12:3-8	58
14:9	89, 117n33
16:1	116n23
16:3	116n23
16:5a	116n23
16:7	108

1 Corinthians

1:18–2:5	66
1:21-29	156f.
2:2	69
3:7	155
3:9	47, 137, 145, 154
9:1	105
10:16f.	58
10:16	58, 114
11–14	130
11:5	108
11:17f.	114
11:20-22	130
11:20, 67	114
11:23	67
11:24f.	114
11:24	58
11:25	85
11:33f.	114
12–14	108
12:10	130
12:12-30	58
13:12	128, 132
14:23	114
14:34f.	105, 108f.
14:35	115n7
15	12, 26, 93, 106, 164
15:3-7	107
15:3-5	45
15:3f.	61
15:3	87
15:5-8	62n8, 105f., 145
15:5-7	107
15:5	105f.
15:6	30
15:8	105
15:15	145
15:17	27, 34
15:20	43, 45, 137
15:23	45, 137
15:28	113, 156
15:35-57	56
15:35	32
15:37f.	32
15:38	33
15:39-44	32f.
15:44	56
15:48f.	56
15:50	33, 52, 53, 56

15:51-53 33
15:54-57 . . . . .34, 85, 128
15:54 . . . . .53, 83
15:57 53
15:58 . . . . . . .53, 92f., 156, 164

2 Corinthians
4:5f. 47, 51
4:8-10 146
4:13f. 51
5:1-5 56
5:1 .57
5:17-21 . . . . . . .44, 85, 87, 113,
 120, 125, 128
5:19f. 87
5:20 . . . . .46, 128

Galatians
1:15-17 46
2:1-10 97
2:19f. 151, 153
2:20 114
3:23-29 153
3:23-28 96-104
3:23-26 68
3:23-25 165
3:28 . . . . .108, 167

Ephesians
1:7 85
1:19-22 . . . . .117n33
1:22f. 59
2:6 . . . . .117n33
2:13 .85
4:8-10 . . . . .117n33

4:15f. 59
5:21-6:9 . . . . .116n16
5:21 . . . . .108, 116n16
5:22-24 108
5:22 . . . . .115n7
5:24 . . . . .59, 115n7
5:25 . . . . .116n16
6:12 .88

Philippians
2:6-11 . . . . .117n34
3:10 113

Colossians
1:15-20 . . . . .59, 117n34
1:18 . . . . .45, 58f., 137
1:20 .85
1:21f. 87
1:22 .85
1:24 .58
2:9 . . . . .128, 134n3
2:12 . . . . .135n9
2:13f. 87
2:14f. 87
2:19 .59
2:20 .87
3:1-4 . . . . .87f.
3:1 . . . . .117n33
3:14 . . . . .116n16
3:18-4:1 . . . . .116n16
3:18 . . . . .108, 115n7
3:19 . . . . .116n16
3:24 . . . . .116n16
4:15 . . . . .116n23

1 Thessalonians
1:10 . . . . .117n3

1 Timothy
2:3f. 128
2:4 . . . . .44, 120
2:5 . . . . .128, 134n3
2:8-15 . . . . .116n16
2:9f. 108
2:11-15 . . . . .105, 108f.
2:11f. 100
2:12 108
2:13 100
3:4 . . . . .116n16
3:7 . . . . .116n21
3:16 . . . .62n8, 117n33, 117n34
6:1f. 116n16

2 Timothy
4:19 . . . . .116n23

Titus
2:1-10 . . . . .116n16
3:1 . . . . .116n16

Hebrews
1:3 . . . . .117n33
2:14 85
4:14 . . . . .117n33
5:5 . . . . .117n33
7:26 . . . . .117n33
8:1 . . . . .117n33
9:11-14 85
9:15 85
9:17-21 85
9:22 85
9:28 85
10:12 . . . . .117n33
10:19 85
12:1f. 154
12:2 . . . . .117n33
13:12f. 79, 159n5
13:12 69
13:20 85

James
2:14-26 . . . . .63n18, 145
4:17 . . . . .63n18, 145

1 Peter
1:2 85
1:3-5 113
1:19 85
1:20f. 117n33
2:13–3:7 . . . . .116n16
3:1-5 . . . . .108, 115n7
3:18-22 . . . . .117n33, 132
3:18-20 89
3:22 . . . . .117n34
4:6 89, 132

1 John
1:7 85
4 164
4:1 130
4:14 126

Revelation

1:5	45, 85, 137
5	69, 80, 156
5:6	85
5:9	85
6:9	145
7:14	85
12:11	85

Gospel of the Hebrews . .42n83
Gospel of Peter . . . . .35f., 38, 42n83, 50f.
Ignatius, Epistle to
 Polycarp . . .4:1–5:1, 116n16
Polycarp, Epistle to
 Philippi . . .4:2–6:1, 116n16

www.ingramcontent.com/pod-product-compliance
Lightning Source LLC
Chambersburg PA
CBHW062216080426
42734CB00010B/1917